Christmas
2011

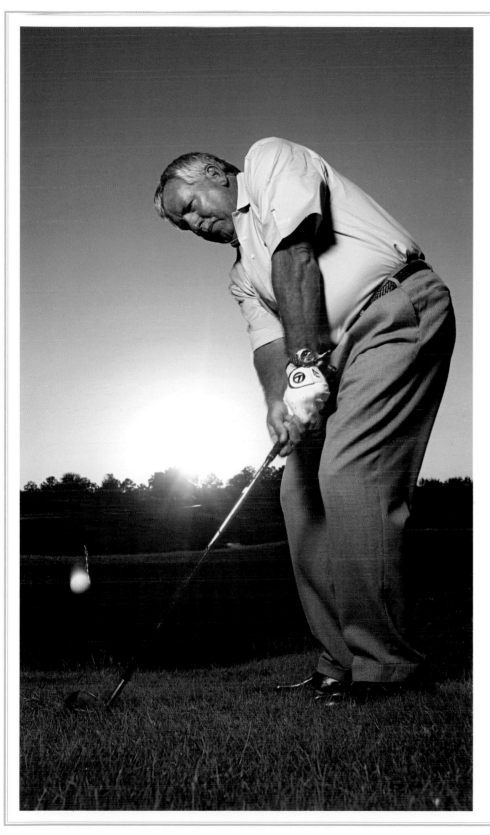

GOLF
MAGAZINE

The Best
INSTRUCTION
BOOK EVER!

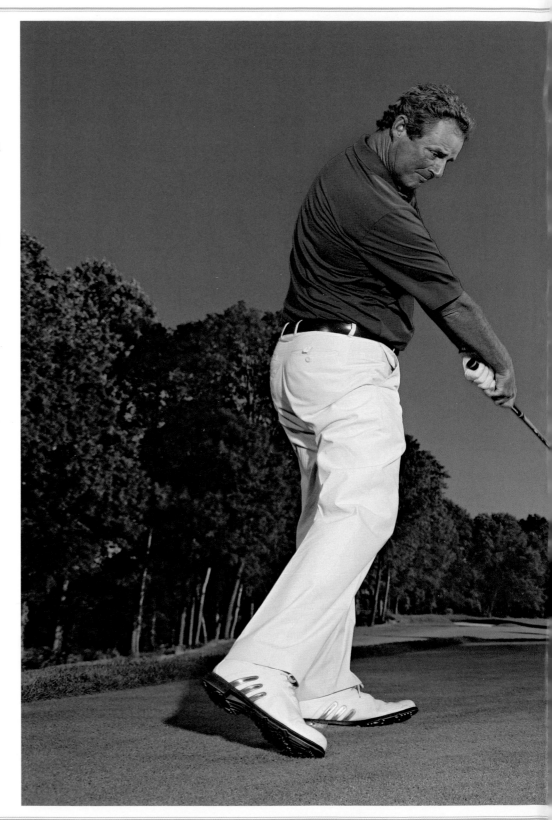

Copyright 2007
Time Inc. Home Entertainment

Some of the material in this book was previously published
in GOLF Magazine, and is reprinted with permission by
Time Inc.

Published by Time Inc. Home Entertainment

Time Inc.
1271 Avenue of the Americas
New York, New York 10020

ISBN 13: 978-1-60320-001-1
ISBN 10: 1-60320-001-0
Library of Congress #: 2007904503

Printed in China

If you would like to order any of our hardcover
Collector's Edition books, please call us at (800) 327-6388.
(Monday through Friday, 7:00 a.m. - 8:00 p.m. or Saturday,
7:00 a.m. - 6:00 p.m. Central Time).

Cover and book design by Paul Ewen
Cover photographs by Bob Atkins and Angus Murray

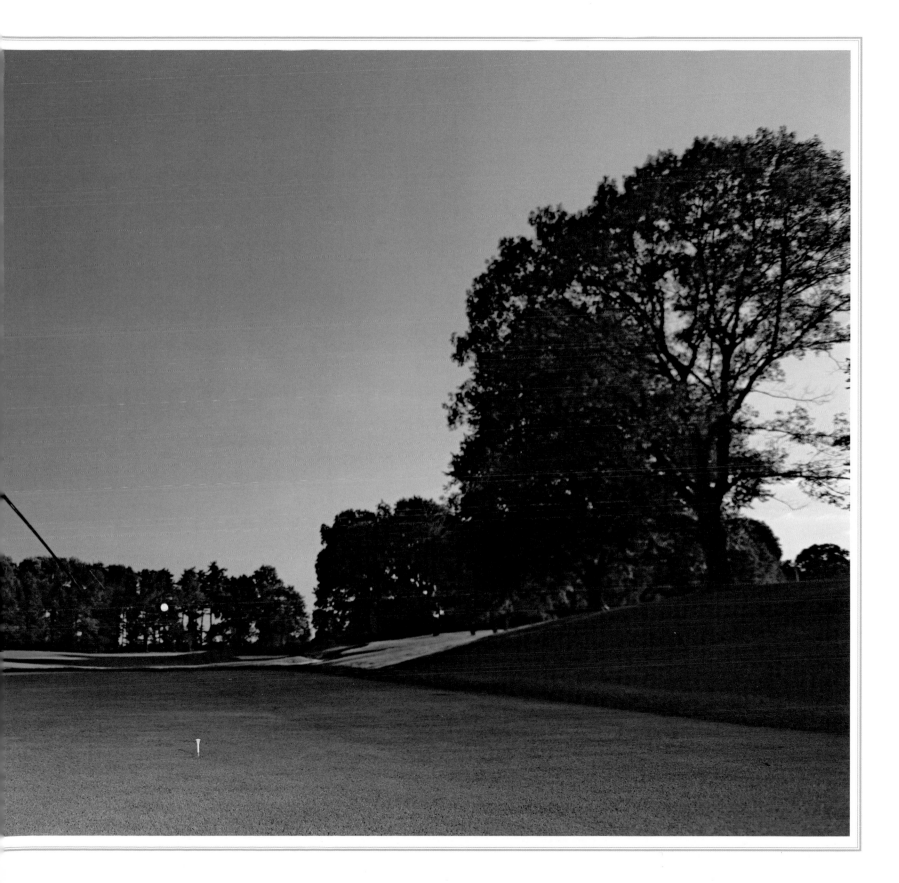

GOLF
MAGAZINE

The Best
INSTRUCTION
BOOK EVER!

From the Top 100 Teachers in America

EDITED BY DAVID DeNunzio

Time Inc.
HOME ENTERTAINMENT

YOUR BEST GOLF EVER!

Despite any success you've had in the past, the book in your hands is going to help you shoot lower scores and better enjoy your golfing experience. Confident claims no doubt, but they're easily made considering the source of the more than 1,000 tips, drills and lessons contained within. Each one comes straight out of the pages of *GOLF Magazine*, the most widely read golf publication in the world. With a almost 50-year legacy of award-winning instruction, *GOLF* has become *the* leader in the way the game is taught and played. Moreover, our instruction is driven by the single greatest collection of teaching experts in the game: the Top 100 Teachers. Members of this elite group are chosen not only for their swing knowledge and experience, but also for their teaching skills and knack for developing methods that make the game easier to learn. Some of the Top 100 Teachers you know by name—the ones that work with the major stars on the professional tours. Others are teaching legends with hall-of-fame status. But all of them are dedicated to helping golfers just like you get better and making sure these changes stick.

Since their debut in 1996, the Top 100 Teachers have produced more than 3,000 pages of instruction in *GOLF Magazine*. This book represents their greatest hits, organized to build your game from the ground up the right way. Use their advice to hit the ball farther, putt better and beat anything the course throws at you. With the help of the Top 100 Teachers, your best golf ever is just around the corner.

DAVID DENUNZIO, INSTRUCTION EDITOR, *GOLF MAGAZINE*

WHAT'S INSIDE

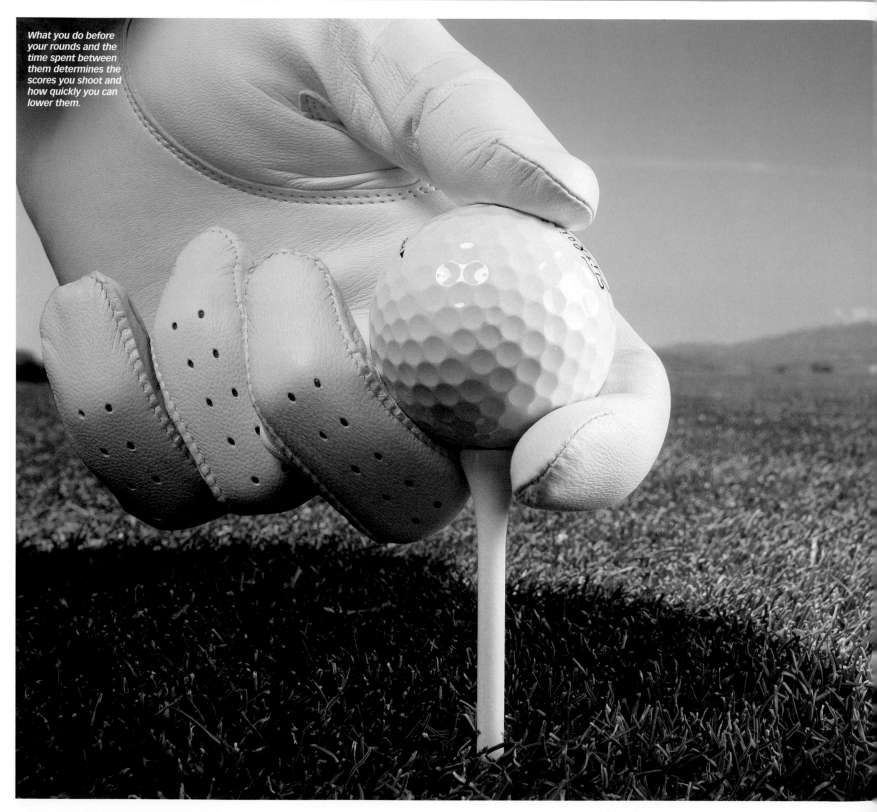

What you do before your rounds and the time spent between them determines the scores you shoot and how quickly you can lower them.

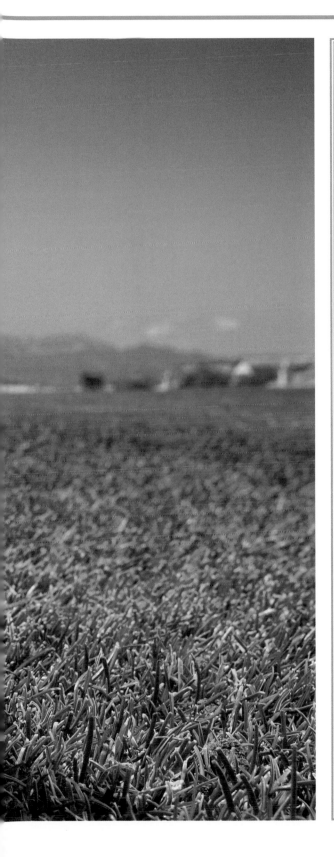

SECTION 1

PREPARING TO PLAY

How to get your round motoring out of the blocks even before you hit your first shot

There are two parts to the game: the playing part and the part that occurs between your rounds. While your typical day on the course lasts roughly four hours, the time from the moment you make your last putt on 18 to when you place your tee in the ground on the first hole of your next round is significantly longer. For some golfers, weeks longer. And although you judge your game by the scores you shoot, it's really what you do between rounds—and just before you tee off—that determines the numbers you mark on your card.

The fact that you're holding this book in your hands means you're serious about your game and about improving. The majority of these pages are dedicated to helping you get around the course in as few strokes as possible. This section, however, focuses on what you need to do between rounds to make sure the lessons stick. With the help of the Top 100 Teachers, you'll learn how to warm up before play to get off to good starts, how to make your practice time serious learning time, how to select the gear that will help you save strokes and how to make your lessons more effective. Armed with this knowledge, you'll optimize the non-playing part of your game so you can put your swing on autopilot and shoot the scores you want.

5 THINGS YOU'LL LEARN IN THIS SECTION

- How to get your swing warm before you play, whether you have an hour to get ready or just 15 minutes
- How to shop for equipment and secure the right mix of clubs to help you score low
- How to select a teacher and get the most out of a lesson
- How to practice with a purpose, make effective practice swings and groove the right moves quickly
- The flaw you must fix first

YOUR GAME

How to be a "Player"

Here are three tricks that only pros know

● Play with the right ball. Most golfers don't know what that is. As a general rule, choose the ball that works best for you when putting and chipping, not the one you can hit the farthest.
—**Bruce Patterson**

● Learn to adapt to different weather conditions with your gear. For instance, if it's cold, use a driver with a lower loft and move the ball a bit back in your stance. When the weather turns, the optimum launch angle isn't 12 degrees. It's more like 8 degrees.
—**Peter Krause**

● You've probably been told to finish your swing with your hands high. But if you want to hit the ball farther, consider finishing low. If you observe the big hitters on the pro tours, you'll notice that the club comes to rest on their left shoulder. This is the result of unhinging, or releasing, the wrists fully through impact. It provides a powerful snap to the swing and produces a low finish.
—**Mike Lopuszynski**

WARM UP AND PRACTICE

How to get loose before play and keep your swing skills fresh between rounds

The 15-Minute Warm-Up

A quick and effective routine to jump-start your round

The situation

You've arrived late to the course and have only 15 minutes to warm up.

The solution

Get your short game and putting warm because you'll need them more than ever while you work out the kinks in your full swing.

What to do

This plan calls for six two-minute segments and allows for three minutes to pick up balls and move between drills. First, stretch your hamstring muscles and twist your trunk all the way right and left to loosen up a bit.

Step 1

Take five swings each with your 7-iron, 5-wood and driver at 3/4 speed. Don't hit balls, just swing the clubs.

Step 2

Grab three balls and your 8-iron, 60-degree wedge and putter, and hightail it for the practice green.

Step 3

Hit the short-game shots described at right in order. If you can squeeze in one full swing before you tee off, hit a 4-wood out onto the range. You'll be ready to start your round with a smooth 4-wood into the first fairway.
—Dave Pelz

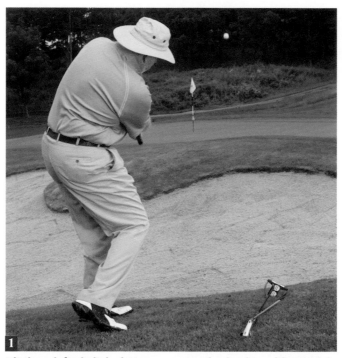

1 Hit three lofted pitch shots over a practice bunker with your lob wedge (or highest-lofted club) to learn how your ball reacts upon hitting the green.

2 Jump into the bunker and hit three short sand shots to a greenside target to activate your hands.

3 Hit three running chips with your 8-iron to a hole 50 feet away to get a feel for distance.

4 Stroke three long lag putts well across the putting surface to dial in the speed of the greens.

5 Hit six three-foot putts to become comfortable with the short ones—these are the score-breakers.

Start With Your Short Game

Most golfers warm up with their longer clubs first. This is why they start their rounds poorly.

Statistical averages show golfers score better on the middle 10 holes than the first and last four. It's easy to see how the pressure to shoot a certain score might make you nervous and result in poor scores at the finish. But poor play on the first four holes? Perhaps this is because you're not prepared to scramble when you miss the first few greens. This data emphasizes the importance of warming up your short-game feel and touch before heading to the first tee. A complete-game warm-up is optimal, but when you're short on time, warm up your scoring game first!

—**Dave Pelz**

Golfers score better on the middle holes than early or late. Warm up your short game first to buck this trend.

Hole #

How to Customize Your Warm-Up

Find the pre-round prep that works best for you

On Tour, I notice that some players take just 40 minutes to get ready, while others warm up for several hours. My point is this: Your pre-round preparation must be tailored to your personality and body conditioning. What gets one player ready to play their best may tire you out. Optimize your scoring potential by trying different warm-up times and techniques, and keeping track of the scores you shoot afterward. Once you learn what works best for you, use it for all of your rounds in the future.

—**Dave Pelz**

DRILL

How to Loosen Up Your Body

Follow these steps for peak performance

Whether your pre-round warm-up time is an hour (ideal) or 15 minutes (typical), you have time to get ready for one of your best rounds. Here's the sequence to follow:

Step 1
Walk briskly to the driving range to get your blood moving, then warm up. Hold two clubs together and swing them in circles, doing 10 reps with each arm. This prepares your shoulders for demands of the golf swing.

Step 2
Rest the clubs on the ground and hold them vertically, securing your hands on top of the grips [above]. Keep your hands there and do 10 squats to warm up your knees, calves and hips.

Step 3
Hit your short irons for a solid 10 minutes. Start with slow, three-quarter length swings and gradually build to full swings. After 10 minutes of hitting balls you can stretch your arm, leg and core muscles however you like without risking a visit to the chiropractor the next day.

Even if you don't hit another ball after this last step, your body will be primed to hit a good drive on the first tee and sustain high performance throughout your round.

—**Dave Phillips**

How to Practice Like a Tour Player

Improve your rhythm—and look cool doing it!

START HERE
Tip over a bucket of balls and, with your club in your right hand, pull a ball out of the pile and drag it over to a spot where you can hit it.

Now "Present" the handle of the club to your right hand, release your left hand, and go back to Step 1. Now you're practicing like a pro!

Stand behind your ball and pick your target. Step into address—first with your right foot and then with your left— while glancing at your target.

The problem

You go through a bucket of range balls like a wave of locusts through a cornfield.

The solution

When you beat balls at a machine-gun pace you're not helping your game much. You need to set up to the ball correctly every time, and also take the time to follow through completely, study your ball flight and landing patterns, and then decompress and get ready for the next shot. In other words, you need to practice like you play.

How to do it

Watch Tour players on the driving range. Most pros follow a six-step procedure that takes them from ball to ball in a deliberate, measured way that mimics how they approach each shot on the golf course. If you copy that procedure, you're guaranteed to become a better ball striker.

—John Elliott

As the ball comes to a stop, remove your right hand from the grip and allow the club to slide down the fingers of your left hand until it feels light and balanced in your hand.

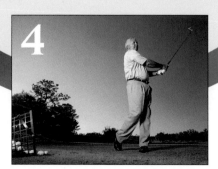

Make a complete, balanced swing so that you're facing the target and most of your weight is on your left foot. Study the flight of your ball, and stay in this position until it has landed.

Once you're comfortable in your address position and have visualized your target line, waggle the club once or twice to loosen your wrists, and then swing away.

INSTRUCTION

How to Practice Your Putting

Six tips for making your time on the practice green pay off

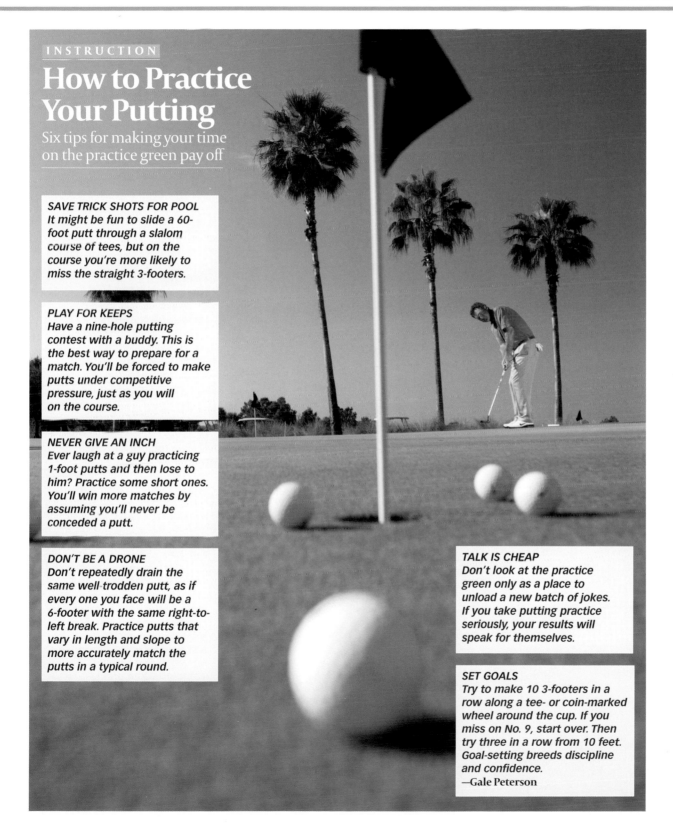

SAVE TRICK SHOTS FOR POOL
It might be fun to slide a 60-foot putt through a slalom course of tees, but on the course you're more likely to miss the straight 3-footers.

PLAY FOR KEEPS
Have a nine-hole putting contest with a buddy. This is the best way to prepare for a match. You'll be forced to make putts under competitive pressure, just as you will on the course.

NEVER GIVE AN INCH
Ever laugh at a guy practicing 1-foot putts and then lose to him? Practice some short ones. You'll win more matches by assuming you'll never be conceded a putt.

DON'T BE A DRONE
Don't repeatedly drain the same well-trodden putt, as if every one you face will be a 6-footer with the same right-to-left break. Practice putts that vary in length and slope to more accurately match the putts in a typical round.

TALK IS CHEAP
Don't look at the practice green only as a place to unload a new batch of jokes. If you take putting practice seriously, your results will speak for themselves.

SET GOALS
Try to make 10 3-footers in a row along a tee- or coin-marked wheel around the cup. If you miss on No. 9, start over. Then try three in a row from 10 feet. Goal-setting breeds discipline and confidence.
—**Gale Peterson**

ASK THE TOP 100

Practice These Major Keys

Other than working on technique, what should I focus on during my practice sessions?

"Practice with the club that allows you to hit the fairway on the most consistent basis, even if it's a 3-wood. Don't feel like your driver is the only club you can hit from the tee box. Also, work on shots around the green, particularly on putts from four feet and in. I've seen it help players drop three strokes in three days."
—**Rod Lidenberg**

"Hit little punch shots with your 7-iron to ingrain the feel of a correct release. Address a ball, and cock the club up so the club shaft is parallel to the ground. Hold it there, get comfortable and start the swing from this point, taking your hands back to chest height. Start down with your hips and finish at chest height. This drill trains your hands and arms to store the power of the downswing for as long as possible."
—**Ron Gring**

"Hit shots with the sole purpose of maintaining your posture from start to finish. You can practice this at home, too. Place a pillow against a wall and rest your forehead against it, then make practice takeaways without moving your head off the pillow."
—**Gerald McCullagh**

HOW TO GET THE RIGHT GEAR

Even if your swing is sound, it won't do you much good if you're playing with the wrong equipment. Here's how to round out your perfect set.

How to Shop Smart

Eight ways to gear up and find value, fit and quality

FLY SOLO
Go alone and let the salesman help you make decisions. Many golfers end up making bad purchases based on advice from a buddy who knows very little about equipment.

CAP YOUR WALLET
Follow a budget to prevent buyer's remorse. Set a price range for the final bill rather than for each individual item. This will give you the flexibility to spend more money on one thing and less on another.

STEP IN IT
Make sure a shoe is comfortable right out of the box. It's not going to fit any better on the course. Also look for a lighter athletic or sneaker-type shoe if you prefer to walk more than you take a cart.

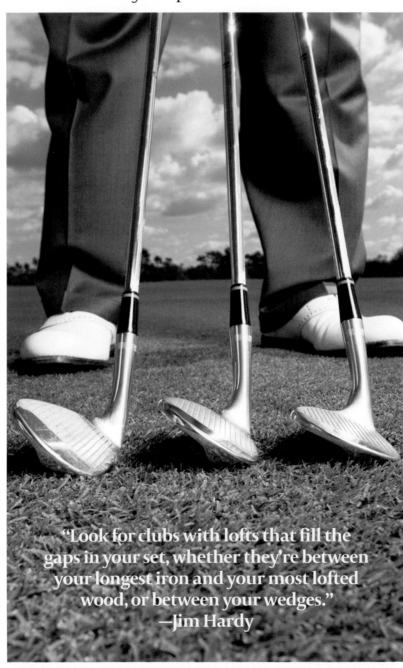

"Look for clubs with lofts that fill the gaps in your set, whether they're between your longest iron and your most lofted wood, or between your wedges."
—Jim Hardy

SUIT UP
Reach for synthetic fabrics that wick away moisture and prevent wrinkles. You'll get the most value from neutral colors you can mix and match without thinking about it.

IRON OUT YOUR BAG
The average golfer needs more hybrids and fewer long irons. Once the salesman knows what type of courses you play, he can tell you what ratio of irons to wedges to hybrids you need.

TEST YOUR EYES
Good sunglasses will have no distortion when you look at the ground through the bottom of the lenses. Take a pair outside for a two-minute test—if they darken up and take the glare out of the parking lot, they're keepers.

GET FIT
A fitting for woods, irons, a driver, grip size and balls takes at most 30 minutes. Most stores have a launch monitor or a simulator so the salesman can fit you and then recommend clubs for your game.

TELL THE TRUTH
Be honest about how you hit the ball, how you strategize and what clubs you favor. Telling the truth about your game is the only way to get a proper fit.

How to Find the Right Mix of Clubs

Follow these rules and you'll always have the right club for the shots you typically face during play

Player's Bag

These specs should suit you if you carry your 5-iron 170-190 yards and your driver 250-275 yards.

SHAFTS

Irons: Steel, stiff flex
Woods: Graphite, stiff or extra stiff

SET

Irons: Hybrid driving iron, 4-iron to PW, Gap, SW, LW
Woods: Driver, Strong 3-wood

BALL

Multilayer, urethane covered model (favoring spin)

YOUR KEY CLUB

Strong 3-wood
With your length, you won't need to pull driver on every tee, especially on short or troublesome par 4s. More fairways mean more birdies.

Low-Handicapper's Bag

These specs should suit you if you carry a 5-iron 155-170 yards and your driver 230-250 yards.

SHAFTS

Irons: Steel, stiff flex
Woods: Graphite, stiff flex

SET

Irons: Hybrid, 4-iron to PW, Gap, SW, LW
Woods: Driver, 4-wood

BALL

Multilayer, urethane covered model (favoring distance)

YOUR KEY CLUB

Lob wedge
You've established a decent long game. Now it's time to learn to save shots around the greens. The L-wedge is a savior from deep bunkers and dense rough.

Mid-Handicapper's Bag

These recommendations should suit you if you carry a 5-iron 150-160 yards and your driver 220-235 yards.

SHAFTS

Irons: Graphite, regular or stiff flex
Woods: Graphite, reg or stiff

SET

Irons: Hybrid, 5-iron to PW, Gap, SW
Woods: Driver, 3-, 5- and 7-wood

BALL

Three-piece performance (distance/spin blend)

YOUR KEY CLUB

Gap wedge
Mastering this club will allow you to take full swings on finesse shots from 100 yards in, a spot you'll encounter since you likely lose some carry on full shots.

High-Handicapper's Bag

These recommendations should suit you if you carry a 5-iron 130-140 yards and your driver 205-220 yards.

SHAFTS

Irons: Graphite, regular flex
Woods: Graphite, regular flex

SET

Irons: Three hybrids, 6-iron to PW, Gap, SW, LW
Woods: High-lofted driver, 4-wood

BALL

Low-compression distance

YOUR KEY CLUB

Hybrids
Lose the long irons and launch the type of high, soaring shots you see more accomplished players hit. The versatile hybrid is also useful around the greens.

"Try one hybrid at a time so you can adjust to the club and see what it can do."
—Ed Ibarguen

HOW TO LEARN

You can do it yourself and take years to get better. Or you can seek out a qualified teaching professional and improve faster than you imagined.

CHECKPOINT

How to Get the Most From a Lesson

Six ways to get what you pay for—a better game

CHOOSE YOUR CLASSROOM
Decide whether you need a range lesson or a playing lesson. If you're looking to improve your swing and ball striking, the range is the best place. But if you want better course management, take a playing lesson.

SET EXPECTATIONS
Before the lesson, tell your instructor what you're looking to improve and how much you'd like to accomplish. Don't expect to drop 10 strokes after one lesson and don't expect 300-yard drives if you're just learning to grip the club.

FIND THE RIGHT PRO
Ask your pals for suggestions—or find one of our Top 100 teachers at golf.com. Call the pros and interview them. Ask them about their teaching style—what you can expect— then pick a teacher who appeals to your needs.

HIT REWIND
Start every practice session with a review of what you've been taught. Start with the basics then go through your last lesson. Don't abandon the teachings if you're not getting perfect results—keep at it and you'll start to see the payoff.

COOL DOWN
Spend another 15 minutes on the range after your lesson. Work on your own to relax and apply what you've just learned from your teacher. Also, take notes, and if your pro tapes the lesson, taking home a video is even better.

DON'T RUSH
Whether you're coming from home or the office, don't blaze into the parking lot and quickly throw on your spikes. To get your mind and body in optimal condition, arrive at your lesson 15 minutes early to loosen up.
—Rick McCord

CHECKPOINT

What You Need to Fix the Most

During lessons, practice and play, correct your most common flaws first. For most golfers, it's a slice.

The problem

Baseball, apple pie and left-to-right shots that defy the laws of physics—no doubt we are a country of slicers. But has America's slice-itis reached epidemic proportions?

A recent poll of the Top 100 Teachers offers hope. According to the Top 100, the slicing problem is improving—but thanks only to gear advances. While it's impossible to gauge technology's effect on accuracy, it's safe to say that our country is slicing less, but we're still a far cry from straight down the middle. We're left just as much as we are right, further proving that correcting your swing path is priority No. 1.

Who slices most?

None of the low-handicap golfers in our poll hit a slice, and 90% of the slices were hit by those with an index of 10 or higher.

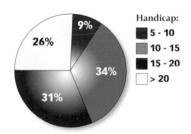

Handicap:
- 5 - 10
- 10 - 15
- 15 - 20
- > 20

Where the shots went

A solid 25% of all shots flew straight. But 43% were either pulled or sliced? We've got some path fixin' to do!

Shot Type:
- Hook
- Pull
- Push
- Slice
- Straight
- Topped/Fat

The experiment

We asked the starter at 69 courses managed by Troon Golf (*www.troongolf.com*) to report on the ball flights of the 9 a.m. foursome on Saturday, Sept. 2, 2006.

The results

More than 70 percent of the 276 tee shots measured failed to fly straight, with more than 38 percent finding the right side. Not exactly "Slice Saturday," but pretty close.

	35.0%		38.6%	
	11.4%	23.6%	20.0%	18.6%
6.4%	.7%	1.4% 2.9%	.7%	.7%
34.3%	2.9%	6.4% 10.7%	8.6%	5.7%
43.6%	6.4%	9.3% 8.6%	9.3%	10.0%
15.7%	1.4%	6.4% 4.3%	1.4%	2.1%

40.7% — 59.3%

300 yds / 275 yds / 250 yds / <225 yds

50 25 0 25 50

Yards left of center | Yards right of center

The most common slice? A big one

Our national driving hot zone is short and right. And while we slice only a third of the time, a half of those slices are landing more than 25 yards from the center of the fairway.

Ball flight of 276 players

Ball flight/Frequency

Hooking and pushing (in-to-out path shots) increase as handicap decreases. Slicing increases as handicap increases.

Shot Type:
- Hook
- Pull
- Push
- Slice
- Straight

<5 | 5-10 | 10-15 | 15-20 | 20> | Handicap

Four Quick Slice Fixes

Point your clubface at the target
Glue a tee to a magnet and place it in the center of your clubface, then make slow-motion swings to learn where your face points during all points of your swing.
—Jane Frost

Use abdominal power
Improve your core stability. This will help you maintain dynamic posture. Without it, your torso and your arms will dominate and swing your clubhead across the target line.
—David Phillips

Hold light and roll
Hold your club like you'd hold a briefcase (in your fingers) with a light grip pressure. Make a baseball swing and feel how your forearms cross over. That's what you're after.
—Carol Preisinger

Hit the sweet spot more often
To learn how to hit the ball in the center of the clubface, use face tape. It's cheap (500' of impact tape costs less than $15 at your local pro shop) and can tell you in an instant if you're missing the sweet spot. Affix the tape to the center of your clubface, and check the mark after each swing. By focusing on the contact point rather than shot shape or distance, you'll learn how to adjust your swing so you catch it flush in the center more often.
—Carl Welty

Elite golfers base their swings on the principle that good positions lead to better positions in the segments of the swing that follow. Do likewise and the lasting improvement you're looking for will come more easily and more quickly than you expect.

SECTION 2

UNDERSTANDING YOUR SWING

How to make it simple and repeatable
for consistent success

The swing is a complex beast. This statement is no surprise to anyone who has tried to build one. Those that excel at it are the ones who commit to constant practice and study to turn the complexities into simple, repeatable actions. Unfortunately, you can't simply learn a swing and expect it to take your game where you want it to go. You must *understand* it. Only when you grasp how your setup and every motion affects what happens next in your swing will you truly be able to hit effective shots, stop bad ones when they occur and own the ability to self-correct and improve.

Like most instruction books, this one starts at the beginning with your address. But unlike the rest, the Top 100 Teachers break down every facet of the swing that follows and provide insights and checkpoints you can use to improve every inch of your motion. It's a simple approach because correcting even just a few positions—or learning how to get into them correctly for the first time—automatically improves the positions that follow.

Follow this guide and you'll quickly become a true student of your swing and learn to recognize breakdowns in your technique. That's when the game you want will begin to take shape.

5 THINGS YOU'LL LEARN IN THIS SECTION

- How to stand at address and hold the club correctly so it can swing itself
- How to swing on the proper plane and make powerful contact on the sweet spot
- Myths to avoid and swing secrets every golfer should know to hit successful shots
- Drills to turn your practice time into quality learning time
- A checkpoint at each moment of the swing to make sure you're doing it correctly

THE FIRST STEP

A fundamentally solid grip allows you to make a natural motion and stops swing errors in their tracks

IT ALL STARTS HERE
Your hands are your only connection to the club, so you better make that connection a good one. As a general rule, hold the club in your fingers, not in your palms.

How to Grip Your Club

Use the creases in your hands to guide
you into the perfect hold

Step 1

Do this without a glove to really get
the feel of how to grip your clubs
properly. Hold the handle against
your outstretched left hand. The
grip should extend diagonally from
the fatty portion of your hand (just
below the pinkie) to the middle
crease of your index finger.

Step 2

Put your glove on and place the
club how you had it in Step 1. Then,
curl your fingers around the handle
so that the fatty portion of your
hand is on top. You should apply
pressure with the last three fingers
of your left hand. (You shouldn't feel
any pressure in your palm.)

Step 3

When you position your right hand,
the handle should rest across the
base of your right pinkie to the top
crease in your index finger. This
ensures that you grip the club with
your fingers, not your palm. Wrap
your fingers around the underside
of the grip and place the fatty
portion of your right hand on top of
your left thumb.

Step 4

Hold your grip out in front of you
and check that the Vs formed by
your thumbs and forefingers point
to the right side of your face.
Depending on your preference, rest
your right pinkie in the crease
between your left index and middle
fingers (overlapping grip) or wedge
it between them (interlocking).

—Brian Mogg

*Whether you like
a strong, weak
or neutral hold,
make sure your
thumb creases
line up.*

Do Your Hands Work Together?

**A lot of golfers can't hit the ball squarely
because their hands work against each
other, not with each other. To make sure
that doesn't happen to you, take the
following test.**

● Grip any club and
have a friend insert two
tees in the creases
formed by the base of
your thumbs and the
back of your hands as
shown above. If one tee
points to the right of
your grip and the other
points to the left, you've
created opposing forces
in your hands and you'll
limit their ability to
square up your clubface
and release the club
with authority.
● Your goal is to
position your hands on
the handle so that the
two tees line up. In this
position your hands can
work as a single unit
and deliver your
clubhead to the ball with
zero wasted energy.
● If you slice, line up the
tees over the right side
of the grip. This gives
you more power to
square up the clubface
through impact. Line the
tees up over the left
side of the grip to keep
the face from closing
too quickly and reel in
your hook or hit a
purposeful fade.

—Jason Carbone

How Much Squeeze Do I Need?

"I recommend that you
grip the club as though
you were gluing your
hands to it. You want
complete contact.
Every bit of the insides
of your fingers should
be touching the handle.
No gaps, no air pockets
and no spaces."

— Bob Toski

"Hold your club over
your right shoulder and
pretend to throw it end
over end without letting
go of the club. The
feeling you have when
holding your club and
going through the
throwing motion is a
good fit for your grip
and grip pressure."

—Craig Harmon

*You'll suffer from a lack of
distance and control with a
misaligned grip.*

SETUP BASICS

The majority of your swing errors—and the need to make compensations—are the result of mistakes in your setup. Get it right here and your swing will take care of itself.

INSTRUCTION

How to Step Into Your Shot

Here's a reliable way to get your stance width correct every time

Step 1
Aim your clubface at your target then step in with your right foot, pointing it behind the ball. This cue is a reminder that you're starting to position the ball. You might even repeat that objective to yourself ("inside left heel," "center of stance," etc.).

Step 2
With your right foot in place, step in with your left. Position it relative to where you want to play the ball. The above is a 5-iron, so the ball goes four inches inside your left heel. A driver, played off your left heel, would require a smaller step.

Step 3
Step out with your right foot, widening your stance until you feel comfortable and stable. With your stance and ball position set, take a quick final look at the target, then return your eyes to the ball and begin your swing.
—**Don Hurter**

INSTRUCTION

How to Take Your Stance

Copy the positions below to build a rock-solid address position and set the stage for a successful swing

DON'T BEND YOUR BACK
Keep your spine straight—
a line should connect the
back of your shoulders
and the back of your head.

THREE-POINT STANCE
The correct blend of
knee bend and hip tilt
will align three points:
the balls of your feet,
your knees and your
shoulders.

HANG OUT
Allow your arms to
dangle freely from
your shoulders (right
arm hides the left).

UNLOCK YOUR KNEES
Bend them slightly
and tilt more from
your hips (keeping a
straight back) to sole
the club.

BUCKLE UP
The shaft points at
your belt buckle
when the club is
soled properly on
the ground.

CHECKPOINT

You should see that your right shoulder is lower than your left, your hands are even with the ball, and the Vs of your grip point to the right side of your face.

CHECKPOINT

Take a balanced, shoulder-width stance using your heels—not your toes—as a guide.

CHECKPOINT

With good posture, your knees, hips and shoulders are spaced equally apart, like the rungs on a ladder.
—**Shawn Humphries**

INSTRUCTION

Adjust Your Grip to Hit Straighter Shots

Experiment with different holds to find the one that works best

When you feel you're aimed correctly but your shots are missing left or right of your target, consider adjusting your grip. A grip that fails to complement your swing style can cause you to miss even if you make a solid swing. Experiment with the following grips and see if a change to either a weaker or stronger hold will help you hit more accurate shots.
—**Kevin Walker**

Weak Grip
Beats a hook
Hands on top of the handle, right V pointing to your nose.

INSTRUCTION

How to Take Aim
Use close targets to prevent shots that fly off line

Step 1
Once you've decided on a target, pick out a divot or another obvious spot on the ground about a foot in front of your ball. The spot should sit on the line that runs from your ball to the target. Imagine a track that extends out from the entire clubhead, toe to heel *[inset photo]*. Thinking of it as a lane instead of a line makes it easier to check that you're aimed correctly.

Step 2
Once you have your aiming lane, hold your club steady and stand with your feet nearly touching. Position your feet so that the leading edge of the club is perpendicular to your toe line. Now your body can accommodate a swing that travels on a plane that correctly matches your line to the target. Widen your stance to address the ball and swing with confidence.
—**Nancy Quarcelino**

Neutral Grip
Best for working the ball
Hands slightly right on the handle, right V pointing to your right cheek bone.

Strong Grip
Beats a slice
Hands resting on the right side of the handle, both Vs pointing to your right ear.

Stand the Correct Distance From the Ball

The lie of your clubs and your posture should dictate how far away you stand from the ball, but here's an easy guide

Fault: You stand too close or too far away from the ball.

Fix: Make a fist. The width of your fist is how much space there should be between your body and the butt end of your 5-iron. The longer the club, the farther you should be from the ball. For a driver, the ideal distance is a fist plus your thumb; for a wedge, about half a fist.
—**Mitchell Spearman**

For a 5-iron, maintain about a fist-width gap from your thighs.

For a driver, it's a fist plus your thumb.

Your Right Foot First

Here's another way to make sure you're aimed at your target

Step 1

As you approach the ball, set the middle of your right foot perpendicular to your target line and even with the back edge of the ball with no knee flex. Set your left-hand grip.

Step 2

Place your club on the ground behind the ball without trying to aim the clubface. The shaft should line up with your left forearm. The clubface will look open, but don't change it.

Step 3

Add your right hand to the club and bring your left foot even with your right. Notice that your hips and shoulders are parallel to each other. Swivel your head, fix your eyes on your target and spread your feet into your regular stance width. When you look back down at the ball, your clubface will still look open. Again, don't change it—that's the adjustment you need to combat what's called "hidden offset" that results when the toe of your iron sits up at address. Trust it, and you'll enjoy more accurate shotmaking, particularly with your short irons.
—**Dr. David Wright**

Pick the Right Ball Position

The trick? Know where your nose is.

Each club in your bag features a unique length and lie angle (the angle the shaft creates when the clubhead is soled on the ground). Because of this, you must vary where you play the ball in your stance to accommodate the dimensions of the club in your hands. As a general rule, the longer the club the more forward you should position the ball in your stance, but the ball should never be left of your left shoulder or right of your nose, regardless of which club you're using for full swings. This photo shows an easy way to remember exactly where to position the ball for every shot.

"You stand taller with a 3-iron than with a 7-iron, so it will bottom out later in your swing—that's why you play the ball forward in your stance with longer clubs."

Putter | PW-7 | 3-6 iron | Hybrid/ Fairway wood | Driver

INSTRUCTION

Use Your Body to Position the Ball

Line up the ball correctly in your stance with this anatomical guide

Driver
Position the ball even with the outside of your left shoulder.

Hybrid/Woods
Position the ball even with the center of your left armpit.

3- through 6-iron
Position the ball even with your left ear for long and mid-irons.

Short irons
Play the ball off your left cheek for short irons and wedges.

Putter
Play the ball even with your nose to sink more putts.

When Is It Time to Use a New Ball?

The modern ball is pretty durable and will hold its properties for a long time. **A top-tier ball will last for about three rounds and a lower quality ball will last slightly less.** Even if you hit down on the ball hard and hit a lot of bunkers and cart paths, the only damage you'll really see will be a duller finish. When the finish wears, your ball flight will be affected and replacing it wouldn't be a bad idea. However, most modern urethane covers make this a slow process and most golfers will lose the ball long before serious wear occurs.

"If you're not hitting many greens in regulation, switch to a ball that's a bit softer to help you more around the greens."
—**Steve Bosdosh**

CHECKPOINT

Once you have your ball position set, make two final checks at address: your weight distribution and your shaft position.

Check 1
For standard full swings with every club, make sure your weight is evenly spread over both of your feet. This provides you with a stable platform to help you maintain balance throughout your motion.

Check 2
If you have difficulty making clean contact consistently, press the shaft slightly forward by moving your hands toward the target (be careful not to move the clubhead as well). This gives you the best chance for ball-first contact and solid strikes.
—**Michael Breed**

WRONG!

WRONG!

The ball position in both photos is in exactly the same position, but my incorrect weight distribution in each photo changes the position of the ball in relation to my head. For the short iron I have here the ball should be positioned off my left cheek. This underlines the need for even weight distribution.

INSTRUCTION

How High Should You Tee the Ball?

Our exclusive test provides the rock-solid answer

The Experiment

Twenty-seven golfers, aged 25 to 71 with handicaps ranging from scratch to 29, were divided into three groups of nine by handicap level: 0-9, 10-19, and 20 and above. Each golfer hit 10 drives at each tee height (low: top edge of ball even with top of clubhead; medium: equator of ball even with the top of the clubhead; and high: bottom of ball even with the top of the clubhead). Each group hit from the three tee heights in varying order to ensure that fatigue and motivation were balanced. Only the best five out of each player's 10 drives at each tee height were recorded so that mis-hits would not skew the data. Participants used their own drivers, with clubheads ranging from 410 cc to 460 cc.

The Analysis

Carry distance and other data were measured by a launch monitor. Accuracy also was recorded: drives that landed in the fairway were scored higher than those that landed in the rough or beyond the rough.

The Results

Carry distance for mid and high tee heights was significantly longer than the low tee height, largely an effect of the higher tees promoting higher launch angles and less spin. The high tee height provided the most distance, giving players an average of 12 yards more carry per drive than the low tee height.

—Eric Alpenfels

HANDICAP	Low tee	Mid tee	High tee
Low (0-9)			
Carry distance (yards)	211.64	219.62	222.92
Launch angle (degrees)	10.5	13.04	13.17
Ball spin (rpm)	4,051	3,875	3,434
Clubhead speed (mph)	98.32	97.08	97.36
Ball speed (mph)	138.59	138.13	138.95

Average carry: 218.06 yards

	Low tee	Mid tee	High tee
Mid (10-19)			
Carry distance (yards)	171.46	177.84	179.84
Launch angle (degrees)	12.4	14.4	14.04
Ball spin (rpm)	3,844	3,794	3,529
Clubhead speed (mph)	86.04	85.76	85.24
Ball speed (mph)	120.9	120.93	120.93

Average carry: 176.38 yards

	Low tee	Mid tee	High tee
High (20 and up)			
Carry distance (yards)	160.85	174.15	178.24
Launch angle (degrees)	11.23	13.7	14.75
Ball spin (rpm)	3,834	3,801	3,591
Clubhead speed (mph)	85.39	85.87	85.01
Ball speed (mph)	120.15	120.92	120.39

Average carry: 171.08 yards

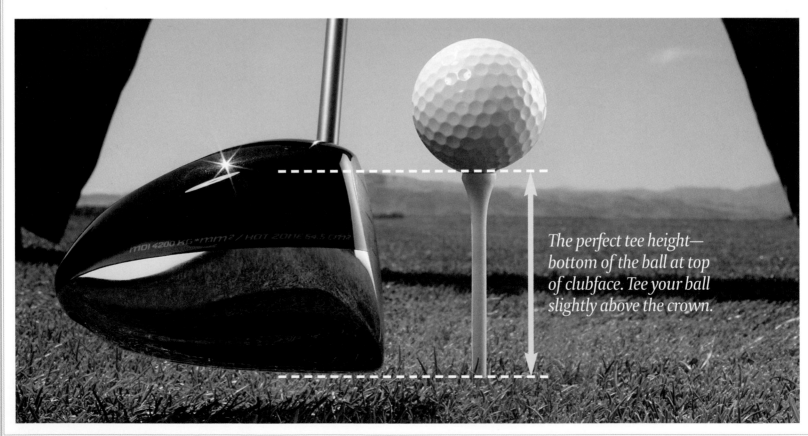

The perfect tee height—bottom of the ball at top of clubface. Tee your ball slightly above the crown.

How to tee up for a...

Scoring iron
For a 6-iron through wedge, bury the tee in the ground so you can see only its head.

Long iron
For longer irons, leave about a ¼-inch of the tee above the ground.

Hybrid club
For hybrids and fairway woods, leave a ½-inch of the tee above the ground.

The Moment of Impact

What happens when you do it right

Catching the ball on the beginning of the upswing produces a higher launch angle and less spin, leading to greater distance.

At impact, the ball compresses because of the force transferred to it from the clubhead. The ball actually sticks to the clubface, sliding and rolling on it for about .0004 seconds.

After impact, the ball leaves the clubface with whatever launch angle, speed and spin your swing has imparted to it. About 1 percent to 2 percent of deformation in the ball remains, causing tiny vibrations inside.

Once clear of the clubface, the vibrations are dampened out, and the ball is on its way.

Striking the ball above the center of the face—the new "sweet spot"—promotes a higher launch angle and less spin. These conditions result in a longer, more efficient ball flight that more than makes up for the clubhead rotation (and loss of ball speed) caused by hitting the ball above dead center.

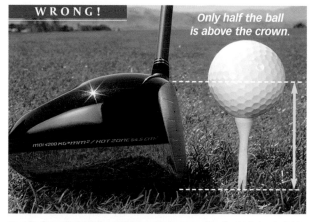

WRONG!

Only half the ball is above the crown.

Results from the mid tee height came in second to the high tee height.

WRONG!

The entire ball is below the crown.

All three handicap groups lost distance on the low tee.

QUICK TIPS TO
IMPROVE YOUR ADDRESS

THE TOP 100 SAY

Kip Puterbaugh
Set up for a level turn

"Take your normal address, and then point your chin toward your right foot. Keep your head in that position and swing back so that your left shoulder turns to your chin. This promotes a stronger move away from the ball and guards against reverse pivoting."

Sandy LaBauve
Pre-set your left hand

"Holding your club in your right hand only, rotate your left hand clockwise until you see at least two knuckles. Curl your left-hand fingers as if gripping a club and then slip it onto the handle in your right hand. This puts your left hand in a neutral position, promoting proper clubface rotation through impact."

Shawn Humphries
Keep your chin up

"Posture is an easy thing to overlook on the course. So when you feel your shoulders start to slouch, take your index finger and push your chin back up. That should get you nice and tall again."

Bill Madonna
Check your stance width

"I recommend an extra-wide stance to increase the role of your lower body and add pop to your swing."

● Set up to the ball with your driver and take an extra step out with each foot.
● Check your stance by dangling your driver down from your right shoulder—it should point to the instep of your right foot.
● Repeat with your left shoulder and have the club point to your left instep.

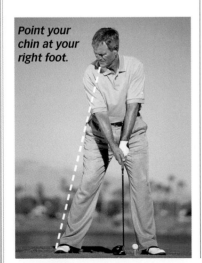

Point your chin at your right foot.

Pre-set your left hand then slide it onto the grip.

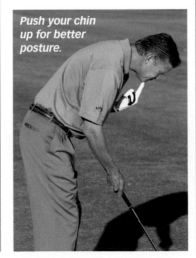

Push your chin up for better posture.

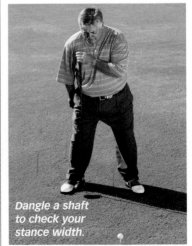

Dangle a shaft to check your stance width.

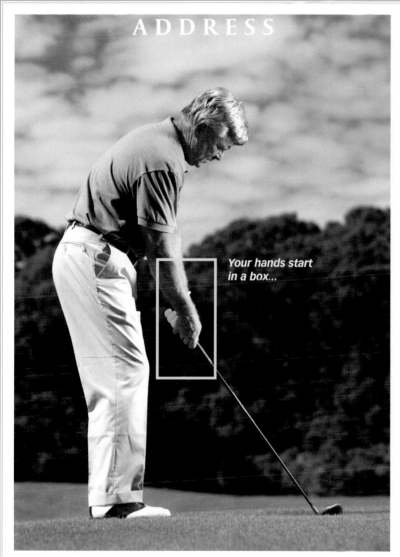

ADDRESS

Your hands start in a box...

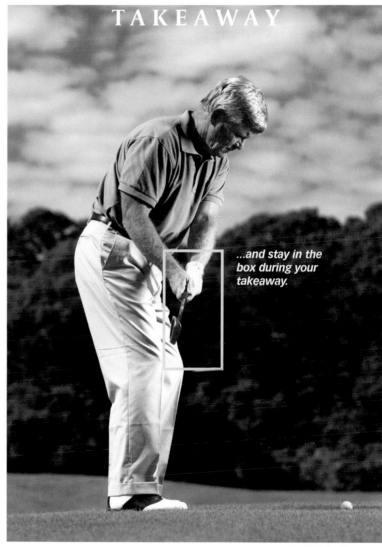

TAKEAWAY

...and stay in the box during your takeaway.

CHECKPOINT

Keep Your Hands "In the Box"

It's a key to getting your swing off to a good start

At address, notice how your hands fit nicely into a small rectangle *[above]*. This is your "hands box," and you'll know it's in the right place if take your stance by bending from your hips so that the shaft is perpendicular to your spine. Make sure that your hands don't leave the box during your takeaway. If they move to the right of the box, you took your club back too far to the inside *[right]*.
—**Michael Hebron**

WRONG!

MAKING YOUR SWING

A solid address position sets the stage for you to create a powerful impact. Here's what to do in each segment of your swing to make good on that promise.

How to Turn Your Shoulders

Tilt as well as turn and get more yards

What you're told to do

Make a big shoulder turn to increase your swing power. However, testing indicates that turning your shoulders too much results in a flat shoulder plane. Flat shoulder turns don't deliver as much speed to the ball as those that are on plane.

What to do instead

Tilt your shoulders as well as turn them. The right amount of turn and tilt will position your shoulder line on the preferred plane line, helping you apply maximum force and speed to the ball.

How to know you're tilting correctly

Place your driver across the front of your shoulders and turn to the top of your backswing. Check the angle of the shaft after you've fully stretched your upper back muscles against your hips. If you've done it right, the shaft (and your shoulders) will point toward the ground slightly above the ball. Now you're set for power and prepped to deliver all of it to the ball.

—Jon Tattersall

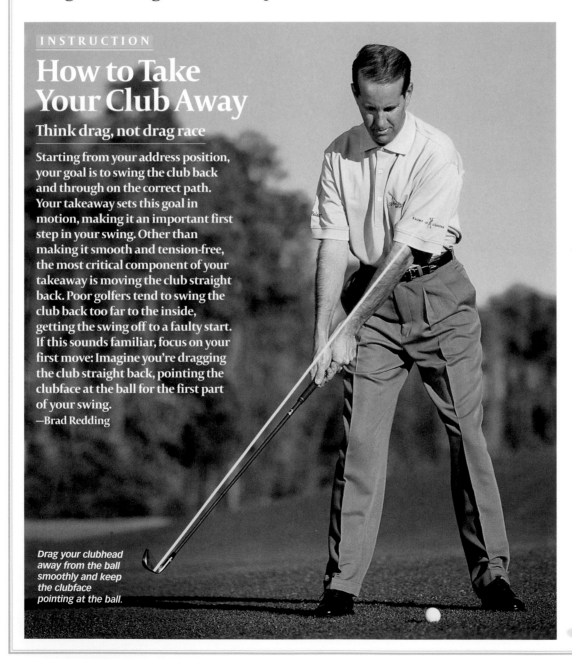

How to Take Your Club Away

Think drag, not drag race

Starting from your address position, your goal is to swing the club back and through on the correct path. Your takeaway sets this goal in motion, making it an important first step in your swing. Other than making it smooth and tension-free, the most critical component of your takeaway is moving the club straight back. Poor golfers tend to swing the club back too far to the inside, getting the swing off to a faulty start. If this sounds familiar, focus on your first move: Imagine you're dragging the club straight back, pointing the clubface at the ball for the first part of your swing.

—Brad Redding

Drag your clubhead away from the ball smoothly and keep the clubface pointing at the ball.

WRONG!

If the shaft looks horizontal then your shoulder turn is too flat and you'll hit a weak shot.

How to Groove a Solid Backswing

Start your swing like a pro with these three drills

A bad backswing is often due to one of three things: a sway away from the target (causing a loss of power), a reverse pivot where you strand weight on your left leg (increasing the chance of a slice) or straightening your right leg (increasing the likelihood of thin contact). Each of these errors makes it nearly impossible to bring your club into the ball on the correct path, giving you little chance for a successful result. Before you spend hours bashing balls on the practice tee or invest your hard-earned money on the latest training aid, try these three drills. A shaft without a head on it can help you determine which problem is affecting your backswing and then show you how to correct it.

—**Brian Mogg**

Fault: Swaying

Fix: Push the shaft into the ground outside your right leg, angled so that it touches your foot and leg up to your knee. Now take your normal backswing. If your right leg pushes the shaft back, you're swaying. Practice until you can turn without moving the shaft.

WRONG!

Fault: Reverse pivoting

Fix: Angle the shaft so that the grip touches your inner right thigh as shown. Now take your backswing. If your right leg pushes the shaft forward toward your front leg, you're reverse pivoting. Practice until you can turn without moving the shaft.

WRONG!

Fault: Losing right-knee flex

Fix: Position the shaft behind you so that the grip presses against the back of your right knee. If your right leg pushes the shaft upward into the back of your thigh on your backswing, you've lost your flex. The grip should remain behind your right knee.

WRONG!

QUICK TIPS TO
IMPROVE YOUR TAKEAWAY

THE TOP 100 SAY

Scott Sackett
Play the angles

"Practice swinging back to hip height while keeping the logo on your glove pointing out. The toe of your clubhead should tilt slightly toward the target line and the leading edge should match your spine angle. That's square."

Brad Redding
Use pad power

"Turn your left hand clockwise on the handle to get the fleshy pad of your hand more on top of the club. This will cup your left wrist and push the club more into your fingers. The resulting grip allows for a better wrist hinge and a straighter takeaway."

Carl Rabito
Turn, don't sway

"Take away the club with your right shoulder while keeping your chin and knees still. This will get your body properly behind the ball and eliminate swaying."

Brad Brewer
Smooth out your takeaway

"Your takeaway should be natural and free-flowing. Practice it by holding the club with only your thumbs and forefingers. This will keep you from whipping your club to the inside or swinging up too steeply."

A two-finger hold grooves a smooth takeaway.

Leading edge matches spine.

Get your pad on top.

Keep your chin and knees quiet.

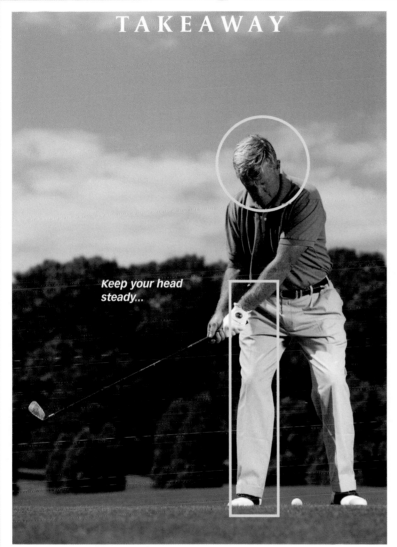

TAKEAWAY

Keep your head steady...

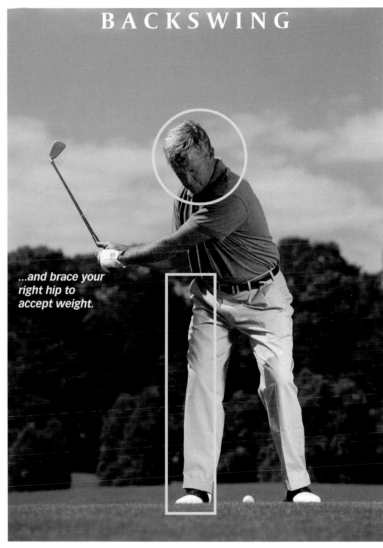

BACKSWING

...and brace your right hip to accept weight.

Don't Lose Your Balance

Brace your right hip to make a stable turn

As you move from your takeaway into your backswing, your main priority is to stay balanced. This means turning *[above]* instead of swaying *[right]*, indicated by the fact your head hasn't moved much from address. Also, monitor your right hip position—keep it in place and braced to accept your weight as it moves from left to right. Think of it as the hub around which your body turns.
—**Michael Hebron**

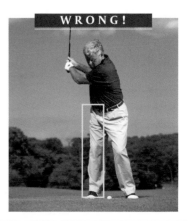

WRONG!

INSTRUCTION

How to Hinge Your Wrists

Do it right and you'll produce power and accuracy

The problem
You know you're supposed to hinge your wrists, but you're not sure how to do it.

The solution
Use the image of a door hinge to guide each of your wrists in the right direction.

Left wrist hinges up.

Right wrist hinges back.

Your wrists hinge in two directions, either up-and-down or back-and-forth. During your takeaway, your left wrist should hinge up, not back. Picture a door hinge on top of your left forearm and thumb with the hinge rod at your wrist to remind you that your left wrist cocks up and down.

Your right wrist does the opposite— it should hinge back on your backswing and forward on your downswing. Imagine a door hinge on top of your wrist and forearm, with the hinge rod in the middle of your wrist. Use that as a guide to direct your right wrist cock both back and through.

During your backswing, picture hinges on both wrists and cock your left wrist up and your right wrist back. That sets your club on the correct backswing plane. If you hinge your right wrist up, your swing will be too steep; if your cock your left wrist back, your swing will get much too flat.
—**Martin Hall**

Correct hinge keeps your club on plane.

INSTRUCTION

The One-Step Power Move

Make an "L" then move it up to achieve maximum width and power

At the end of your takeaway, rotate your forearms and hinge your wrists to create an L. Then, simply move the L to the top by turning your shoulders. This maintains the width of your swing and increases your power.

CHECKPOINT

Your left wrist should be flat and your right wrist bent—the perfect anti-slice position.

TOP 100 POLL

Q Should I think about hinging my wrists on my backswing, or should it happen naturally?

Hinge happens naturally: 71%

You control hinge: 29%

A "Your wrists can and will hinge in response to the momentum of the club, but if you grip the club too tightly that's not going to happen."
—Scott Sackett

1

Set the club parallel to the ground and your target line by rotating your forearms and hinging your wrists.

2

Keep turning your shoulders and make sure the back of your left hand matches the angle of the clubface.

3

Lift your arms as you continue to turn—this is what maintains the L.

KEY MOVE

4

You've done it right if the angles of your left hand and clubface still match and you've created separation between your right side and your right elbow.

How to Sync Up Your Backswing

Try this quick drill to match your arm swing to your turn

Fault: Your arms outrace your shoulder turn on your backswing, throwing your club off plane.

Fix: Feel like your left arm is connected to your chest as you swing your club to the top. This links your arm swing to your shoulder turn so you can keep your swing on plane.

Drill: Take practice swings with a glove tucked under your left armpit. Try to complete your backswing without the glove falling to the ground. At first it will feel like you're going to lose power, but by limiting the length of your arm swing you'll hit the ball better.
—**Donald Crawley**

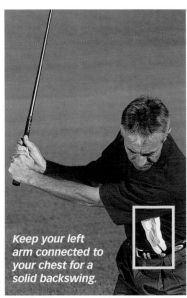

Keep your left arm connected to your chest for a solid backswing.

Keep Your Tilt to Increase Your Coil

Here's how to power up behind the ball for big-time yards

Spine-tilt basics

In a fundamentally sound setup, your spine should tilt away from the target (to your right) about 5 degrees. This side bend is just as critical as your forward bend from your hips. If you're not bent to the right at address, you're bent left, and that's trouble.

How to tilt for power

As you swing to the top, increase your side bend by tilting your upper body to the right at least 10 degrees. A good way to think about it is to feel like you're moving the top of your spine farther away from the target than the bottom as you make your backswing turn. If you try to keep your spine constant in this sense—that is, don't tilt it to the right—you'll end up with a reverse pivot and a possible slice.

—Martin Hall

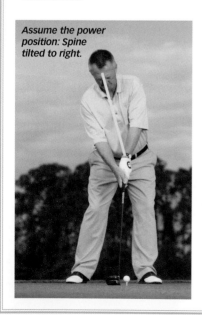

Assume the power position: Spine tilted to right.

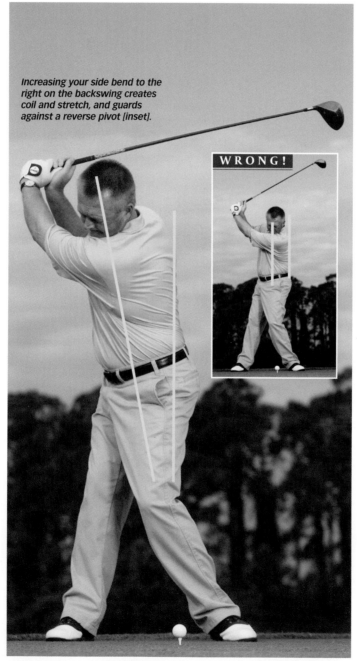

Increasing your side bend to the right on the backswing creates coil and stretch, and guards against a reverse pivot [inset].

WRONG!

Get Dressed to Get Bent

Tie on a tie to learn how to get behind the ball at the top

1

Put on a shirt and tie, or at least imagine that you have. Now bend forward into your golf stance and bump your hips to the left so that your belt buckle moves to the left of the tie. The idea is to move the bottom of your spine, not the top.

2

Swing to the top and check your tie: It should hang farther away from the target than your belt buckle (if the tie is inside your belt buckle you've made a reverse pivot). As you swing back down, try to keep the base of your spine closer to the target than your tie.

—Martin Hall

DRILL

How to Control Your Turn

Use this simple drill to prevent overturning and destroying your backswing coil

Fault: You overturn on your backswing, making your downswing very difficult to control.

Fix: Stop your backswing at its natural stopping point. Try the drill at right to learn where that is. If you catch Tiger Woods during a practice round, you'll see him do this from time to time. This drill proves that your natural backswing length is determined by how far your can turn your left shoulder. If you feel you need more turn, get into the gym and start stretching.
—Bruce Hamilton

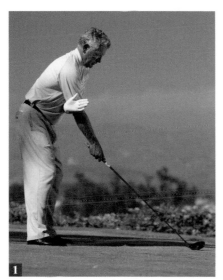

Get into your golf posture and address a ball. Take your left hand off the club and move your left arm under your right, placing the back of your left hand against your right elbow.

Take your backswing, keeping your left hand firmly against your right elbow the entire way to the top. Feel the muscles in your left shoulder tighten as you swing to the top.

When you can't turn any more, stop. Now you're loaded and in control. If you removed your left hand, you'd still be able to turn your right shoulder. That's overturn and it's bad for your game.

INSTRUCTION

Swivel Your Head for Power

Keeping it still just cheats you of distance

The problem
You drive the ball straight, but not very far.

The solution
Move your left ear toward the ground during your backswing.

Why it works
When you try to keep your head still during your full swing, you restrict your ability to make a full turn. Swiveling your head, on the other hand, allows you to make a bigger shoulder turn, and that's a quick way to hit longer tee shots. Watch Tiger Woods when he swings. As he takes the club back, he moves his chin from left to right so that his left ear is closer to the ground at the top. Jack Nicklaus did the same thing, although he swiveled his head before he began his backswing. The key to this move is to keep it natural—allow your head to be carried along by your body turn.
—Brady Riggs

WRONG!
Keeping your head still blocks your upper body from turning as much as it can.

RIGHT!
Allowing your head to swivel with your body turn actually increases rotation and coil.

QUICK TIPS TO
IMPROVE YOUR BACKSWING

THE TOP 100 SAY

Peggy Kirk Bell
Watch your weight

"Don't allow your weight to get outside your right foot on your backswing. This inhibits the move back to your left side on your downswing. Make practice swings with a sand wedge placed under the outside of your right foot to remind you to keep your weight on the *inside* of your right foot."

Roger Gunn
Use your shoulders as a guide

"Start your backswing with your shoulders. Your shoulders swing your arms, and your arms move the club. All of this happens around a steady head, with your left shoulder turning under your chin."

Jason Carbone
The right path to the top

"Picture and feel how you would throw water from a bucket over your right shoulder. That syncs your arms with your body so you can remain in control of your clubhead."

Gerald McCullagh
How to stay on plane

"Set up with your rear end against a wall and swing your club to the top. If you're too inside, the club will almost immediately hit the wall. Practice going halfway back without hitting the wall to ingrain a better backswing plane."

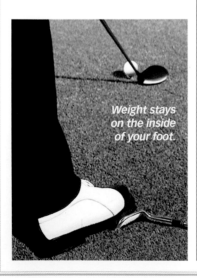

Weight stays on the inside of your foot.

Lead with your shoulders.

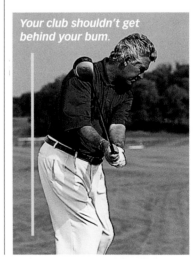

Your club shouldn't get behind your bum.

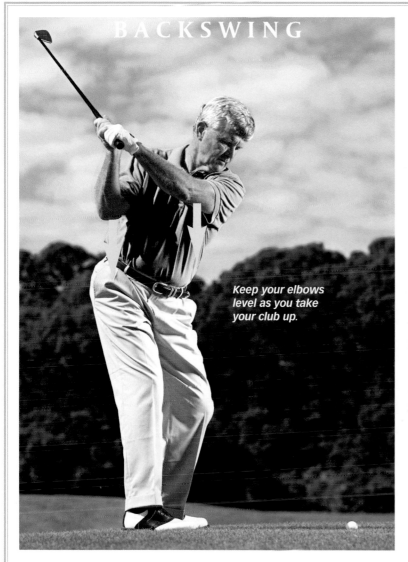

BACKSWING

Keep your elbows level as you take your club up.

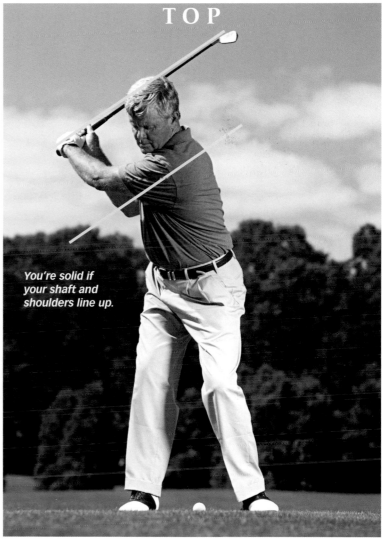

TOP

You're solid if your shaft and shoulders line up.

CHECKPOINT

Use Your Elbows to Swing on Plane

They should point down at the end of your backswing

The goal of your backswing is to get your club up and around you. Your turn takes care of the around part and your arms take care of the up. But simply lifting the club skyward won't get the job done *[right]*. To keep your club on plane, strive for level elbows as you lift your club to the top. Both elbows should point to the ground when you've completed your backswing. You've done it right if your shoulder angle and shaft angle match up.

—Michael Hebron

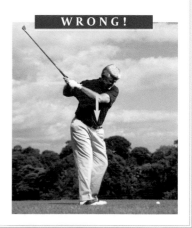

WRONG!

Get Square at the Top to Get Square at Impact

Dial in the correct face angle by bowing or flexing your left wrist

Slices, hooks and everything bad in between result from your clubface not squaring up to the ball at impact. This happens because you're not square at the top of your backswing, either. Good ball strikers know that if you're square to your path at the top (same clubface and shoulder angles), chances are you'll be square again at the bottom.

To check if you're doing it right, swing to the top and hold. If you're a slicer, the clubface is probably pointing at the target. **Try varying amounts of left and right wrist bend to match the face angle to your swing path.** Ultimately strive for a flat left wrist at the top of your swing. This will take care of what's happening at impact.
—**Tim Mahoney**

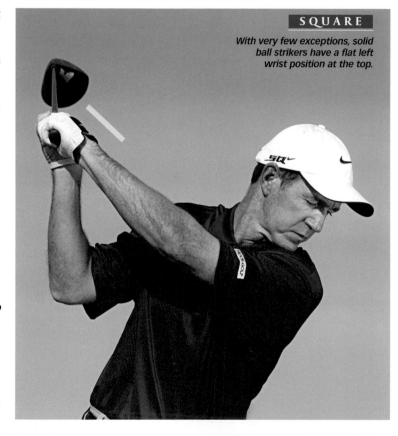

SQUARE

With very few exceptions, solid ball strikers have a flat left wrist position at the top.

OPEN

Adding left wrist cup opens the face and requires perfect timing to get square at impact.

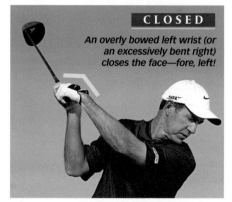

CLOSED

An overly bowed left wrist (or an excessively bent right) closes the face—fore, left!

How to Stay on Plane

Try the "hit the wall" drill

Fault: You turn your shoulders too aggressively to start your downswing and end up pulling the ball or hitting a wicked slice.

Fix: Take your address position with your back to a wall and swing your club to the top. With your clubhead barely touching the wall, bring your arms down to the mid-downswing position and stop. If you're guilty of turning your shoulders too hard, you'll lose contact with the wall *[far right photo]*. This drill helps you "slot" the club by sliding your left arm down and across your chest.—**Darrell Kestner**

Swing to the top...

...maintain contact...

...and never do this.

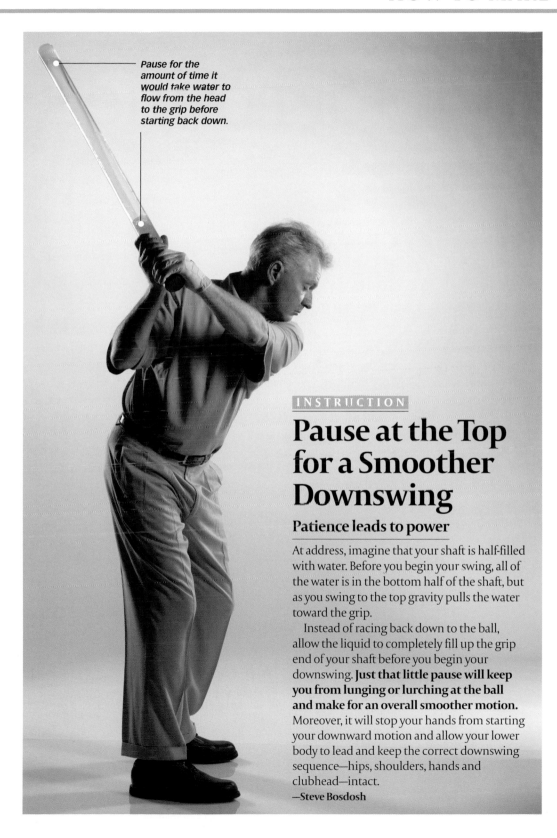

Pause for the amount of time it would take water to flow from the head to the grip before starting back down.

Pause at the Top for a Smoother Downswing

Patience leads to power

At address, imagine that your shaft is half-filled with water. Before you begin your swing, all of the water is in the bottom half of the shaft, but as you swing to the top gravity pulls the water toward the grip.

Instead of racing back down to the ball, allow the liquid to completely fill up the grip end of your shaft before you begin your downswing. **Just that little pause will keep you from lunging or lurching at the ball and make for an overall smoother motion.** Moreover, it will stop your hands from starting your downward motion and allow your lower body to lead and keep the correct downswing sequence—hips, shoulders, hands and clubhead—intact.

—Steve Bosdosh

DRILL

How to Build Up "Lag Power"

Save your swing's energy for impact

Here's how to retain your right-hand angle so you don't release the club too early and rob your swing of precious potential energy.

Stop.

1 Swing any club up to the top and stop. Check that your left shoulder has turned behind the ball with your weight over your right foot. Also, make sure that your left arm is firm and that your right arm is bent 90 degrees.

Stop.

2 Swing the club down until your left arm is parallel to the ground and stop. Make sure your right arm is still bent 90 degrees. Don't simply "pull the handle." This important first move down must come with a forward bump of weight.

Swing!

3 Straighten your right arm and fire your club through impact. Feel how the piston move puts outward pressure on the handle and keeps your wrists from losing their hinge. The only time both arms are straight is after impact.

QUICK TIPS TO
IMPROVE YOUR TOP POSITION

THE TOP 100 SAY

Dr. Gary Wiren
Swing to your right shoulder

"Try to turn back as far as your flexibility allows, feeling resistance in your left side. If you do this correctly, then all you need to do is get your hands over your right shoulder and the club will be on plane."

Mike Davis
Don't collapse at the top

"Swinging your club past parallel doesn't mean extra power—it just means you're overswinging, usually because you collapse your wrists and left elbow at the top. To fix this, firm up your grip and try to keep your left arm straight. This doesn't shorten your swing—it strengthens it."

Bruce Hamilton
Get out of the way

"Set up in your golf posture, and imagine you're standing at home plate. The pitcher throws a fastball at your head. Your natural reaction is to quickly spin your left shoulder away from the pitcher, with your right shoulder moving behind you. That's the kind of turn you need for power."

Tom Stickney
Do the bump

"Once you're set at the top, find something to jump-start your move back down. Try 'bumping' your left hip to the right of your target. It's an excellent way to trigger your hip turn as well as keep you from coming over the top."

Hands to right shoulder.

Folding your left elbow is a no-no.

For the correct amount of turn...

...get out of the way of an inside fastball.

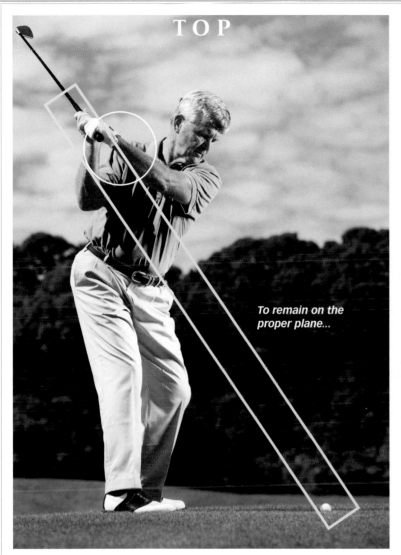

TOP

To remain on the proper plane...

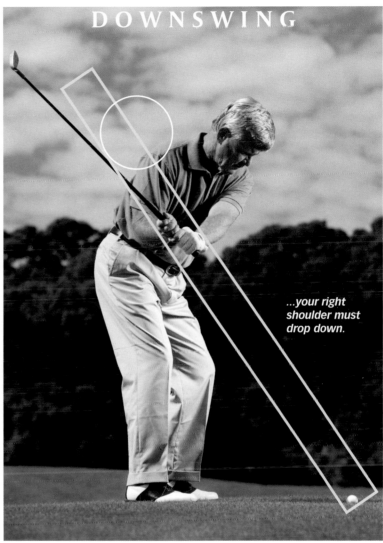

DOWNSWING

...your right shoulder must drop down.

Do You Have the "Magic Move"?

Drop your right shoulder down to keep your club on plane

If you're solid at the top, most of your work is done. But you can lose it all in an instant if you make the wrong first move down. Check what's happening with your right shoulder. Does it drop down at the start of your downswing? If it does, you're in a great position to deliver the club on plane [yellow box]. If your right shoulder stays at the same height [right], your downswing will be above plane and your chances of a pull or slice will skyrocket.
—Michael Hebron

WRONG!

INSTRUCTION

How to Make a Solid Downswing

Keep it simple for sweet contact

Your goal should be to hit the sweet spot more consistently with every club in your bag. The best way for you to achieve it is to properly sequence your downswing. By that I mean following the four Hs: hips, handle, hands and (club)head. Thinking of your downswing in this order simplifies your thoughts, reduces the amount of effort you make, and produces more yards and purer strikes. The sequence of hips, handle, hands and clubhead is paramount for success. Here's how to get it.

Your hips should stay in line with the tee.

1

Rotate your hips to start your swing

Stick a tee in the butt end of a 5-iron, hold it across your hips and get into your address position. The tee should point toward your target *[inset]*. Now shift onto your left leg, turning the tee to the left *[above photo]*—this is the motion your hips should take as you start your downswing motion.

2

Lean the handle forward

The handle has to beat the clubhead to the ball in order to get powerful and consistent impact. Again, use your 5-iron with the tee in the grip. Swing to the top and, as you start down, immediately get the tee to point to the ground *[above photo]*. This will allow the grip to reach the ball first.

3

Keep your hands cocked

Your wrists should remain hinged throughout your downswing. A common flaw is to release your hands too early and throw the clubhead at the ball. Instead, keep your hands cocked until after the handle has passed the ball.

DRILL

Drop the Clubhead Down

Here's the secret to solid ball striking

Since the handle of the club leads the way to impact, the clubhead will descend on a slight arc when it contacts the ball. To get a feel for that sensation, try this drill.

1. Push a row of three tees into the ground two clubhead widths behind the ball as shown.

2. Address the ball with a 6-iron and swing. You want to barely nip the tees on the backswing and then completely miss them on the downswing.

3. Swing all the way through to the finish. If you miss the tees coming down, the clubhead correctly lagged behind the handle, and you should be admiring a high, straight shot.
—**John Elliott**

DRILL

Hit Correctly From the Inside

Trace an in-to-out path and you'll never slice again

Fault
You swing across the ball. Ideally, your clubhead should approach the ball on a path that's slightly inside of your target line.

Fix
Place three balls diagonally as shown and swing. Try to contact only the center ball. The only way to do this is to swing on an inside-out path. If you come over the top, you'll definitely hit the ball on the left, and maybe even all three balls. This drill works with every club in your bag.

Bonus
The "gate" created by the three balls is excellent for turning that slice-causing swipe into a powerful hit.
—**Darrell Kestner**

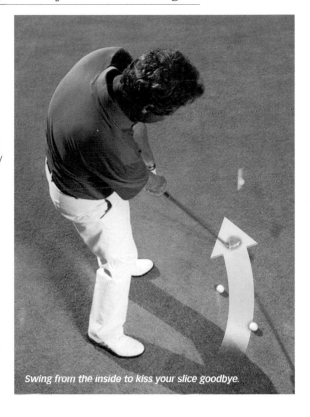

Swing from the inside to kiss your slice goodbye.

Swing From Seven to One

Groove a power-rich inside delivery by picturing a clock at your feet

Swing to the one o'clock position on a clock face to groove the right path.

Imagine your feet rest at the 9 o'clock position on a clock face. As you swing down from the top, try to sweep your clubhead on a path that crosses 7 o'clock on its approach to the ball, and crosses 1 o'clock after impact. If you slice, you're likely swinging from 5 o'clock to 11 o'clock.
—**Michael Breed**

QUICK TIPS TO
IMPROVE YOUR DOWNSWING

THE TOP 100 SAY

Don Hurter
Shift, don't slide

"Many players try to create power by sliding their hips toward the target. Instead of sliding, make a slight shift and then rotate. To feel the right move, swing a 6-iron with your left arm only. As you start down, shift and rotate your hips and legs forward. You'll feel your left arm fall down your chest. That's the drop you need."

Rick McCord
Make a heads-down move

"From the top, flex your knees and lower your head to pull your arms down. This pulling motion is what brings the club into impact with the clubhead lagging behind your hands. As you do this, continue to rotate your hips toward the target."

Dan Pasquariello
Forget your legs

"Too much hip and leg action leads to an open clubface at impact. Your downswing should mirror your backswing, and since your arms take away the club, they should swing it down into the ball, too."

Dana Rader
Keep it tucked

"Tuck your right arm against your right side on your downswing—it helps you drop your right shoulder, putting the club on the correct path into impact. If your right arm stays away from your side, your shoulders will turn horizontally, causing an outside-in swing path and weak slices."

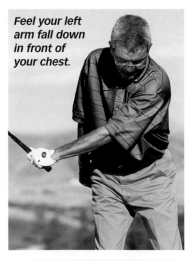

Feel your left arm fall down in front of your chest.

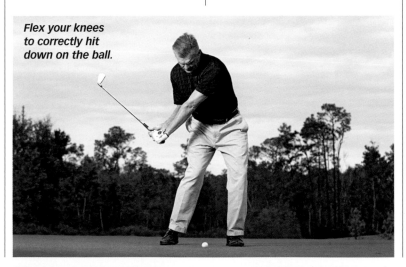

Flex your knees to correctly hit down on the ball.

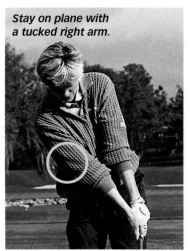

Stay on plane with a tucked right arm.

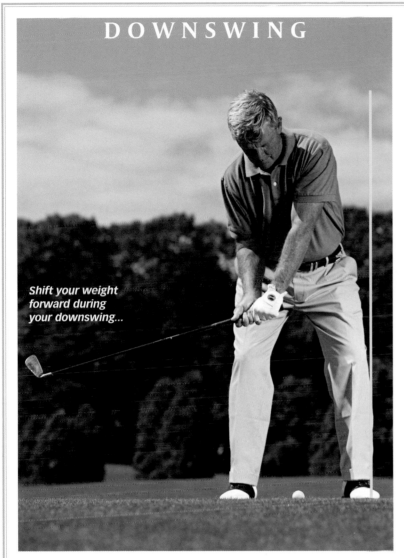

DOWNSWING

Shift your weight forward during your downswing...

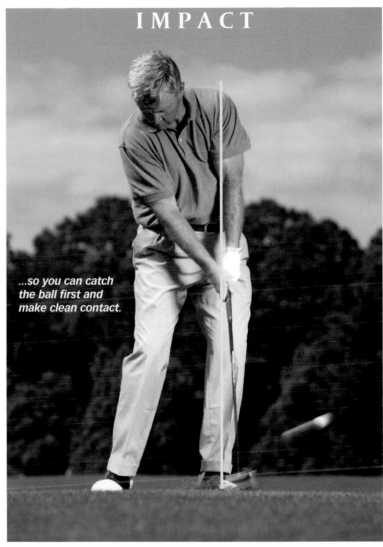

IMPACT

...so you can catch the ball first and make clean contact.

Bottom Out in the Right Spot

Move forward to make make ball-first contact

If you often hit fat or thin shots, pay attention to how far your lower body moves toward the target on your downswing. This forward motion allows your hands to get to the ball before your clubhead, and moves the bottom of your swing arc toward the target so you contact the ball before the ground. If you hang on your right side *[right]*, you'll make contact behind the ball (fat) or after your swing has already bottomed out (thin).
—**Michael Hebron**

WRONG!

How to Make a Powerful Impact

Strive for these positions and your shots will rocket off the clubface

If you've followed the plan to this point, quality impact will happen by itself, but knowing where you should be when you strike the ball is an important step in improving the other elements of your swing.

While they're not mirror images of each other, address and impact positions do share many common traits. You'll always make solid contact if your spine and the back of your head are aligned just like they were at address, and if the shaft angle at impact is the same as it was at setup.

RE-CREATE ADDRESS
Copy your setup posture—imagine someone holding your head up (but not still) before impact.

REMAIN BALANCED
Keep your knees unlocked and stay balanced over the balls of both feet.

KEY MOVE
The clubface should point in the same direction as the back of your left hand—at the target.

STAY IN-LINE
The butt of the club points at your belt buckle. If it points behind, you released too early.

GET SHIFTY
Shift your weight from the inside of your left foot to the outside and keep your right foot stable.

Open the Door

Turn your hands like you're opening a door to square up the clubface through impact

1 Retain the hinge in your wrists deep into the downswing. That saves energy for impact.

2 Continue to move your hands while keeping your right shoulder back.

3 Rotate the back of your left hand as if you're turning a doorknob.

4 Open the door so that the back of your left hand faces the target.

5 Keep your arms extended through impact (so you don't chicken wing).

6 Maintain the triangle formed by your arms, hands and shaft.
—Shawn Humphries

How to Avoid Scooped Shots

Keep your right wrist bent for solid strikes

Fault

You try to scoop the ball into the air with your irons and wedges. This instinct to lift leads to mis-hits and missed greens.

Here's how to strike your irons pure so you can hit your targets.

Hit punch shots with one arm to learn how to keep your right wrist bent into impact.

Fix #1: Slap your hand

Hold your left hand out as shown. Now slap it with your right—see how you make that angle with your right wrist? That angle is the key to a crisp hit. It happens naturally when you slap something because your focus is on the slap, not on getting the ball airborne.

Fix #2: Hit a punch

Take a 7-iron and hit half-swing punch shots with your right arm only. To make solid contact, you'll need a descending blow, which comes from that right-wrist angle mentioned at left. Add your left hand and some weight shift back and through and hit some longer shots. Your ball striking will improve in no time.
—Charlie King

Which Slice Is Your Slice?

Finding the answer is the key to fixing your impact

The predominant ball flight of most recreational players is a slice (a shot that curves wildly from left to right). The first step to stopping your slice is to determine which type of slice is destroying your game. That way you'll know if you have to correct your face angle at impact, your downswing path or both.

POLL 52% of you hit a straight slice

POLL 18% of you hit a pull slice

POLL 30% of you hit a push slice

Straight slice
Your path is solid but your clubface is open at impact. The ball starts straight, then curves.

Pull slice
Your path is outside-in and your clubface is open. The ball starts left, then curves right.

Push slice
Your path is too inside-out and your clubface is open. The ball starts right, then curves farther right.

QUICK TIPS TO
IMPROVE YOUR IMPACT

THE TOP 100 SAY

Todd Anderson
Let your hands win

"Picture a finish line at the ball. Try to get your right knee to that line at impact with your hands leading the clubhead. Shifting your right knee toward the target helps keep your clubhead on a downward path, and if your hands stay ahead of the club, you'll get the most power out of your swing."

Mike Bender
Lean the shaft forward

"This drill teaches you to make contact with a forward lean to the shaft. Draw a line in the sand down the middle of your stance. Using your left hand only, swing across the line, blasting out several divots in front of it. The object is to hit the sand and stop, so the grip stays ahead of the clubhead."

Brady Riggs
Stack up at impact

"Set up to the ball with a 7-iron, then pull your left foot back 18 inches and rest it on your toe. Make half-speed swings and note how the awkward stance forces your upper body to remain on top of your lower body (otherwise you'll fall off-balance). That's the sensation you're looking for."

Fred Griffin
Shake hands with the target

"From some angles it looks like your forearms cross shortly after impact—but that's an illusion. In a proper release, your right hand remains to the side of the shaft. Halfway into the follow-through, it should look like you're shaking hands with someone to your immediate left."

Hands reach the ball first.

Lean the shaft forward.

Stack your upper body over your lower.

Shake hands with the target.

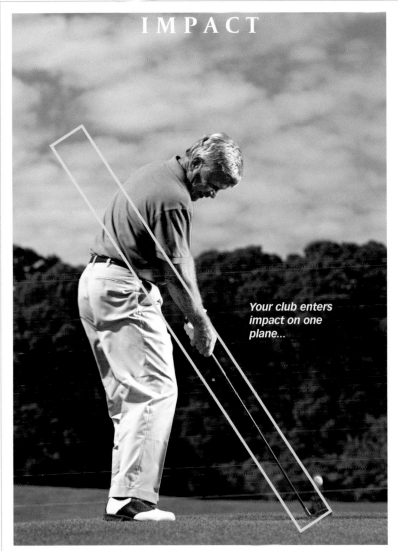

IMPACT

Your club enters impact on one plane...

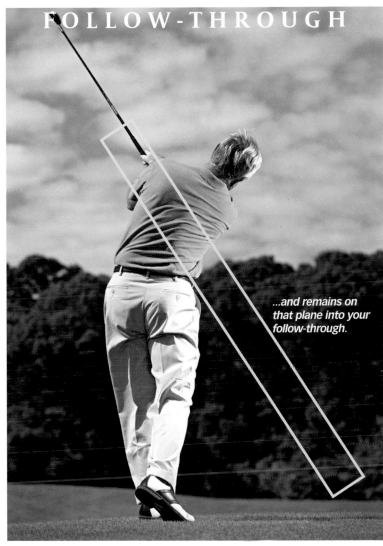

FOLLOW-THROUGH

...and remains on that plane into your follow-through.

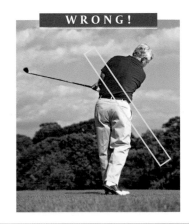

CHECKPOINT

Mirror Your Downswing Path After Impact

Take the right (plane) exit

Very few golfers consider what happens after impact very important. But the plane on which your club exits the hitting area says a lot about the path you took on your backswing and downswing. If it's to the left [*see photo at right*], you swung outside-in and hit a slice or pull. Try to re-trace your backswing on your through-swing. You'll have to maintain your forward bend until the force of your swing causes you to straighten up in your finish.

—**Michael Hebron**

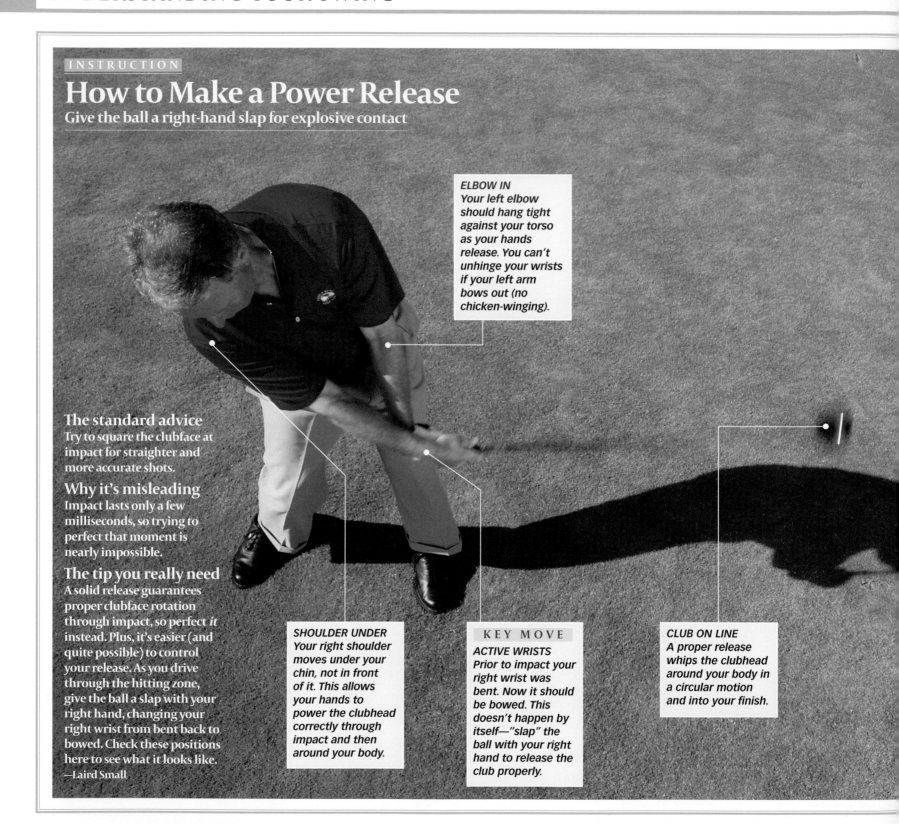

How to Make a Power Release

Give the ball a right-hand slap for explosive contact

ELBOW IN
Your left elbow should hang tight against your torso as your hands release. You can't unhinge your wrists if your left arm bows out (no chicken-winging).

The standard advice
Try to square the clubface at impact for straighter and more accurate shots.

Why it's misleading
Impact lasts only a few milliseconds, so trying to perfect that moment is nearly impossible.

The tip you really need
A solid release guarantees proper clubface rotation through impact, so perfect *it* instead. Plus, it's easier (and quite possible) to control your release. As you drive through the hitting zone, give the ball a slap with your right hand, changing your right wrist from bent back to bowed. Check these positions here to see what it looks like.
—Laird Small

SHOULDER UNDER
Your right shoulder moves under your chin, not in front of it. This allows your hands to power the clubhead correctly through impact and then around your body.

KEY MOVE

ACTIVE WRISTS
Prior to impact your right wrist was bent. Now it should be bowed. This doesn't happen by itself—"slap" the ball with your right hand to release the club properly.

CLUB ON LINE
A proper release whips the clubhead around your body in a circular motion and into your finish.

DRILL

Wristy Business

Try this drill to improve your release

Settle into your stance without a club and take a mock grip with your hands. Flex your right wrist back. Your left wrist will bow automatically. This is exactly where you want to be as you approach impact, with your hands leading the clubhead.

Create your release by hinging your right wrist into a bowed position at half speed. Notice how your left wrist bends back as a result and how your body turns and opens slightly to the target to support this action.

Continue this drill, picking up speed each time. The faster you do it, the more you should feel like you're "slapping" the ball with your right hand, or flexing it forward like you do when you shoot hoops. That's the feel you're after.

INSTRUCTION

Control Every Shot

You can create any ball flight you want by turning your left-hand knuckles either up or down

Knuckles down is good for...

All full swings, rough escapes and fairway-bunker shots

Knuckle down for power

For maximum speed and distance, gradually rotate your forearms (right over left) and turn your wrists through the hitting zone so that your left-hand knuckles and left elbow point toward the ground in your release.

Why it works

Maximum clubhead acceleration occurs when your hands give in to the force of your downswing and turn over to release your clubhead toe over heel. You know you've reached your power threshold when your left-hand knuckles and left elbow point down in your release.

How to do it

Through the hitting zone, sling the club smoothly past your left thigh by trying to "flick" an imaginary object off your left thumb. Or, think of how you'd turn your left hand out to hitch a ride.

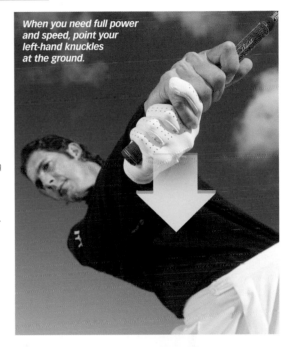

When you need full power and speed, point your left-hand knuckles at the ground.

Knuckles up is good for...

Greenside bunker shots, chips and pitches, knock-downs, bump-and-runs and punch shots.

Knuckle up for control

For shots that require control over raw distance, keep your hands ahead of the clubhead at impact and the back of your left hand pointed up in your follow-through.

Why it works

You're basically holding off your release, which is the fastest part of your swing. While you'll lose distance (which you don't need on these shots), you'll gain extra accuracy because you're squaring your clubface with your body turn instead of your hands, and big muscles are easier to control than little ones.

How to do it

Through impact, cup your left wrist slightly and lift the back of your left hand toward the sky. This usually produces a scoopy impact, but if you set up with your hands ahead of the ball, your contact will be crisp.

—Robert Baker

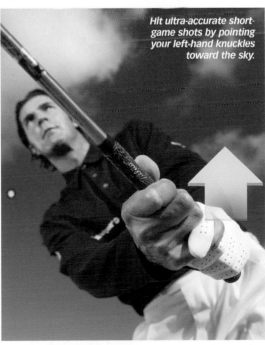

Hit ultra-accurate short-game shots by pointing your left-hand knuckles toward the sky.

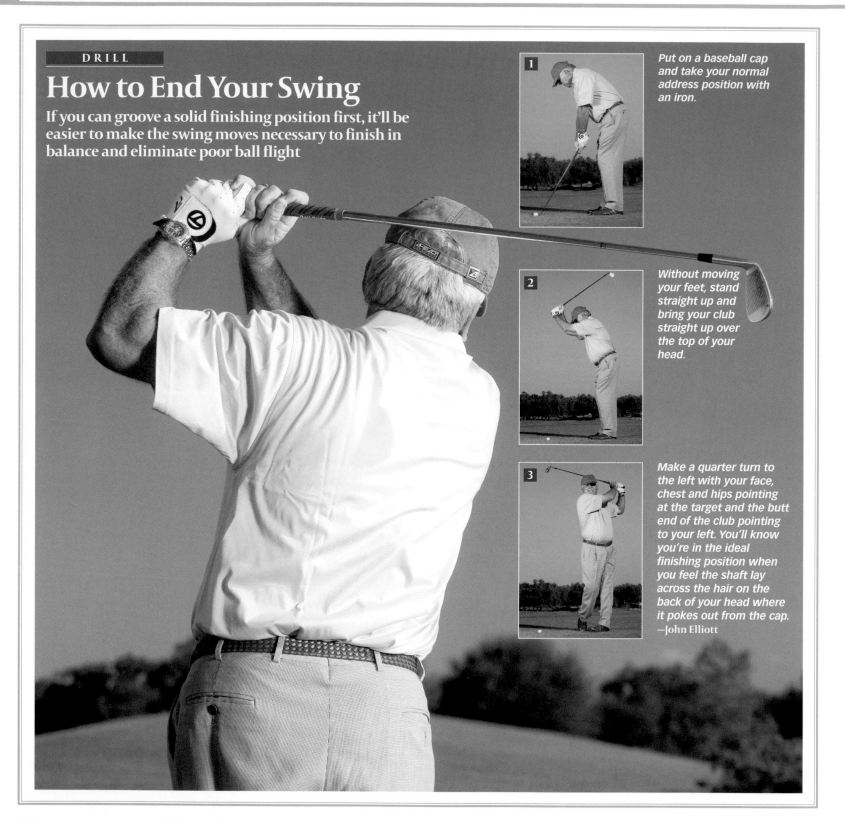

DRILL

How to End Your Swing

If you can groove a solid finishing position first, it'll be easier to make the swing moves necessary to finish in balance and eliminate poor ball flight

1 Put on a baseball cap and take your normal address position with an iron.

2 Without moving your feet, stand straight up and bring your club straight up over the top of your head.

3 Make a quarter turn to the left with your face, chest and hips pointing at the target and the butt end of the club pointing to your left. You'll know you're in the ideal finishing position when you feel the shaft lay across the hair on the back of your head where it pokes out from the cap.
—John Elliott

Use Your Finish to Shape Shots

Pre-set your club to hit draws and fades on command

How to hit a draw

Get into your address position and swing to waist-high in your follow-through. Move your arms and club so that...

● Your club points 10 yards right of the target.

● Your right arm is fully extended and in line with your clubshaft.

● The toe of your club points up.

● Get a feel for this position and swing back to the top of your backswing. Notice how your club automatically moves to the inside and around you *[inset below]*. This is the perfect position from which to attack the ball from the inside out.

● When you proceed to play the shot, swing your club in an effort to re-create the feel of the backswing and release that you just rehearsed.

Start here to hit a draw.

Fade top position

How to hit a fade

Swing to a waist-high follow-through from address and move your arms and club so that...

● Your left arm is fully extended and creates an "L" with the clubshaft.

● The toe of your club points right.

● The shaft points 10 feet left of your target.

● Ingrain this feel and then swing back to the top of your backswing. This time, your pre-set fade release automatically makes you take the club more up and to the outside *[inset below]*, which is the perfect position to produce left-to-right spin at impact.

● When you proceed to play the shot, swing your club in an effort to re-create the feel of the backswing and release that you just rehearsed.

—**Mike Adams**

Start here to hit a fade.

Draw top position

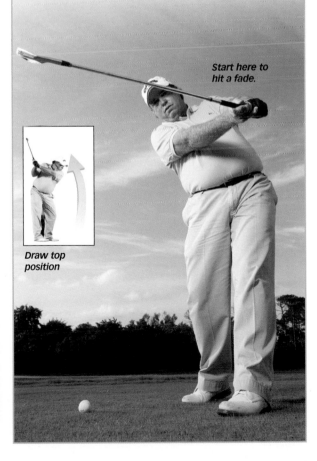

Here's Proof That Your Finish Means Everything

Recently, a Swedish woman came to me to learn how to play golf. She didn't speak English and had never even touched a club. I tried to use pictures and video to explain the swing, but since she only spoke Swedish she couldn't understand me.

Step One was to physically place her into a sound address position. Only when she had ingrained this position into her muscle memory was she allowed to make a backswing

Step Two was to physically take her up to the top of the backswing and pause her there.

Step Three was to hit the ball from her static top position. After each swing, I physically adjusted her into a proper finish position and made her hold it for a few counts. I did this for every swing, during every lesson, an hour a day for six days in a row. By the end of the sixth day she was hitting her 7-iron 130 yards with a nice, high draw. It was incredible to see how quickly muscle memory took over her swing. In just under a week she was able to feel if and when she was correct in each spot.

The key to this lesson was pausing at each position. This allowed her to feel what was correct, especially the end point, to give her the feeling of where she needed to be.

Most golfers never truly know if what they feel in their swings is right or wrong, especially when they're finishing their swings off balance and out of control.

—**Mike Bender**

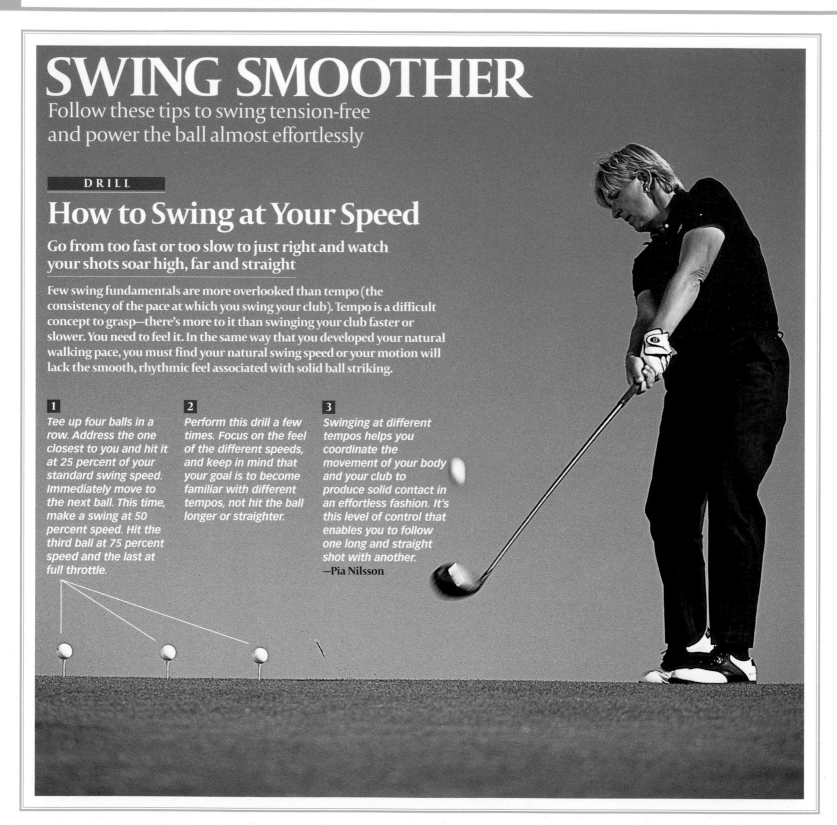

SWING SMOOTHER

Follow these tips to swing tension-free
and power the ball almost effortlessly

DRILL

How to Swing at Your Speed

**Go from too fast or too slow to just right and watch
your shots soar high, far and straight**

Few swing fundamentals are more overlooked than tempo (the
consistency of the pace at which you swing your club). Tempo is a difficult
concept to grasp—there's more to it than swinging your club faster or
slower. You need to feel it. In the same way that you developed your natural
walking pace, you must find your natural swing speed or your motion will
lack the smooth, rhythmic feel associated with solid ball striking.

1
*Tee up four balls in a
row. Address the one
closest to you and hit it
at 25 percent of your
standard swing speed.
Immediately move to
the next ball. This time,
make a swing at 50
percent speed. Hit the
third ball at 75 percent
speed and the last at
full throttle.*

2
*Perform this drill a few
times. Focus on the feel
of the different speeds,
and keep in mind that
your goal is to become
familiar with different
tempos, not hit the ball
longer or straighter.*

3
*Swinging at different
tempos helps you
coordinate the
movement of your body
and your club to
produce solid contact in
an effortless fashion. It's
this level of control that
enables you to follow
one long and straight
shot with another.*
—Pia Nilsson

Get Smooth With the Right Hinge

Time your wrist cock with your body pivot

The problem

You often lose the timing of your swing because you either delay or quicken your wrist hinge in your takeaway. These errors destroy the natural momentum of your club going back, and can do the same on the way back down via a late release or one that occurs far too early in the downswing.

The solution

Hinge your wrists at the correct time, which varies depending on the iron you have in your hands and the shot you need to play. Adjust the timing of your hinge to create perfect rhythm and tempo.

For full swings with your mid - and long irons...
Simply maintain the hinge that you established at address during your takeaway. Full swings require a longer body pivot, so hinge less and turn more as you bring your hands to waist height. You know you've done it right if your chest points away from the target and the butt of the club is outside your right leg when the shaft is parallel to the ground.

WRONG!

A late hinge creates a late release and poor tempo.

Error on the quick side

You've been told to keep the clubhead low in your takeaway, which is good advice unless you overdo it and remove the hinge in your wrists that was established at address [photo above]. Now you're late on your hinge going back, which means you'll be early on your hinge going forward, and you'll hit the shot fat. As a general rule, hinge your wrists sooner and you'll hear the sweet sound of crisp contact more frequently.

CHECKPOINT

For half-swing shots inside 50 yards, your right wrist should hinge before your hands pass your right knee.

For half-swing shots...
Make a full hinge before your hands pass your right knee. Short swings from 30-60 yards require much less body pivot, which means your wrists must hinge sooner in your backswing. You've done it right if your chest points at your right foot and the butt of the club is on top of your right leg when the shaft is parallel to the ground.
—**Dom DiJulia**

Be Loose, Not Lazy

Use "downtime" on the course to your tempo's advantage

Fault: You make casual, right-hand only swings while waiting on the tee box or in the fairway for the group ahead to clear away. While most of these mini-swings are made with the sole purpose of passing time, they'll ingrain bad habits since you're likely just flipping your club back and through— a big no-no.

Fix: Continue to make your mini-swings when the course backs up, but do so with a purpose. Repeat a solid back-and-forth motion with an eye toward removing tension in your arms and hands. Take it a step further and make sure you're rotating your right hand as the club sweeps beneath you. Turn into your follow-through with the toe of your club pointing up. When it comes time to play your shot, you'll be loose and ready to deliver a smooth, powerful strike.
—**John Elliott**

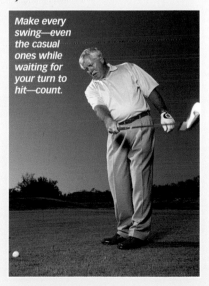

Make every swing—even the casual ones while waiting for your turn to hit—count.

HIT STRAIGHTER

Try these teacher tricks to find the fairway or the green with laser-like accuracy

INSTRUCTION

One Minute to Straighter Shots

Watch your watch to create perfect impact every time

In order to control the direction of your shots, you must control the position of the clubface at impact. Unfortunately, knowing exactly where the clubface is pointing throughout your swing is difficult, but you can do it if you focus on something you can see, such as your wristwatch.

Unless your grip is way too strong or very weak, the face of your watch points in the same direction as the clubface. So your goal is to get into the habit of pointing your watch at the target at impact. The position of your watch at impact also can help you discover errors in your swing and clubface position. During your next practice session, watch your watch and you'll find out how to hit straighter shots.

—John Dahl

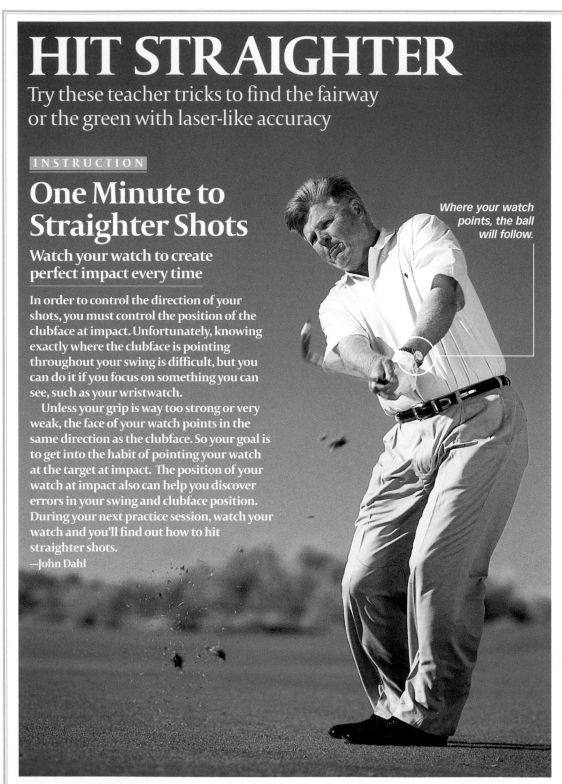

Where your watch points, the ball will follow.

Solid
Straight shots result from squared impact, evidenced by your hands leading the clubface into impact and your watch facing the target.

Hook
If your watch points behind you, your swing is guilty of too much arm and hand rotation. The clubface is closed at impact, and the ball is heading left.

Slice
If your watch points to the right of the target (or even remotely skyward), the clubface is open, and you're looking at a banana ball.

Cast
Great ball strikers have a flat left wrist at impact. If your knuckles get in front of your watch, that's an early release, and you won't know where the ball is going.

INSTRUCTION

How to Tame Your First-Tee Jitters

Mental tips for getting your round off to a solid start

If you get nervous standing over your first tee shot, relax. Even Tour players feel opening-tee jitters at major tournaments and other big events. The best way to beat first-tee pressure is to use your warm-up time to get into a playing mode rather than just bashing balls with no goals in mind. Here are three keys to becoming a cool customer on the first tee.

1 Make sure your pre-round warm-up is exactly that, and not practice. Don't work on swing keys or ask for tips when you have 30 minutes or less until your tee time. Any confusion about technique will only heighten the pressure you feel later.

2 Vary your clubs and distances often, never hitting more than three shots in a row with the same club. Take a cue from well-coached basketball teams. The players don't take countless free throws before a game, but instead hit shots from various spots around the court.

3 Spend the last 10 minutes of your warm-up "playing" the first three holes of the course you're about to tackle. Hit the club you plan to hit off the first tee and then hit the appropriate club for your approach. Go through your pre-shot routine and try to execute the shots exactly as you would on the course. Repeat this for the next two holes. This drill heightens your visualization and helps you narrow your targets. You'll arrive at the first tee ready to play, which will lessen the pressure.

Richard Coop, Ph.D., *GOLF Magazine's* mental-game consultant

CHECKPOINT

Be a Palm Pilot

Your right hand controls the clubface

If you've taken a proper grip, your right palm should mimic the angle of your clubface. So instead of trying to control your clubhead, control your right hand. Make sure your right palm points down at the ball once it reaches your right thigh in your downswing. This forces you to properly hit down on the ball and is a good start to squaring the clubface.

—David Glenz

A square clubface at impact doesn't guarantee success, but it gives you a much better chance for it.

Point your right palm down at the ball as your club reaches the hitting zone to make powerful contact on the sweet spot.

HIT PURER SHOTS

You know when you've crushed it—here's how to get that feeling time and again

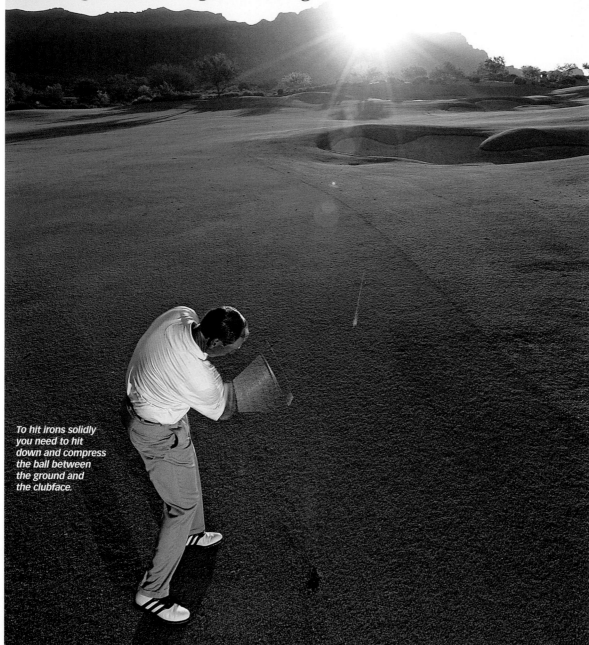

To hit irons solidly you need to hit down and compress the ball between the ground and the clubface.

Learn From Your Divots

It's the first step to ball-first contact

Good iron players hit the ball first, then the turf. Next time you're at the range, press a tee into the ground about one inch from the ball outside your target line *[top photo]*. Hit the ball with your 7-iron. **If you make ball-first contact, the divot will be on the target side of the tee** *[bottom photo]*. If the divot starts slightly behind the tee, you hit it a little fat and sacrificed distance. If the entire divot is behind the tee, you chunked it. Try to hit 10 shots in a row with your divot starting on the target side of the tee.

Place a tee opposite your ball to test your divot pattern.

Your divots should be in front of the tee and point to the target.

DRILL

Do You Extend or Flip?

Only one is good for your game

WRONG!

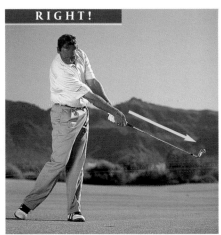

RIGHT!

Flip is not hip

If you hit low-flying skulls, chances are your clubhead is whipping ahead of your hands as you try to scoop the ball into the air [above]. That puts the leading edge of the club into contact with the ball. You'll know you're doing it if your clubhead is higher than your hands in your release.

Hit down and through

Hit a series of balls and stop the clubhead below the level of your waist [above]. You'll find it impossible to scoop at the ball—and necessary to hit down on it—to achieve this shortened finish. Don't be afraid to shorten your follow-through if you mis-hit a few irons in the middle of your round.

DRILL

Drop Your Foot Back

It helps you get your weight on your front foot

Address a ball in the middle of your stance while holding a 5-iron. Bend your right knee, point your toe into the ground and hit the ball. By dropping your right foot back, away from the target line, you can't lean away from the target—a classic reverse pivot—as you make your downswing. Instead, you will rotate around your left foot and make a descending blow on the back of the ball.
—**Mike Malaska**

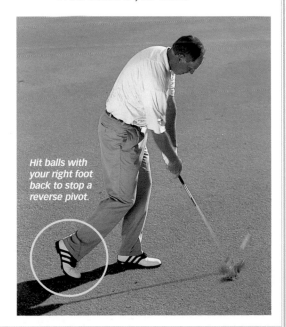

Hit balls with your right foot back to stop a reverse pivot.

INSTRUCTION

Slot the Club for Solid Drives

Keeping your right arm tucked against your side is the key

Fault: You prematurely release (or cast) the clubhead.

Fix: Take your driver to the top of your swing with your right arm. Hold a plastic bottle against the right side of your torso as shown, then bring your club down to impact. If you squash the bottle before you unhinge your wrists, you delay your release until the moment when it creates the perfect blend of power and accuracy. If you don't, you allowed the clubhead to outrace your hands to the ball, which costs you in yards and missed fairways.
—**Robert Baker**

1

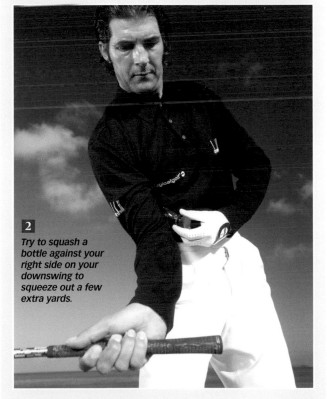

2

Try to squash a bottle against your right side on your downswing to squeeze out a few extra yards.

CHECK YOUR TECHNIQUE

You know what to do, but are you doing it right? Here's how to find out.

Mirror the Perfect Swing

Use your reflection—and hip turn—to stay on plane from start to finish

Your goal

To create the perfect swing plane. The perfect plane is described as a circle tilted to match the angle of your clubshaft at address. That's a good visual, but you can't attach a hula-hoop to your 7-iron. All you need to perfect your swing plane is masking tape and a mirror.

How to achieve it

Let's assume that your address position is solid, with your back straight, knees flexed and ready for action, and your arms hanging underneath your shoulders. Find a full-length mirror and take your address position in front of it. Study your reflection and note the angle of your clubshaft. Place tape on the mirror along this line (we'll call this *Line 1*), and then another in the opposite direction (*Line 2*), so that the two lines intersect at 90 degrees. These lines hold the key to grooving an on-plane swing because they help you get your body and club in the correct positions on both the backswing and the follow-through.

—Mike LaBauve

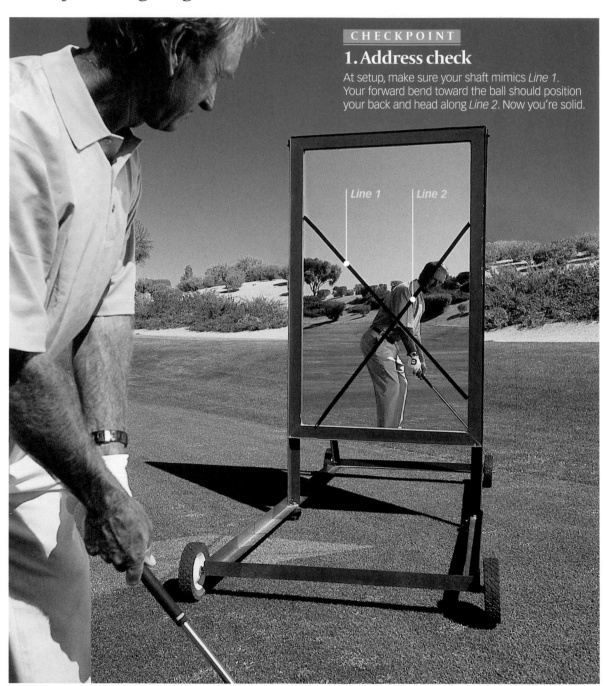

CHECKPOINT

1. Address check

At setup, make sure your shaft mimics *Line 1*. Your forward bend toward the ball should position your back and head along *Line 2*. Now you're solid.

Line 1   Line 2

2. Backswing check

Take your club back to just above waist high and stop. Look at the mirror and make sure your back and head still lie on *Line 2* and that your shoulder turn and wrist hinge have placed the clubshaft along *Line 1*.

If you're not on the correct backswing plane, it's because you lifted the club with your hands more than you turned your upper body (shaft above *Line 1*). Or you whipped the club too far to the inside by turning your shoulders too level and not raising the club at all (shaft below *Line 1*). To get your club correctly on plane, all you need to do is turn your left shoulder under your chin and gently cock your wrists a full 90 degrees.

3. Follow-through check

Swing through impact and stop when your hands reach just above waist height. Study your reflection to make sure that the shaft rests on *Line 1*, and your head and back haven't strayed from *Line 2*.

The common error here is a clubshaft that lies above *Line 1*, because most golfers don't swing enough to the left, or if they do they don't execute enough hip turn. You really need both: an aggressive and full hip rotation, along with hand movement that brings your club across your chest (not away from it). Although most swings finish with the shaft over the left shoulder (above *Line 1*), the shaft goes left after impact before it travels up.

6 Plane Errors to Avoid

Do any of these swings look familiar? If so, it's time to get back on plane.

It's very difficult to hit solid shots once your club gets off plane. Make a point to check your swing plane in a mirror often to avoid grooving bad habits.

Upright
Hands way above shoulders

Hitting under
Shaft below shoulder plane

Trapped
Club too far behind the body

Over the top
Club above shoulder plane

Across the line
Shaft points right of target

Laid off
Club points way left of target

Get the Perfect Finish

Stretch your left hip flexor to the max to maintain proper posture and keep your club on the correct exit plane

With your hands on your hips, make a mock swing and hold your finish. Make sure your weight is over your front foot and your belt buckle faces directly at the target.

With everything else in place, bend your upper body to the right until your torso matches the angle of Line 2 on the mirror, and hold it. Ouch! But performing this stretch just a few times will instantly loosen your hip flexor and allow you to swing on plane with greater ease.

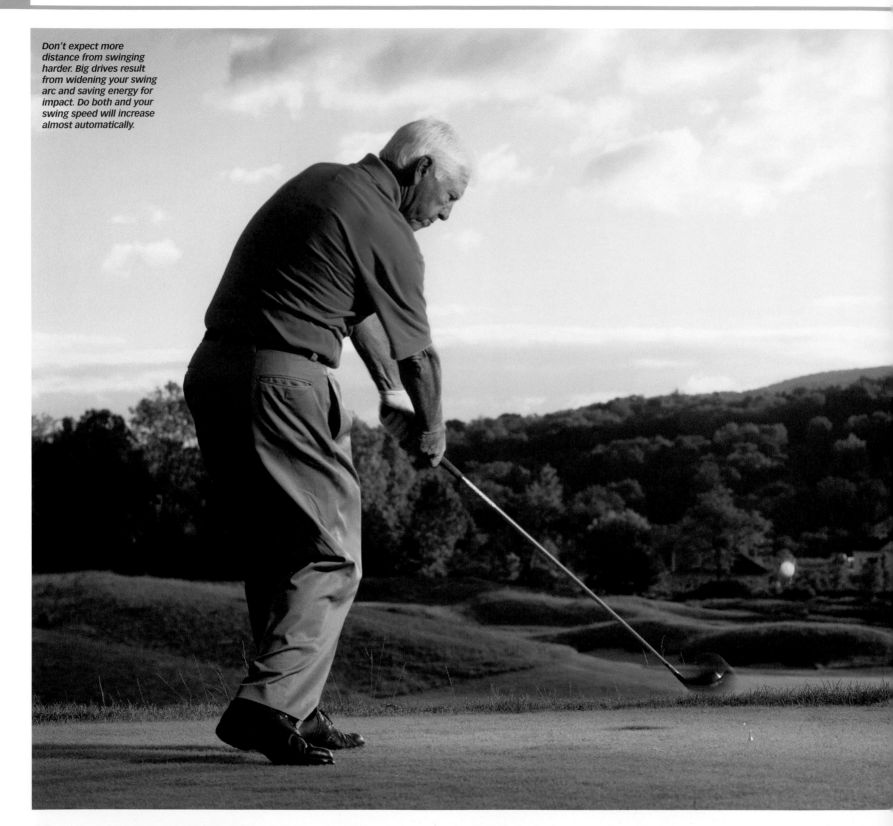

Don't expect more distance from swinging harder. Big drives result from widening your swing arc and saving energy for impact. Do both and your swing speed will increase almost automatically.

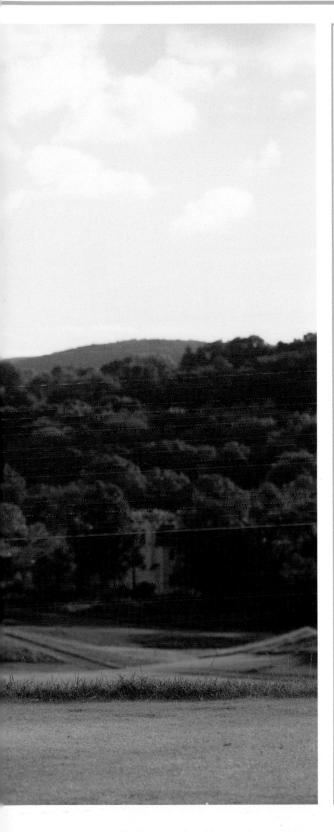

SECTION 3

YOU AND YOUR DRIVER

How to turn a love-hate relationship into a beautiful friendship—and massive yards

T he key to the modern game is to hit the ball as far as you can and then go find it. Technology provides you the tools to knock it out there, but do you know how to use them? Your driver can't swing itself, nor can you simply move your arms or hips faster to create yardage that isn't there. There are hard, fast rules you must follow. And since your driver is the longest, largest and potentially most dangerous club in your bag, neglecting them pays off in a triple-whammy of lost yards, lost balls and lost strokes.

Once you harness the power of your driver, however, you'll find that playing by the big dog's rules makes the game a whole lot easier. Approach shots become shorter, par 5s become reachable and your confidence soars when you know you can bust one out there anytime you like.

There are three main things you must do to improve your driving distance: increase the width of your swing, sequence your downswing to add club speed, and learn how to make consistent contact in the center of the clubface. This section touches on all three, with tips to not only make you the big hitter in your regular foursome, but the most accurate one, too.

5 THINGS YOU'LL LEARN IN THIS SECTION

- How to widen your swing arc—the primary ingredient for power-packed drives
- How to swing faster without swinging out of your shoes
- How to hit more fairways—even the narrow ones
- Why an expert clubfitting session can give you more yards in an instant
- Power drills that give you extra speed at the exact point where you need it most

What Are Your Weak Spots?

Here's what *GOLF Magazine* readers had to say about their driving game in a recent survey.

What's your most common driving mistake?

Not enough distance: 37%
Hooking: 21%
Slicing: 33%

What club do you replace most often?

Driver: 42%
Putter: 21%
Something else: 26%
Fairway woods: 11%

WIDEN YOUR ARC

Big swings begin with a big arc, and the wider the path your clubhead traces from start to finish, the more speed and power you can create to launch the ball deep down the fairway

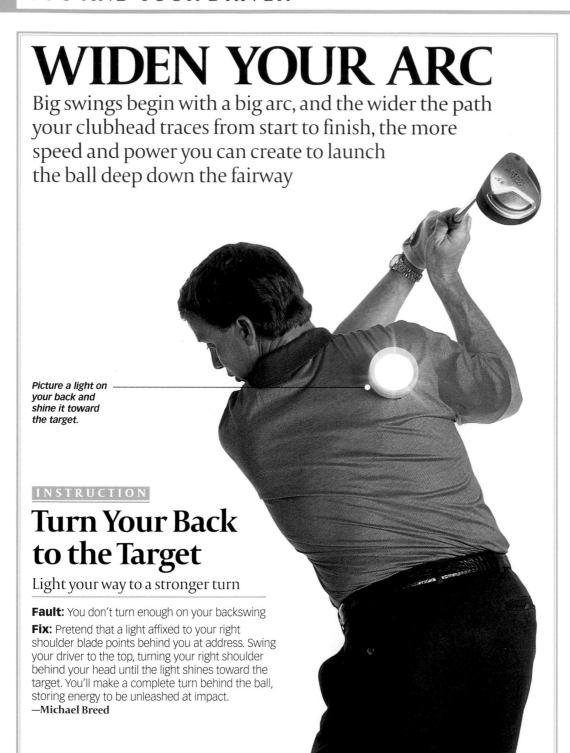

Picture a light on your back and shine it toward the target.

Turn Your Back to the Target

Light your way to a stronger turn

Fault: You don't turn enough on your backswing

Fix: Pretend that a light affixed to your right shoulder blade points behind you at address. Swing your driver to the top, turning your right shoulder behind your head until the light shines toward the target. You'll make a complete turn behind the ball, storing energy to be unleashed at impact.
—**Michael Breed**

Three Drills to Get Wider

1. Reach for it

Place your driver on the ground, straight back from your right foot, and put a chair at the other end. Pick up the club and swing it back slowly, trying to nip the chair as you pass it. If the clubhead clears the chair, you're not getting enough extension. If you move the chair on the way back, you're overreaching. A perfect extension just grazes it. Once you've extended to the chair, check that your weight is on your right side.
—**Fred Griffin**

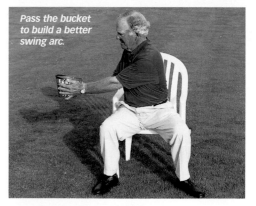

Pass the bucket to build a better swing arc.

2. Do the sit and spin

Hold a bucket of range balls (or fried chicken or anything of similar weight) while sitting forward in a chair. Now turn to your right, as if you were handing the bucket to someone seated beside you. Notice how your head, shoulders and torso all turn together. That's what a full turn feels like, with your body rotated away from the target and your weight balanced over your right side.
—**Craig Shankland**

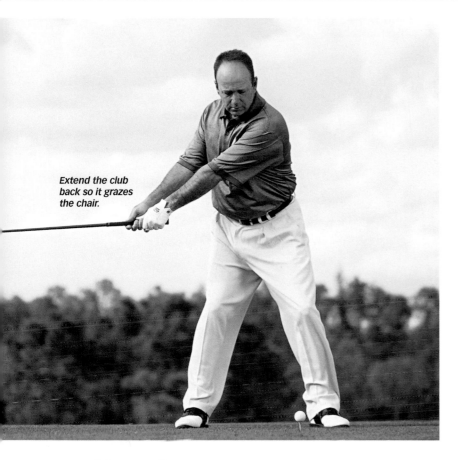

Extend the club back so it grazes the chair.

3. Add some hip power

To understand the role your hips play as you coil behind the ball on your backswing, try this drill made popular by Julius Boros. If you have a stocky build like Julius (or me!), this drill will help you hit the ball a ton.

Step 1

Set up in your regular driving stance, and then swing your driver back to hip height using only your right arm. Extend your right arm as far as you can.

Step 2

Now try to reach over and put your left hand on the grip. Your body gets in the way, right? In order for your left hand to reach the club, you have to rotate your right hip back, which gives you enough room to reach the club. Copy this position to build more power.

—Bill Madonna

Spread Your Wings

Go from narrow to wide by flexing your back

Look at any great driver of the ball and you'll see that the space between his shoulders is the same at impact as it is at address. You'll never see hunched shoulders or bent arms as the club swings through the hitting zone. **Maintaining the distance between your shoulders creates the necessary room for you to swing through impact** and, more importantly, helps you maintain the width of your swing arc for enhanced speed.

To establish and better retain width, use the muscles in your back. At address, bring both hands to ear height with your palms facing outward. As you do, sense how the large muscles of your back bring your shoulder blades closer together and pull your shoulders farther apart. Now, bend from your hips into your normal address posture, keeping your back engaged and your blades pinched together. Now you're set for power.

—Mike Malaska

Pinch your shoulder blades together to get wide at address.

Keep your shoulders apart as you settle into your driving stance.

Re-create wide—not shrugged—shoulders at impact.

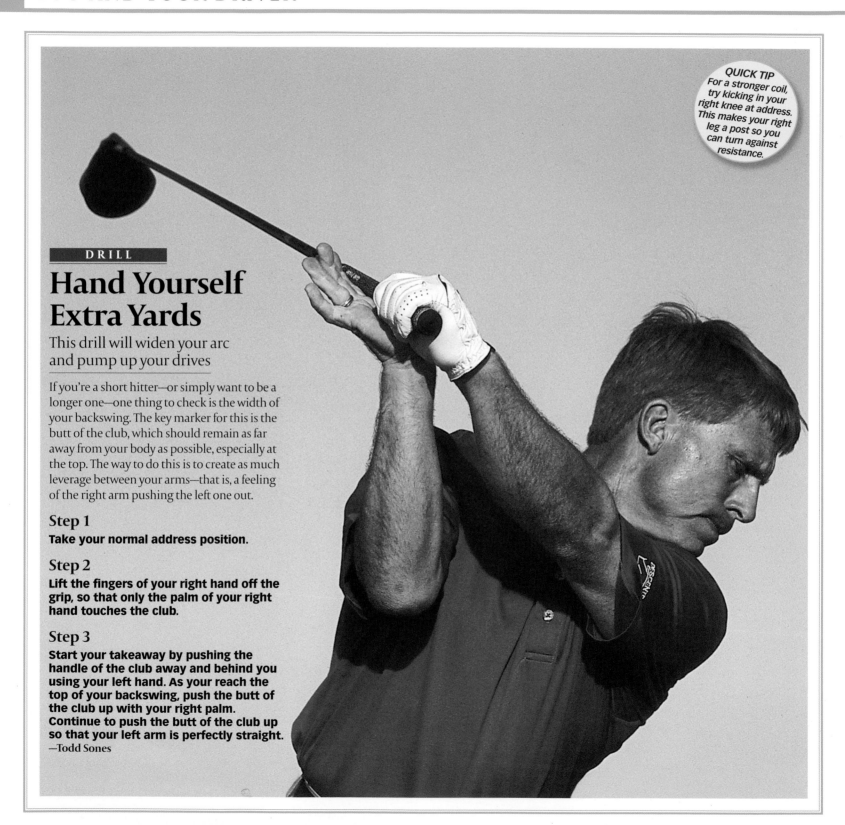

DRILL

Hand Yourself Extra Yards

This drill will widen your arc and pump up your drives

If you're a short hitter—or simply want to be a longer one—one thing to check is the width of your backswing. The key marker for this is the butt of the club, which should remain as far away from your body as possible, especially at the top. The way to do this is to create as much leverage between your arms—that is, a feeling of the right arm pushing the left one out.

Step 1

Take your normal address position.

Step 2

Lift the fingers of your right hand off the grip, so that only the palm of your right hand touches the club.

Step 3

Start your takeaway by pushing the handle of the club away and behind you using your left hand. As your reach the top of your backswing, push the butt of the club up with your right palm. Continue to push the butt of the club up so that your left arm is perfectly straight.
—Todd Sones

CHECKPOINT

Once you're comfortable with this wider and freer takeaway, grip the club as you normally do and try to re-create that same feeling of leverage and width as you take the club to the top. Note in the sequence below how this leverage and width is maintained at every point: takeaway, top, downswing, impact and follow-through. That's what you should strive for.
—**Todd Sones**

"Create as much leverage between your arms as possible— that is, a feeling of the right arm pushing the left one out."

The lie of your club sets the path.

Leverage begins in the backswing.

Hands as far away from the body as possible.

Club re-traces wide backswing arc.

Arms pulled from the shoulder sockets.

Width maintained in the release.

Width is still evident at the end.

INSTRUCTION

Stretch to 10:30

Move the butt of your club far away from your body

The more distance there is between the butt of your club and the ball when you reach the top, the more room your clubhead has to accelerate on the downswing. When the grip is at 10:30, it's the farthest it should be from the ball. To get it there, swing back while keeping the triangle formed by your shoulders and arms intact. If your grip hits 12:00, your arms probably have folded, collapsing the triangle and reducing your power.—**Martin Hall**

CHECKPOINT

How to Get Wide From the Start

Pre-set your hips for an upswing

Set up to a ball with a driver, then pick up the club and hold it across your hips. You want the club to point up slightly (about a 10-degree angle) from your right hip to your left hip. If your club is parallel to the ground or sloping down, your swing path will be too steep and you'll lose yards. If it's pointing up as shown, you'll set up your swing to trace a wider arc, approach the ball from the inside and sling the club through impact with explosive results.
—**Rick Martino**

DRILL

Take a Hike!

Another way to add leverage

Without a club, set your hands like a quarterback ready to receive the snap from center, with the lifeline of your right hand placed firmly on top of your left thumb. Make a mock backswing and try to maintain the pressure from your right hand on your left thumb all the way to the top. You know you've done it right if you feel your right hand push your left arm outward.
—**Tim Mahoney**

HOW TO ADD SPEED

Even just a few miles per hour of extra clubhead speed can be the difference between hitting a mid-iron and a long iron on your approach

INSTRUCTION

Nail Drives With the O-Factor

What is the O-Factor?
The angle of your hips in relation to horizontal.

How to use it
Turn your left hip up and to the left of the target immediately at the start of your downswing—and keep turning it!

What it does
The move is so powerful that it literally pulls your shoulders and arms along for the ride. And since your hips move first, everything else must accelerate to catch up at impact. Using your hips like this is what allows you to hammer the ball without swinging hard.
—**Robert Baker**

Address
Set your body like an airplane coming in for a landing, with your left shoulder and left hip above their right-side counterparts, and your spine tilted away from the target.

Backswing
Turn against the resistance of your right thigh, not your entire lower body, and make sure you rotate your shoulders and your hips. This allows you to create maximum energy.

O-Positive
At address, your O-Factor should be slightly positive. As you settle into your stance, bump your left hip up to set your body at the correct angle.

O-Neutral
You're balanced and loaded up with power if your hip angle shifts back to zero while your spine remains tilted away from the target.

Downswing

From the top, turn your hips immediately to the left and, as the club approaches impact, pull your left hip up. This creates whip-like speed and helps drop your club onto the correct plane.

O-Positive

Kick in your right knee to get your left hip moving up and your right shoulder moving down.

DRILLS

How to Groove Your O-Factor

Perform these drills to improve your hip action and gas up your swing

Make a hip swing

To learn the feeling of powering your downswing with your hips, place your driver behind your back as shown, make your backswing turn and, as you rotate through impact, keep your upper body as quiet as possible. Make a level turn going back and use "butt power" to whip your left hip up and around on your downswing.

Whip your hips and let your left arm fold in your follow-through.

Angled shaft matches angled hips.   *Level shaft matches level hips.*   *Left hip up, right shoulder down.*

Fling your headcover

With your left hand, swing a headcover over your right shoulder and slap your back, then use your hips to whip it forward. Keep your left arm in and try to smack your back with the headcover on your follow-through.

—**Robert Baker**

CHECKPOINT

Fingers First

A palm grip slows you down

Your hands represent one of three power sources in your swing (your arms and your pivot are the other two). To use them correctly, start by gripping the club in your fingers. Think about a major league pitcher: When he wants to bring the heat, he grips the ball in his fingers. When he wants to take something off a pitch, he holds the ball in his palm. When you hold the club in your palms it limits your ability to release the club. A palm grip also creates tension because you have to squeeze tighter to hold the club, and that dramatically decreases clubhead speed. How important is a finger grip? It's the first thing you should consider in the search for more power.

—**Sandy LaBauve**

WRONG!

A palm grip robs you of speed.

RIGHT!

A finger grip adds speed.

1

At the top of your swing, strive for a flat left wrist and a right elbow set squarely on the shaft plane established at address.

2

Allow your arms to drop down without moving your shoulders while you start to shift your weight forward and unwind your hips.

3

Now you're trapped. The shaft is below the preferred swing plane and the clubhead is behind your right hip.

4

From this position, aggressively turn your shoulders. What pulls this move together is a full, powerful release of your hands through impact.

INSTRUCTION

Make a Bad Swing to Gain 25 Yards

One beautiful mistake leads to more power

The "mistake"

Very few players swing the club on plane, even though that's the goal. It's much more common to have the clubhead and your hands and arms "trapped" behind your body in the middle of your downswing, a position you find yourself in when you get too quick with your lower body during the transition from backswing to downswing. This forces you off plane and into a position where you're coming at the ball from too far inside the target line.

How you know you do this

Big pushes and killer push-hooks are the norm.

How to make it work for you

All you need to do is turn your shoulders hard at impact. Get trapped, then rip your shoulders through impact and your clubhead speed will go through the roof.

Smash Factors

Drills to teach you to explode through impact

Get from "inside" to "on fire!"

While holding a ball in your right hand, extend your left arm and place your driver's head on the ground as shown at right. Now swing your right hand back to its normal position at the top of your swing. From this point, try to throw the ball through the gate created by your left arm and driver shaft (like you'd skip a rock across a lake). Notice how far from the inside you need to come—and how you must keep your spine angle intact—to get the ball through the gate.

Groove a big-time shoulder turn

To feel what a strong shoulder turn feels like, grab a medicine ball. Assume your address position and, with your hands on both sides of the ball, make a backswing. At the top, hold it for a count of one, and then try to toss the ball as far left of your target line as possible. The only way to perform this drill correctly is to aggressively rotate your shoulders and, once again, to hold your spine angle.
—**Tim Mahoney**

Throw the Hammer Down

Picture a nail to drive the ball like a Tour pro

Picture a nail stuck into the back of your ball. As you swing down, try to drive the nail through the core. You'll accelerate through the ball instead of to it, generating extra clubhead speed. Focusing on a small target like the head of a nail can also help you deliver the club's sweet spot to the back of the ball more often.
—**Michael Breed**

Accelerate the club through the ball as if you were driving a nail.

Is Custom-Fitting Really Necessary?

Haven't been fit yet? Here's why you need to do it—stat!

Q: Have you been fit for a driver?
45%—Yes   55%—No

If you read *GOLF Magazine* even infrequently, you know that custom-fitting really works. Finding the right loft, lie angle and shaft flex for your swing will trim strokes off your game. The following reader was a classic slicer with a weak grip and poor swing path. Now he hits his driver in the fairway and 34 yards longer.

Age: 29
Handicap before: 25
Handicap after: 22
Old driver: 360 cc, 9.5°, graphite shaft, regular flex, 45.5", standard grip
New driver: 460 cc (draw biased), 9.5°, 65-gram graphite shaft, stiff flex, 45.5", standard grip

This reader switched to an offset, draw-biased head and a lower-spinning ball, and he strengthened his grip. A stronger grip takes some sidespin off his ball and straightens his ball flight. The offset head has extra weight in the heel to promote a right-to-left flight.

NEW DRIVER
OLD DRIVER
216 yards   250 yards

The Clubfitting: Test Result for Driver

	BEFORE	AFTER
Clubhead speed	92 mph	97 mph
Ball speed	137 mph	148 mph
Launch angle°	14°	15°
Height (apex)	89 feet	120 feet
Backspin	3,300 rpm	3,500 rpm
Sidespin	611 rpm	597 rpm
Avg. dispersion	21 yards right	15 yards right
Carry distance	216 yards	250 yards

1
Feel the apple slide down during your downswing...

2
...and sling it pass the ball after impact.

Turn Your Swing Into a Sling

Sling apples to release all the power in your swing

To feel the proper acceleration and rhythm of the clubhead in your downswing, use this image made famous by Sam Snead. Imagine there's an apple stuck to the center of the shaft. (Snead used to cut out the core of an apple and slide it over a hickory stick.) As you start down from the top, feel the apple begin sliding down the shaft until it flies off the end just after impact. You should feel like you're slinging the apple at or beyond the ball. This image delays the clubhead at the start of the downswing just enough so that your arms and body can work in sync and transfer full energy to the ball at impact.
—**Martin Hall**

QUICK TIP
Try to contact the lower inside quadrant of the ball. You'll create a more inside delivery, and maybe hit a draw.

INSTRUCTION

Go Wide for Speed

This right-foot trick gives you extra yards

Sometimes you have to carry the ball 10 or 15 yards farther than usual to clear a hazard or to position your drive on a reachable par 5. To get that boost, try this: Widen your stance by sliding your right foot about a foot's width away from the target. This will set your upper body well behind the ball, promoting an ascending strike. It will also give you more time to release the clubhead and crush the ball.
—**Michael Breed**

Widening your right foot gives your swing more time to accelerate.

DRILL

Pull Down for Power

This drill helps you release with max power

Most golfers throw the clubhead at the ball, which reduces leverage too soon. You want to keep the clubhead away from the ball for as long as possible on your downswing. To help you accomplish this, try gripping a club as you normally would, but with about two inches of separation between your hands. **Take a few swings with this split grip, pulling down with your left hand on the downswing while pulling back with the fingers of your right hand.** This creates the latest release possible—you can't release the club early—and tremendous clubhead speed.
—**Phil Ritson**

INSTRUCTION

How to Stripe Your Opening Tee Shot

Ask yourself these three questions to find the right fix for you

Don't aim at a target 300 yards away; pick one three inches away instead.

READER POLL

Q: Do you get more nervous over the first tee shot of the day or a pressure putt late in the round?
53%—First tee shot
24%—Pressure putt
15%—Don't get nervous

1
IS IT FIRST-TEE JITTERS?
It's common to feel nerves on the first tee, which can make you guide your shot, instead of making an aggressive swing.

2
AM I TRYING TO MAKE A PERFECT SWING?
The fairway looks extra small on the first tee before you're into the round. You may try to make a perfect swing, which causes tension.

3
AM I PULLING THE WRONG CLUB?
Golfers often hit driver with trouble left and right, when a nice little 5-wood would be perfect.

You know if...
You kill it on the range, but you feel like the whole world is watching when you stand on the first tee.

You know if...
Check your recent scorecards. If you struggle on the first couple of holes, you're making the shots harder than they are.

You know if...
Your instinct is to go with a safer club, but you pull driver to keep up with your buddies. You're giving in to peer pressure.

How to fix it
Make pre-round range bets with your pals—wager, say, a beer, that you can hit a distant green, or nail the ball picker-upper. That gets you used to playing with pressure so the first tee shot is a piece of cake.

How to fix it
Be like Jack. Nicklaus liked to pick a target three inches in front of his ball—a blade of grass, a leaf—and aim at that *[see illustration, left]*. Don't even bother looking down the fairway once you're aimed.

How to fix it
Obey your inner caddie, not your inner Daly. Hit the club that gives you the best chance of finding the fairway. Better 220 from the fairway than 180 from the trees.
—**Rick Grayson**

HIT IT LONGER

A wider swing arc and greater clubhead speed help the yards add up. Here's what you need to put the two together to make you consistently—and scary—long.

DRILL

Try a Power Shift

Drive your weight toward the target

Want distance? Make sure you're shifting your weight toward the target on the downswing. To check your weight shift, take your address with a driver, then tee a second ball just inside your back ankle [*inset photo, right*]. Make your normal swing, moving your weight away from the target going back and toward it coming down. If you transfer your weight correctly, your back ankle will roll inward on the downswing, knocking the second ball off the tee. If you don't bump the ball, you're leaving yards on the table.
—**Ted Sheftic**

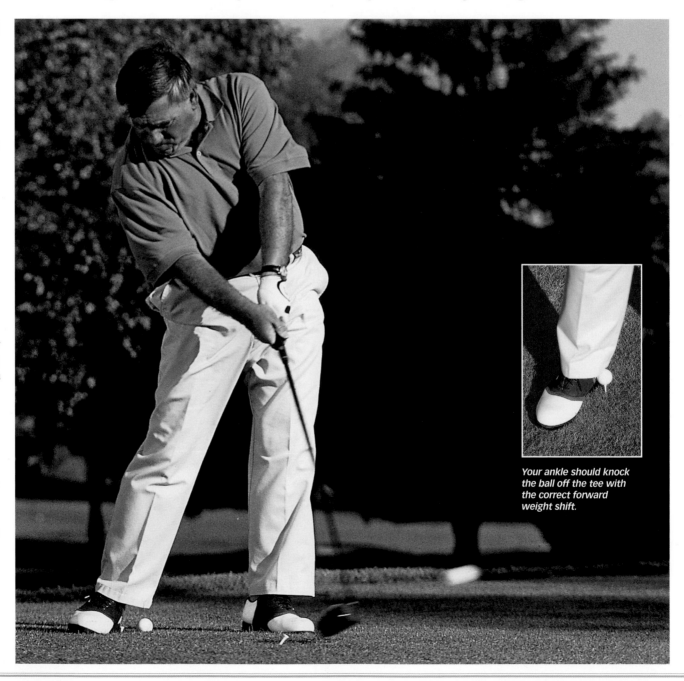

Your ankle should knock the ball off the tee with the correct forward weight shift.

INSTRUCTION

Try a Narrow Stance—It Works!

Keep your feet at hip width to bust big drives

The prevailing wisdom
A super-wide stance creates the support you need when you're swinging for the fences.

Why the prevailing wisdom is wrong
When you take a stance with your feet outside your shoulders, your lower legs angle in from your feet to your knees. This is a power-bracing position, not a power-delivering position.

What to do instead
Place your feet under your hips. This "stacks" the upper part of each leg on top of the lower, allowing you to tap the power of your entire leg.

The extra benefit
A hip-width stance makes it easier to pivot around each hip. This is a fundamental of any striking motion. If your stance is wider than your hips, you'll need to move laterally to get either hip where you need it, and with all that sliding you're bound to reverse pivot and hit a major-league slice. A hip-width stance negates the need to slide and the likelihood you'll slice.
—**Mike Adams**

An extra-wide stance encourages sliding.

A hip-width stance improves your pivot.

What's the Best Stance Width?

For swinging a driver, the feet should be positioned…

Under your shoulders: 58%

Outside your shoulders: 17%

Under your hips: 25%

"A narrow stance can certainly give you extra rotation. But if you're a hard swinger, place your feet outside your shoulders."
—**Jon Tattersall**

CHECKPOINT

Know Your Driver

Look for design options that can help your swing

Before you purchase the same souped-up, high-performance driver used by your friends or your favorite Tour professional, be aware of the major design elements that could help—or potentially hurt—your swing.

CLUBHEAD
Most drivers are 460 cc in size. Smaller heads are available but, in general, larger ones offer more resistance to twisting and added forgiveness.

WEIGHTING
Clubheads with a low, deep center of gravity (CG) produce a higher ball flight than those with a high CG and/or a CG closer to the clubface.

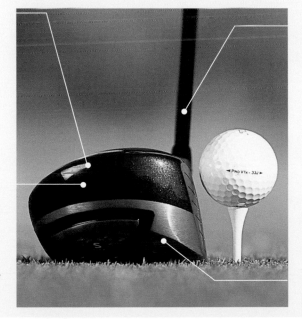

SHAFT FLEX
Flexes range from extra-stiff to ladies. Finding the proper flex, based on your swing speed and tempo, will help you max out distance and improve control.

BALL FLIGHT
If you slice, look for a clubhead with "draw bias" weighting. If you fight a hook, you may find relief with a "fade bias" club.

"*Start your downswing by 'firing' your right side. Kick your right foot and knee toward the target. This shifts your weight to your left side and sets your hip turn in motion.*"
—**Jimmy Ballard**

How to Make a Power Pivot

It's all about staying on plane

How can you hit it flush time after time? The simplest way is to rotate your shoulders on a consistent plane from setup through impact. That means no rising or dipping. Try this drill.

Tee a ball and take your address. Then cross your arms and hold a club against your chest with the grip end at your left shoulder. Turn as if you were swinging to the top and point the grip at the ball. Then mimic your downswing and point the clubhead at the ball.

This power drill will train you to turn your shoulders on a single plane for consistent contact—the first step toward booming tee shots.
—Jim Murphy

Turn your shoulders on a single plane for consistent power off the tee.

Hit the Hot Spot

Make contact high on the face and spot yourself 10 extra yards

You've almost certainly heard Tour players and TV commentators talking about how the sweet spot on drivers has moved from the center to nearer the top of the clubface. The name for this 21st-century sweet spot is the hot spot.

The discovery of the hot spot signals a new era in the evolution of the golf swing. It has happened before: Hickory shafts changed to steel, blade irons changed to cavity back, and wood clubheads changed to metal—all these changes produced shifts in how players strike the ball. In short, the way the game is played largely depends on the equipment of the day. The huge-headed drivers are here to stay, so here's how to reap their benefits and start hitting your longest drives ever.

1
Mark your ball with a dot the size of a shirt button, and place it on the tee so you'll make contact with it.

2
Note where your longest shots make a mark and tee the equator of your ball to that spot every time.

Find Your Hot Spot

Why are the world's best players hitting the ball longer than ever before? Their secret is clear—In some cases, contact is being made on the top scoring line of the clubface! This produces the high-launch, low-spin ball flight that translates into extra yards.

No matter which brand of driver you hit, the hot spot is above the center of the clubface. But it's slightly different for each driver. To find yours, take an erasable marker and put a circle on your ball [top photo]. Tee it up with the circle pointing straight back at your clubface at address.

Now hit some drives. After each one examine the clubface to see the circular mark [bottom photo]. When you catch one flush, the mark will be high. That's your new sweet spot.

Align the equator of the ball with your hot spot every time and you'll hit long drives more consistently.
—Peter Kostis

Long, but not Wrong

Conventional wisdom says the longer your shaft, the longer—but more off-target—your tee shots. Turns out that's not the case.

Test

We gave a foursome (handicaps: 7, 8, 12 and 14) the following test clubs—460 cc head at 43.5 inches (the old industry standard), 45 inches (the new standard), 46.5 inches and 48 inches (the maximum length allowed by the Rules of Golf). Players hit the drivers in a precisely varied order. Shots had to land within the grid (320 yards long x 35 yards wide) to be counted. With the assistance of the experts at Golf Laboratories in San Diego, Calif., we tracked the results with a launch monitor and also measured by hand exactly how far off target each drive landed.

Results

Holy fairways, Batman! The two longer-shafted drivers were not only long, but also relatively straight. Stunningly, they were actually up to two yards more accurate than the shorter drivers. (In real terms, shots were straight enough to stay in the fairway.) Our suggestion: At the very least, give a longer shaft a try.

Longer shafts equal longer drives and (surprise!) straighter shots.

Shaft test: Tale of the tape				
Shaft length	**43.5 in.**	**45 in.**	**46.5 in.**	**48 in.**
Head speed (mph)	97	98	99	101
Ball speed (mph)	138	143	144	146
Launch angle (degrees)	10.19	11.97	11.03	12.96
Back spin (rpm)	3,617	3,694	3,289	3,457
Carry distance (yards)	204	217	211	223
Total distance (yards)	241	248	245	252
Dispersion (yards from center line)	15.75	15.93	13.40	14.47

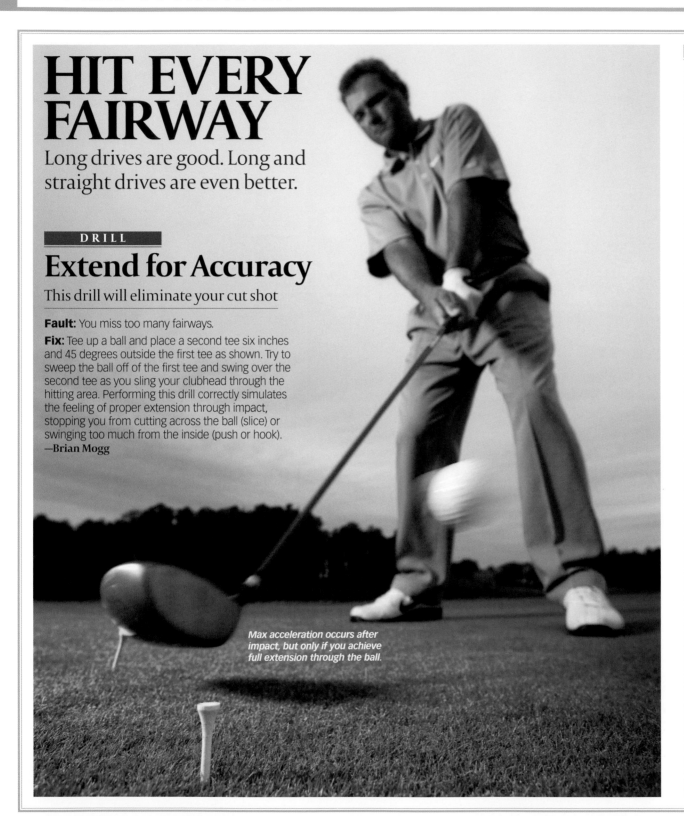

HIT EVERY FAIRWAY

Long drives are good. Long and straight drives are even better.

DRILL

Extend for Accuracy

This drill will eliminate your cut shot

Fault: You miss too many fairways.

Fix: Tee up a ball and place a second tee six inches and 45 degrees outside the first tee as shown. Try to sweep the ball off of the first tee and swing over the second tee as you sling your clubhead through the hitting area. Performing this drill correctly simulates the feeling of proper extension through impact, stopping you from cutting across the ball (slice) or swinging too much from the inside (push or hook).

—Brian Mogg

Max acceleration occurs after impact, but only if you achieve full extension through the ball.

What Starts Your Move Back Down?

On the downswing with a driver, should the legs move the hips or should the hips move the legs?

Hips move the legs: 57%

Hips and legs work together: 7%

Legs move the hips: 36%

"Your backswing and forward swing start from the ground up and, as the old song goes, 'the hip bone's connected to the thigh bone.' Your legs move your hips, not the other way around."

—Rick McCord

"Your legs are like the legs on a tripod—they hold up the top. Legs react, they do not act."

—Mike Perpich

"Your hips should lead. In fact, they should begin to turn forward before you finish your backswing."

—Jon Tattersall

Shorten Your Finish for Safer Driving

Try this quick tip to split the fairway every time

The problem
Not only do you spray your drives, but you take the anxiety over your sprayed drives to every tee.

The solution
Instead of swinging into your normal full follow-through, finish your drives when the clubhead reaches about waist high after impact. Call this spot "Checkpoint Charlie," and go through the following list when you reach it:

● *The clubshaft and your left arm are more or less still in line*

● *Your right wrist is still bent back slightly*

● *Your right arm is across the middle of your torso*

● *Your chest is facing the target*

● *The toe of the clubhead is pointing up, neither too open nor too closed*

If you work on finishing your driver swings with a short follow-through that satisfies the five conditions above, you may lose a little distance, but you'll also land a lot more shots on the short grass.
—**Martin Hall**

Don't Flex Toward the Ball

Proper knee movement makes flush contact easy

If you kick your back knee toward the ball on your downswing, solid contact becomes nearly impossible. Instead, drive your back knee toward the target as you start down, and begin to post your front knee by straightening it. This creates a wall that everything slings past with maximum force and helps produce flush contact with less sidespin.
—**Paul Trittler**

WRONG!	RIGHT!

As you swing to the top, strive to retain the flex in your right knee.

Drive your right knee toward the target on your downswing, not toward the ball.

Choke Down for Control

When you absolutely must find the fairway, your 3-wood is the best bet. The shorter shaft of a 3-wood gives you greater control. But if you insist on hitting driver, grip down an inch or two on the handle. This effectively shortens the club, making it play more like a fairway wood, but gives you the advantages of the larger clubhead.
—**Michael Breed**

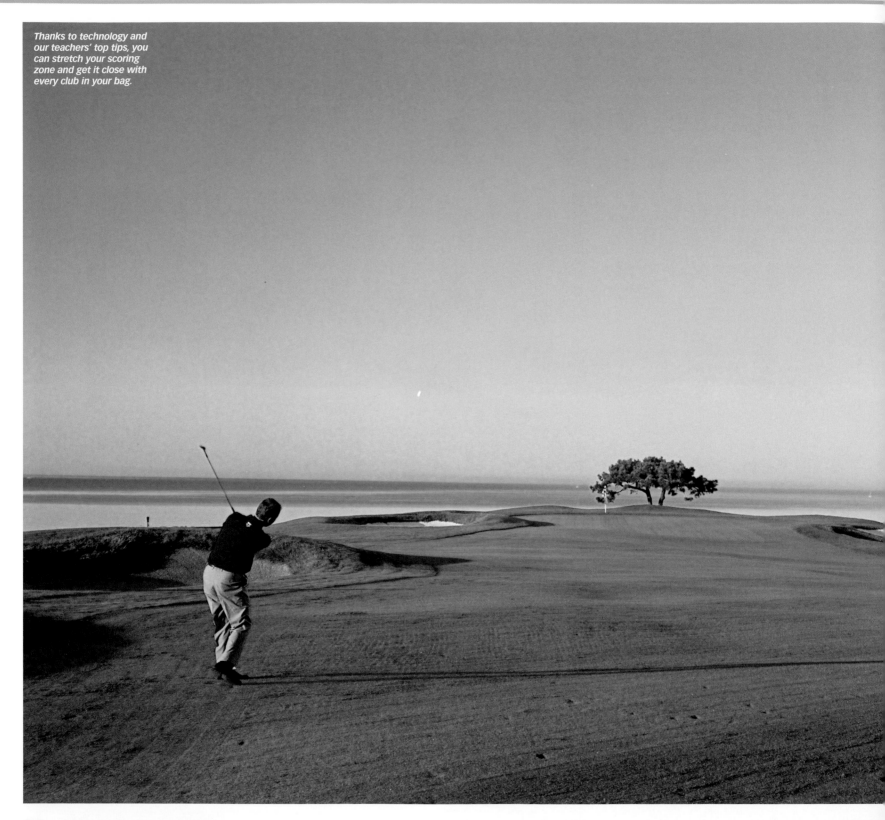

Thanks to technology and our teachers' top tips, you can stretch your scoring zone and get it close with every club in your bag.

SECTION 4

HYBRIDS, WOODS & LONG IRONS

They're easier to play than ever. Here's how to use them to make more long-range birdies.

Y ou expect to get the ball close to the flagstick with your short irons and wedges. With longer clubs, however, you're happy with just getting the ball close to the green. It's time to change that line of thinking. Technology has made long irons, fairway woods and hybrids much easier to play, and the swing to get you to birdie range from long distance is the same you'd use with your 8-iron, minus a few adjustments to your setup to create a more sweeping type of impact. The Top 100 Teachers show you the quick way to make that happen on the following pages, so there's no reason you shouldn't expect to hit shots with longer clubs as close to the pin as you do with your more traditional scoring irons.

The main challenge is to plan your attack in such a way that minimizes the damage when you do miss with your woods and long irons. That means choosing the right landing spot, selecting the right club and using the lay of the land to shape the shot once the ball hits the ground. The Top 100 Teachers have you covered here, too, with strategic ways to get the most out of your long game.

5 THINGS YOU'LL LEARN IN THIS SECTION

- How to hit long irons on the sweet spot consistently
- How to get the most out of your hybrids
- The setup and swing changes necessary to sweep the ball powerfully off the turf with your fairway woods
- How to hit long-iron "stingers" off the tee and from the fairway to control spin and trajectory
- Drills to help you hit your long irons and woods farther and with greater accuracy

The Lowdown on Hybrids

What confuses you most about golf equipment?

31% — Hybrids
20% — Balls
10% — Wedges
7% — Drivers
7% — Irons
25% — Confused? Not me!

What makes hybrids work

In a word, gravity. The simple physics behind the hybrid's success is its low, deep center of gravity (CG). Because the club's CG is below that of the ball's, the collision of the club and ball at impact produces a higher launch angle and spin rate. A deep CG also directs the clubhead to the ball at a higher effective loft angle, which again increases launch angle and spin rate.

One other element helps the club get the ball up quickly: a flexible shaft bending forward just prior to impact.

The guts of a hybrid reveal the secret to its success: a low, deep center of gravity.

LONG-IRON SECRETS

Use these special swing adjustments to knock down the flagstick with your 3-, 4- and 5-irons

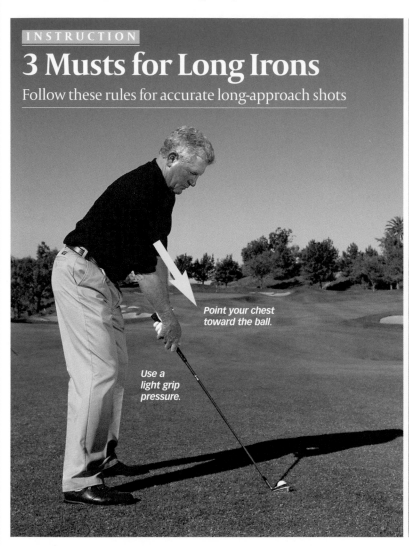

INSTRUCTION

3 Musts for Long Irons

Follow these rules for accurate long-approach shots

Point your chest toward the ball.

Use a light grip pressure.

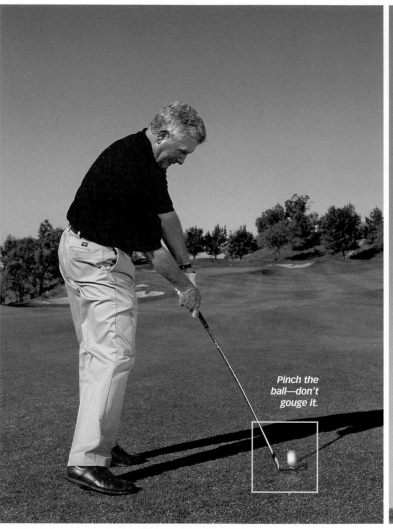

Pinch the ball—don't gouge it.

1. Address for success

Long irons can be intimidating. But a solid setup will help ease your fears. Keep your back straight and bend forward from your hips so your chest points toward the ball. Don't put a death grip on the club; light grip pressure will keep your swing smooth. Aim so that your natural shot shape will take the ball over safe portions of the fairway, which in the photo above is down the right side.

2. Compress the ball

Good long-iron players make a slightly descending blow, compressing the ball against the clubface as the leading edge skims the turf. At impact, your hands should be slightly ahead of the ball, pinching it off the ground—don't gouge it out like you do with your wedges. Ensure the right type of strike by rolling your right ankle inward and getting your weight on your left side.

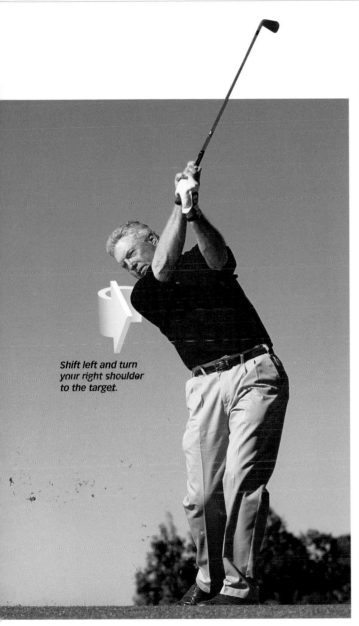

Shift left and turn your right shoulder to the target.

3. Finish strong

Uncoil your upper body until your right shoulder points at the target. Your hands should finish high, near your left ear, with almost all of your weight over your left foot. Don't cut your follow-through short in an effort to assert more control. This makes your hands and arms rigid, and tension kills the smoothness you need for distance and accuracy. So don't hold back at impact—finish strong.

—Bruce Hamilton

CHECKPOINT

Swing Flatter With Longer Clubs

Make a plane adjustment to ensure crisp contact

The problem
You slice your long irons.

The solution
The longer irons in your bag have longer shafts and decreased lie angles, so you need to produce a flatter swing plane so you can sweep more and gouge less. As you take the club back, try to swing your hands under your shoulder plane. If you swing them above your shoulders like you would with a short-iron, your downswing will be too steep. You'll hit down on the ball instead of sweeping it, most likely with an out-to-in path.

—Mark Wood

NO! YES!

Long-iron, hybrid and fairway-wood shots require a shallower, more sweeping swing plane [right photo].

INSTRUCTION

Take It Away in Two Pieces

Explode the myth of the "one-piece takeaway" for explosive long irons

The myth
You should take away your club by moving your arms, shoulders, hips and club together.

The truth
Your club has a greater distance to travel than your arms, shoulders and hips.

How to do it
Most golfers let their shoulders work too much and the clubhead too little. To correct this, think about your takeaway as a sequence called CASH—where, in order of speed, the Clubhead moves the fastest, then your Arms, your Shoulders and your Hips. As you can see from the photos below, my hands have moved about a foot, my shoulders just inches and my hips barely at all, but the clubhead has moved about 4 feet! If you take away your club in this sequence, you'll reach the optimum position for power at the top of your backswing.

—Mitchell Spearman

Check where the hips start...

...and notice how little they move compared to the hands.

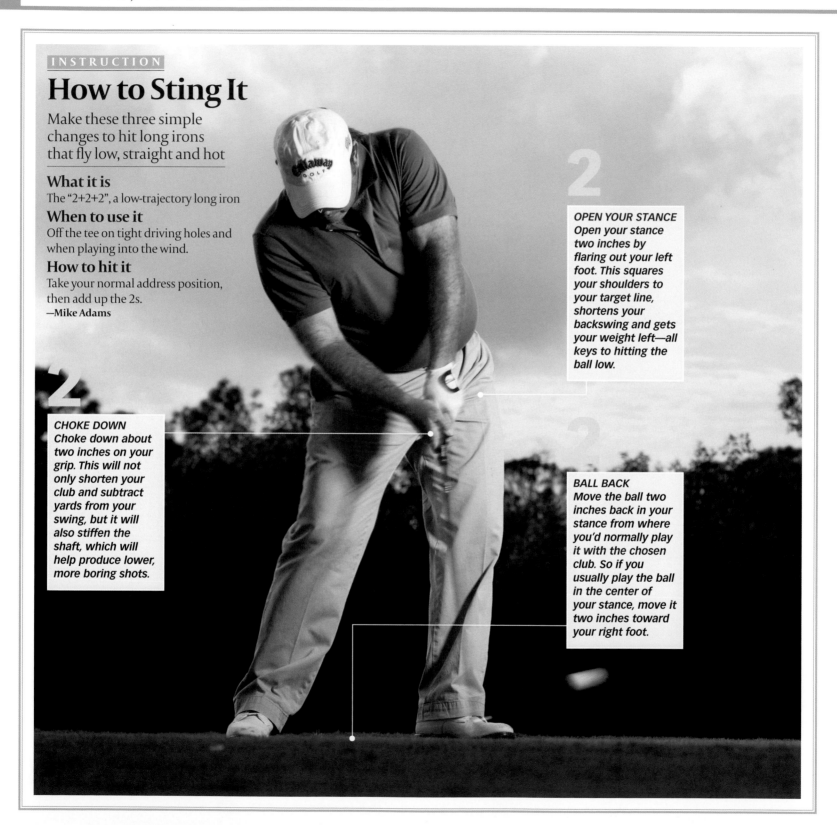

How to Sting It

Make these three simple changes to hit long irons that fly low, straight and hot

What it is
The "2+2+2", a low-trajectory long iron

When to use it
Off the tee on tight driving holes and when playing into the wind.

How to hit it
Take your normal address position, then add up the 2s.
—Mike Adams

OPEN YOUR STANCE
Open your stance two inches by flaring out your left foot. This squares your shoulders to your target line, shortens your backswing and gets your weight left—all keys to hitting the ball low.

CHOKE DOWN
Choke down about two inches on your grip. This will not only shorten your club and subtract yards from your swing, but it will also stiffen the shaft, which will help produce lower, more boring shots.

BALL BACK
Move the ball two inches back in your stance from where you'd normally play it with the chosen club. So if you usually play the ball in the center of your stance, move it two inches toward your right foot.

How to Catch Long Irons Flush

Try this tip to make contact on the sweet spot more often

Fault
You hit long irons super thin.

Why you're doing it
You're making a big backswing shift to power up behind the ball *[photo, right]*, but you're getting stuck there on your downswing. This moves the bottom of your swing arc back so you catch the ball on the upswing.

Fix
Get balanced at address and maintain that balance throughout your swing.

—Tim Mahoney

WRONG!

Keep your head still.

Keep your arms extended as long as you can during your backswing. This will help you maintain your balance.

Turn to the top while keeping your weight evenly distributed over both legs.

How to Hit Your Long Irons Farther

We studied five iron distance drills—this one works the best

Take your normal address and then pull your feet together. Try to make swings without losing your balance. This drill boosts distance by improving the quality of impact. It also helps you avoid an out-to-in swing path, since it's hard to swing out-to-in from this position without falling over. While the test results showed a statistically insignificant increase in clubhead speed, an improved path contributed to more center-face hits and a 13-yard average increase in carry distance.

—Eric Alpenfels

Set your feet together to make better contact and add yards.

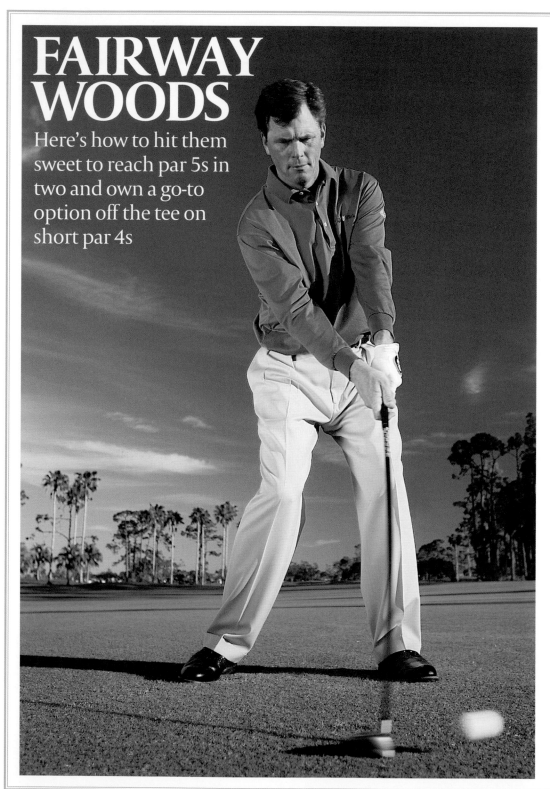

FAIRWAY WOODS

Here's how to hit them sweet to reach par 5s in two and own a go-to option off the tee on short par 4s

Three Musts for Fairway Woods

Follow these rules to sweep the ball powerfully off the turf

1. Position it

Set up with the ball just inside an imaginary line that stretches down from your left armpit. This ball position helps create the sense that you're setting up "behind" the ball at address and allows you to…

Position the ball at your left armpit.

2. Sweep it

One of the biggest mistakes you can make when hitting fairway woods is to feel like you're picking up the club on your backswing and then hitting down on the ball through impact.

Sweep the clubhead back, don't lift it.

To avoid this mistake, sweep the clubhead along the ground to create extension in your backswing, until your natural hip and shoulder turn lifts it off the ground (instead of your arms). As you continue your backswing, concentrate on bringing your left arm over your right shoulder. This motion will help you swing the club around your body, rather than bringing it straight up and down. Once you do that, relax and…

3. Let the loft do its job

The shallow path you established during your backswing puts the club into a position where you don't have to "help" the ball into the air—the loft on the clubface will do that for you. Once the ball is airborne, continue to sweep the club along the ground until your body lifts the clubhead into your follow-through.

—**Todd Anderson**

Left arm over right shoulder.

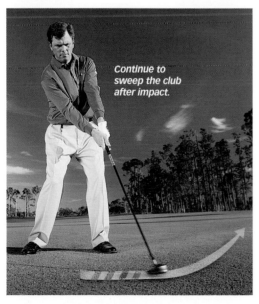

Continue to sweep the club after impact.

Start from a high tee and work down to hitting off the turf.

DRILLS

Practice Your Sweep Move

It only takes 30 swings to get the move down right

If you're uncomfortable trying to pick the ball cleanly off the turf with your fairway woods, grab a bucket of 30 range balls and do the following.

● Hit 10 shots with your 3-wood, teeing up each ball so that half of the ball is above the top of the clubhead.

● Lower the tee to just above ground level and hit 10 more balls.

● Finally, hit 10 3-wood shots off the turf.

By gradually lowering the ball height, you'll learn that the sweeping swing that works when the ball is teed up can do the trick when it's on the ground.

—**Bryan Gathright**

Roll It Away

Here's another way to make your fairway woods a sweeping success

You've already learned that the wider your swing, the more clubhead speed you can generate. This applies to your fairway woods as well as your driver and irons. Practice making a wider arc by placing a ball behind your 3-wood at address, then initiate your swing by rolling the ball straight back. Starting low and slow will help you establish more width and crank up your fairway woods.

—**Carol Preisinger**

How to Crush Your Woods

This tip turns your clubs into cannons

Fault
You're not hitting your fairway woods as long as you'd like.

Why it's happening
You're shortening your swing radius in the hope that a more compact swing will help you sweep the ball cleanly off the fairway turf.

Fix
Keep your left arm straight during your backswing and feel both arms being pulled from their sockets through impact. Try increasing your right-hand grip pressure. If you maintain pressure from your right hand on your left thumb, your left arm will remain straight. This creates a wider arc and allows you to extend fully and catch the ball powerfully at impact.

—**Tim Mahoney**

WRONG!

A loose grip makes for short arms and thin contact.

RIGHT!

Keep your hands connected for a wide arc and flush contact.

HOW TO HIT YOUR HYBRIDS

They're the most versatile clubs in your bag, but only if you use the right technique

Hybrid Off the Tee

Think ankles and hips to generate power and control

Why it works

A hybrid is shorter than a driver, which makes it inherently easier to control. It also features more loft, and more loft creates more backspin and less sidespin (the spin that sends your ball off to the left or right). A long iron used to be a good driving alternative, but a hybrid beats even that. Its face has the same bulge and roll features of a driver that add corrective spin and draw or fade your ball back into the fairway.

Tilt your head slightly behind the ball to further encourage an upward strike.

Get in your reverse K by dipping your right shoulder and right hip.

Distance between heels = distance between shoulders.

Position the ball just back from where you'd play a fairway wood.

Tee the ball so half of it is lies above the top edge of the club.

Roll and sweep it off the tee

The tilt you establish at address with your "reverse K" [photo, left] must be maintained until impact since it's what allows you to catch the ball on the upswing. Lose your tilt and you'll hit down on the ball—exactly what you don't want.

From the top, roll your ankles toward the target. This simple move has powerful implications. It shifts your weight forward, drops the club into the perfect delivery position, keeps your head behind the ball and, most importantly, saves the energy of your core section for impact. Notice how rolling your ankles whips your knees into action and opens your hips.

After you roll your ankles, drive through the ball by turning your right shoulder and hip toward the target. At the same time, pull your left shoulder toward the sky. This move helps you maintain the tilt you established at address so you can catch the ball on the upswing.

—Robert Baker

Roll your ankles toward the target.

Hybrid From the Fairway

Coil behind the ball like you're hitting a driver

Get your pants pocket behind you

There's a saying that when the ball is down, hit down. Not so fast. A hybrid from the fairway requires the same sweeping motion as the tee shot. Contact with the ground is OK; divots, however, are not.

To make a solid sweep you must rotate your body behind the ball with your right side on your backswing. Use the classic Greg Norman tip: "Get your right pants pocket behind you." As you turn to the right, feel how your left hip and knee are pulled away from the target. That's the sensation of coil—the stored energy that you release into the ball at impact.

During the takeaway, coil your left shoulder, hip and knee against the resistance of your right thigh.

How to Kick-Start Your Downswing

Your knees are the key to bring every green into range

Kicking in your right knee on your downswing is an easy move that "breaks" your right leg, making your entire right side shorter and positioning your right shoulder below your left. This sets you up to get your hybrid club under the ball and launch it high toward your target.

To practice this move, place your clubhead with the face slightly open just below your right knee and grab the hosel. Now, kick your knee in (while raising your right heel) and close the face. That's the action you want on your downswing when swinging a hybrid.
—Robert Baker

Soaring to New Heights

Results from our exclusive launch-monitor test will convince you that it's time to buy a hybrid

It's no secret that hybrids are easy to rip high and long. But how exactly do they stack up against other clubs of similar loft?

The Test

Four of our testers—handicaps 0, 8, 14 and 25—hit dozens of balls with four Nike Golf clubs: a 3-iron, a 7-wood, an iron-based hybrid and a wood-based hybrid. All had 21 degrees of loft, except for the 3-iron, which was 20 degrees. Hooked up to a launch monitor, the testers hit the clubs in varying order. Only well-struck shots were recorded, and we averaged the testers' totals. Here's how the clubs fared.

Type of Club	Shaft length (inches)	Clubhead speed (mph)	Ball speed (mph)	Launch angle (degrees)	Apex (feet)	Flight time (seconds)	Backspin (rpm)	Sidespin (rpm)	Carry (yards)
3-iron	39	91	132	7.6	33	4.2	3,269	691	175
Iron-based hybrid	40¾	93	134	8.8	49	5.0	3,889	798	187
7-wood	41½	94	134	9.4	55	5.3	4,219	707	197
Wood-based hybrid	39¾	94	132	9.6	61	5.6	4,647	420	199

What Hybrid Works Best?

There are wood-based and iron-based hybrids. Wood-based hybrids often have larger faces, for a bigger effective hitting area and added forgiveness, and in general, have a lower and deeper center of gravity than iron-based ones. That means wood-like hybrids get the ball airborne higher and with less effort, to maximize carry distance. By contrast, iron-like hybrids offer you more workability and trajectory control (which is why better players gravitate to these clubs).

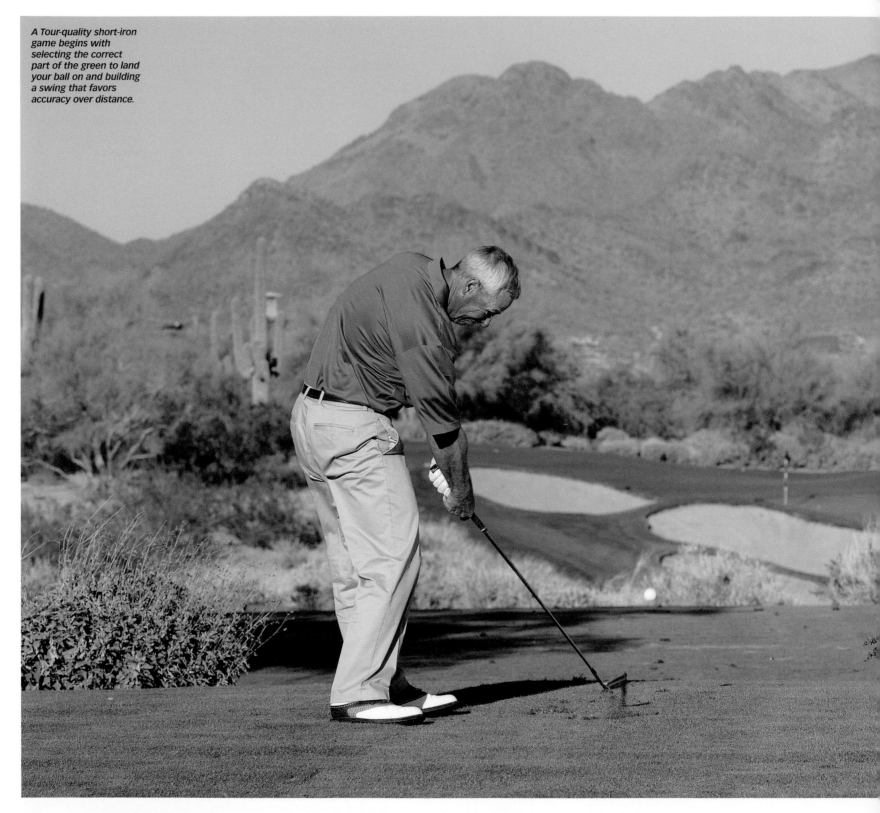

A Tour-quality short-iron game begins with selecting the correct part of the green to land your ball on and building a swing that favors accuracy over distance.

SECTION 5

SCORING SHOTS

You should attack the pin with your short irons. Here's how to do it with max control.

Even if you hit every fairway you won't do your scores much good if you miss on your approach, especially from scoring range (any distance you can comfortably hit with a 7-iron or less). Here is where you have the easiest chance to knock the ball close. After all, these are short irons with lots of loft that give you more backspin and less sidespin (with fewer hooks and slices as a result). The trick is to build a short-iron swing that favors accuracy, not distance. If you need to hit the ball farther, switch to a longer club.

Swinging a short iron is no different than swinging your driver or fairway woods. But since your short clubs are shorter and sit on a steeper angle at address, you must make a more upright swing. In this section, the Top 100 Teachers share their secrets on how to get the job done right.

While a great short-iron swing doesn't guarantee more birdies, it certainly helps. You also must pick the right part of the green to hit to and learn how to adjust when caught at those tricky distances inside 100 yards. The Top 100 have plenty to say on that, too, so get ready to go low.

---

5 THINGS YOU'LL LEARN IN THIS SECTION

- How to correctly swing your short irons and wedges
- What to look for on the green to choose the spot that will give you the easiest birdie putt
- How to hit four distances with every wedge in your bag and add spin to make your short approaches bite
- An easy trick to help you make pure contact in the center of the sweet spot and with a square clubface
- When to attack the pin and when to play it safe

Tighten Up Your Weak Links

What area of your game would you like to improve most? Here's what *GOLF Magazine* readers had to say in a recent survey.

Here are your trouble spots

Driving: 19%

Approach shots: 30%

Chipping: 15%

Something else: 21%

Putting: 15%

"Don't be intimidated by the complexity of the golf swing. It's similar to some everyday tasks. Think of chopping wood or hammering. You hold the implement with your hands and use your arms to apply the power. Same for golf. As you swing, picture one of those activities. You won't think technique; you'll swing the club back with your hands and then forward with your arms as though it were one motion."
—**Manuel de la Torre**

THE SHORT-IRON SWING

From scoring range, use a swing that favors accuracy over distance

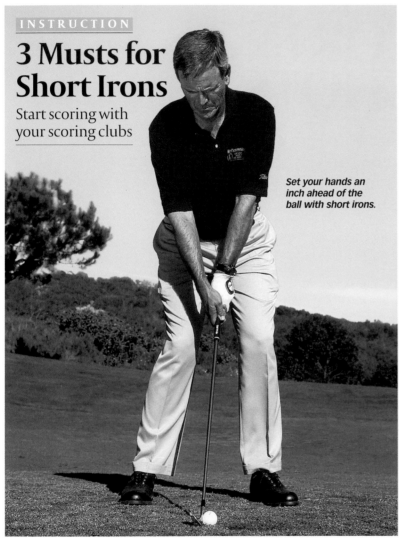

INSTRUCTION

3 Musts for Short Irons

Start scoring with your scoring clubs

Set your hands an inch ahead of the ball with short irons.

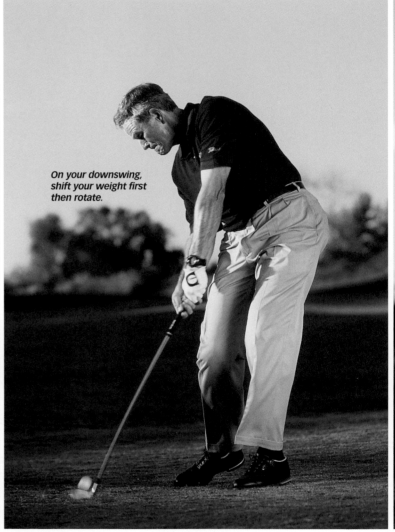

On your downswing, shift your weight first then rotate.

1. Quit pressing

The loft on your 8- and 9-irons is enough to produce towering approach shots. However, many players press their hands too far forward at address, which delofts the clubface. Instead, try this: Play the ball in the middle of a narrow stance and set your hands about an inch ahead of the ball. Also, flare your front foot slightly to pre-set your turn through the shot.

2. Shift and turn

The best players rotate their hips and shoulders as much with short irons as they do with the driver. Start your downswing by shifting your lower body toward the target, then turn your hips through. You may feel the clubhead lagging—that's OK. By shifting first, then rotating, you'll create room for your hands and arms to sling the club through last.

Pick the Right Club

Run through this checklist every time you're at an in-between distance

You're in the fairway and thinking birdie, but the sprinkler head says you're between clubs. Which one should you hit? This chart will give you the answer.
—Jerry Mowlds

Swing your clubhead toward the target for extra accuracy.

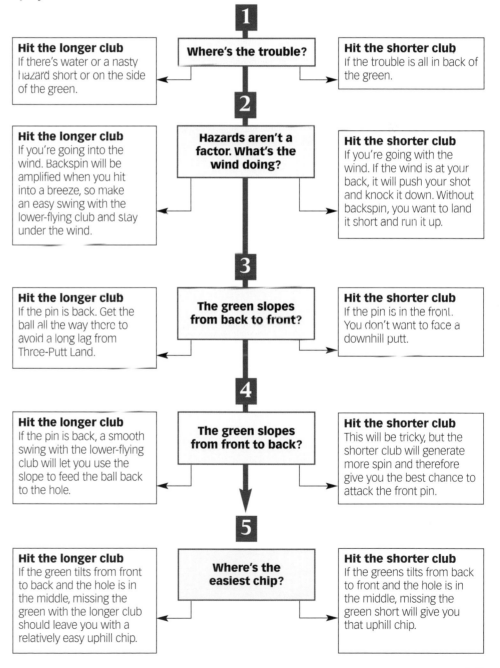

1

Where's the trouble?

Hit the longer club
If there's water or a nasty hazard short or on the side of the green.

Hit the shorter club
If the trouble is all in back of the green.

2

Hazards aren't a factor. What's the wind doing?

Hit the longer club
If you're going into the wind. Backspin will be amplified when you hit into a breeze, so make an easy swing with the lower-flying club and stay under the wind.

Hit the shorter club
If you're going with the wind. If the wind is at your back, it will push your shot and knock it down. Without backspin, you want to land it short and run it up.

3

The green slopes from back to front?

Hit the longer club
If the pin is back. Get the ball all the way there to avoid a long lag from Three-Putt Land.

Hit the shorter club
If the pin is in the front. You don't want to face a downhill putt.

4

The green slopes from front to back?

Hit the longer club
If the pin is back, a smooth swing with the lower-flying club will let you use the slope to feed the ball back to the hole.

Hit the shorter club
This will be tricky, but the shorter club will generate more spin and therefore give you the best chance to attack the front pin.

5

Where's the easiest chip?

Hit the longer club
If the green tilts from front to back and the hole is in the middle, missing the green with the longer club should leave you with a relatively easy uphill chip.

Hit the shorter club
If the greens tilts from back to front and the hole is in the middle, missing the green short will give you that uphill chip.

3. Swivel to the finish

Don't try to steer the club into the ball. Instead, concentrate on swinging the clubhead toward the target. You should also allow your head to swivel forward to encourage momentum down the target line. Your torso and hips should point just left of the target at the finish, and your weight should be over your front foot.
—**Kip Puterbaugh**

INSTRUCTION

How to Stop Missing the Sweet Spot

Practice cross-handed to groove solid contact

The problem

You thought you had your swing grooved, but a rash of poor shots proves otherwise.

The solution

Using a 7-iron on the practice tee, switch the position of your hands on the grip (left below right) and swing cross-handed. It will feel awkward at first, but if you stick with it you'll ingrain the following swing keys that are difficult to perfect using a normal grip.
—John Elliott

1 Needed hinge
Since your right hand is on top, your right wrist will hinge sooner in your backswing and establish an extra lever for power.

2 Proper arm positioning
The cross-handed grip forces your right arm to follow the lead of your left—it will fold correctly as your left arm remains straight.

3 The power approach
You'll also feel a bent right elbow and an extended left arm deep into your downswing —both are vital to compress the ball and add power.

INSTRUCTION

Set Your Short Clubs Correctly

Hit it purer with a little forward press

There's no way to hit solid iron shots consistently if your hands don't lead the clubhead into the ball. That's the ideal position, and most of you aren't getting there. One reason is a faulty shaft angle at address—hands set behind the clubface—which causes all sorts of mis-hits. If you tilt the shaft toward the target at address, it'll go a long way toward helping you hit it pure.

—J.D. Turner

WRONG!

Address: Hands ahead

Take your grip, then push your hands toward the target so the butt of the club points just in front of your belt buckle *[above right]*. Make sure to keep the clubface square to the target line as you do this, rather than turn the face open. Placing your hands ahead should feel more powerful; it puts the club in a "trapping" position. This is probably a new sensation, as most golfers are used to setting the shaft back *[above left]* and swinging up on the ball to help get it airborne.

Backswing: Pre-set your hinge

Setting up with the shaft leaning forward has another benefit: It pre-sets your backswing wrist hinge. In fact, your right wrist is already slightly hinged by virtue of the shaft leaning forward. Starting from this position gives your backswing a head start and guarantees a full and power-rich hinge. By contrast, when the shaft leans back at address, the clubhead has a lot of catching up to do. With the wrists hinged at the top, you have the best chance of a solid, hands-ahead strike at the bottom.

INSTRUCTION

Punch Your Way to Lower Scores

This low power play checks up quick

Why you need it
The punch flies with a piercing, lower-than-normal trajectory that, amazingly, stops with more spin than a shot hit with your standard full swing.

When to play it
The classic punch-shot situation is into a headwind. The lower trajectory allows your ball to maintain its flight pattern without ballooning and falling short of your target.

How to do it
You can hit a punch shot with any iron. (Plan for a loss in distance equal to one club.) Your primary goal is to get your clubface as square to your target as possible at impact with your weight firmly on your left side. It's a 3/4 swing, which is easier to produce than a full one. Here are the specifics to keep your ball low when you have to.

—John Dahl

Two musts: Weight forward, hands forward.

Lead the club back to the ball with your turn.

Don't stop turning and keep your club low.

Address
Play the ball slightly back of center and forward press your hands so they're in line with your left thigh. Pre-set about 70 percent of your weight on your front foot.

Swing
Make a 75 percent backswing with a tiny shift of weight to your right foot. On the downswing, use more body turn than arm swing to bring the club back to the ball.

Impact
Keep your left wrist firm at impact and your clubhead low to the ground after impact. This ensures that your left wrist will lead the way through the hitting zone.

PLAN YOUR APPROACH

How to be aggressive while avoiding costly mistakes

INSTRUCTION

How to Attack When the Pin Is Back

Here's your plan to get it close

The situation

125-yard par 3, pin cut in the middle of the third tier on a green that slopes back to front. A stiff 20-mph wind is in your face.

THE TOP 100 SAY

48%—Play for the back tier with a punch/knockdown shot

38%—Play a safe low shot to the middle of the green and let your putter do the rest.

14%—When's the last time you practiced a punch? Make your regular swing and play to the middle of the green—always the smartest play.

20-mph wind

If you're an aggressive player...
Hit a knockdown to the pin

Club selection: If the card says the hole is 125 yards and the pin is back, figure you have 135 to the hole. The general rule for playing into the wind is one more club for every 10 mph. So if you normally hit a 9-iron from 135 yards, you should drop down to a 7-iron here. But since you're going to play a knockdown, drop down one more club to a 6-iron.

Swing tip: Trust that you have enough club and make a three-quarter swing back and through. Lead the club into impact with the shaft leaning toward the target.

Target: Aim at the middle of the second tier. Your knockdown shot should skip forward to the third tier before it grabs.

"Ben Hogan said, 'Never hit a high ball to a back pin.' That's great advice."
—**Charlie Sorrell**

If you're not confident with the knockdown shot...
Hit a regular full shot to the middle tier

Club selection: Drop down two clubs for the wind and make your normal swing. If you pure it you might reach the back tier. If you don't, you'll still have an excellent chance of a two-putt par.

Swing tip: Forget the wind and make a relaxed swing. Don't try to "power" the ball or juice up your tempo, because even if you pure it you'll just create more backspin and the ball will fly higher (and shorter) into the wind.

Target: Even though you're planning to land your ball on the middle tier of the green, you should still aim for the top of the pin.

"How many clubs is a 20 mph wind worth to you? Most golfers come up short even without wind. Ask yourself: can you hit the club you select over the green? If not, then you aren't swinging enough club."
—**Shawn Humphries**

If you tend to slice or hook your irons...

Play a low shot to the middle tier, because low shots spin less.

You need to keep spin to a minimum because wind exacerbates backspin, and if you hit your normal shot you'll end up short.

Club selection: Plus two for the wind.
Swing tip: You don't need a pure knockdown—just something slightly lower to keep the ball under the wind. Think of hitting a long chip—play the ball back of center and think of squaring the clubface with your body, not your hands. That means rotating your hips and shoulders to the left of your target from the top of your backswing to well past impact.
Target: Center of the green.

"If you tend to cut or hook the ball, wind can spell disaster, especially on a tee shot on a par 3. A headwind magnifies any curving ball flight, so controlling the shot shape is a critical factor. An intentional punch is ideal in this situation because it's easier to control both the distance and direction and it keeps spin to a minimum."
—**Keith Lyford**

Stop Leaving Yourself the Wrong First Putt

For more one- and two-putts, think about splitting the green into quadrants

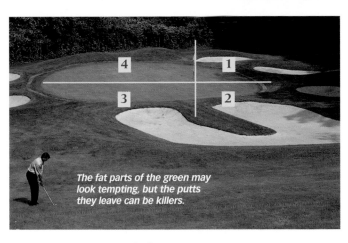

The fat parts of the green may look tempting, but the putts they leave can be killers.

The situation
You have a decent lie and you're in definite scoring range, but you're not sure if you should shoot straight for the flagstick.

The common mistake
You play to the fat part of the green to avoid trouble, but this puts you in three-putt territory.

The right play
Before you set up for any approach shot, take the extra time to divide the green into numbered quadrants, using the flagstick as the midpoint. Then examine each quadrant to determine which one is the most likely to leave you with the easiest uphill putt.

How to do it
When you divide the photo above into quadrants, you're left with two large areas to the left of the pin and two smaller ones to the right. Moving clockwise from the back right, number the quadrants 1, 2, 3 and 4. At first glance, you might be tempted to aim at quadrant 3 or 4, but each of those will leave you with a downhill putt, and you can't be aggressive when putting downhill. Quadrant 1 will also leave you a downhill putt, so you're left with quadrant 2. This may be a tougher shot, but from inside 100 yards you should be able to get your ball there and have the easiest putt on the green: straight uphill.
—**Michael Breed**

Don't Hold Back

You have a better chance of hitting the ball solidly by swinging with your normal tempo rather than trying to hold back and swing easy.

A typical green is about 30 yards deep, so if your yardage is 150 to the center, that means 135 is your number to the front of the green. Assuming there isn't a water hazard guarding the front, choose the club that gets you to that 135-140 distance and make a confident swing through impact.
—**Keith Lyford**

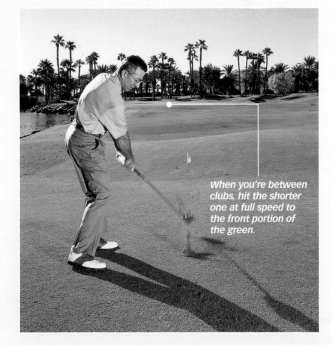

When you're between clubs, hit the shorter one at full speed to the front portion of the green.

SPECIAL PLAYS

You won't always get a perfect lie at your favorite short-iron distance. Here's how to adjust for slope and hit close to the target from anywhere inside 100 yards.

How to Hit From Any Distance

Change your club, not your tempo

After extensive testing and research, I discovered that the best way to control distance is with the length of your backswing. Make it shorter for short shots and longer for long shots, all with the same rhythm and a full follow-through. Imagine a clock, with the 12:00 position above your head. When your hands reach 12:00, you're set for full power. The 10:30 position generates 80 percent of your full-swing distance, while the 9:00 and 7:30 positions produce 60 percent and 40 percent distances, respectively.

The 7:30, 9:00 and 10:30 swings, paired with four wedges in your set, give you 12 unique distances. This system guards against the biggest short-shot killer of them all: deceleration. Find the yardage, select the club/swing combination, and pull the trigger.

—**Dave Pelz**

64° XW	60° LW
55 YARDS	**70** YARDS
55° SW	49° PW
85 YARDS	**100** YARDS

Groove three backswings (7.30, 9.00 and 10.30) and everything in between becomes easy.

10.30

64° XW	60° LW
42 YARDS	**53** YARDS
55° SW	49° PW
64 YARDS	**75** YARDS

9.00

7.30

64° XW	60° LW
28 YARDS	**35** YARDS
55° SW	49° PW
43 YARDS	**53** YARDS

Slope School

How to pick the right club when hitting to an elevated green

The situation
You're 130 yards from the pin, but the green is elevated and you don't know how many yards to add to the actual distance so you can swing the correct club.

The solution
Look at the flagstick and calculate how many flagsticks you'd have to stack up on top of your ball until the top one was even with the hole. Take this number and multiply it by eight (roughly the height of a flagstick in feet), and then take that total and divide it by three to give you a number in yards. Add that number to the listed yardage to give you the real distance to the hole and club down accordingly.

This trick also works when the green is below you. This time, stack up the flagsticks on the real one until the top flag is even with the ball. Subtract the calculated yardage from the listed distance and club down accordingly.

—**Dana Rader**

INSTRUCTION

Make Clean Contact From Sidehill Lies

Save strokes from uphill and downhill situations with this easy foot move

The problem

You're having trouble making solid contact and staying in balance when your lie isn't perfectly flat.

The solution

From these lies, you tend to lean into the hill, which almost always results in an inconsistent array of fat and thin shots, as well as poor balance in your backswing and/or finish position.

The key

The secret to avoiding this error is to make sure that your shoulders match the slope of the hill. Easier said than done—after all, how do you make your shoulders even with the slope of a hill without tipping over? The answer lies in your downhill foot.

> **QUICK TIP**
> When the ball is above your feet, take more club and choke down. When the ball is below your feet, try to maintain posture.

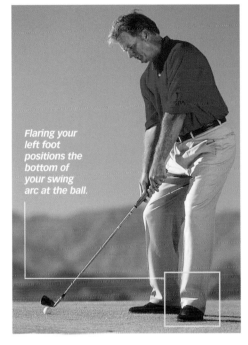

Flaring your left foot positions the bottom of your swing arc at the ball.

A flared right foot will give you more freedom to swing from an uphill lie.

Downhill lie

Club selection
A downhill lie subtracts loft from your shot, so you should take a more lofted club when you're hitting a ball down a slope.

Ball position
Play the ball in the middle of your stance or even slightly toward your back, or uphill, foot.

Stance
Flare your left foot about 45 degrees. Flaring your left foot gives your left side a more stable platform, so you can tilt your shoulders to match the slope and swing without losing your balance.

Swing
Make your regular swing with your normal tempo.

Flare your left foot and play the ball back for clean contact on a downhill.

Uphill lie

Club selection
An uphill lie adds loft to your shot, so you should take a less lofted club when you're hitting a ball up a slope.

Ball position
For an uphill lie, move your ball an inch or two farther toward your uphill foot than you normally would.

Stance
Flare your right foot about 45 degrees to even out your stance from this lie and position the ball at the bottom of your swing arc so you don't slam your club into the hill.

Swing
Make your regular swing with your normal tempo.

Play the ball forward and flare your right foot for clean contact on an uphill.

Make Your Mark (But Don't Leave It Behind)

Most of the golfers at my local daily fee don't bother fixing their ballmarks. I'm tired of putting on pocked surfaces. Can you explain how to repair marks? I'll post the answer in the locker room.

Fixing ballmarks makes the world a smoother, prettier place, but a lot of golfers didn't learn how the right way. It's basic etiquette to do this—something every golfer should learn early on. When marks aren't repaired, the damaged grass grows back slowly, causing burn marks. To fix a mark the right way, follow these simple steps:

Take a tee, key or pronged repair tool and insert it at the edge of the mark, not in the middle.

Twist the edges gently toward the center, trying not to tear the grass. Don't lift the center.

Use your putter to tamp down the surface so it's flat again.
And remember, you should be happy to fix your ballmark because it means you've hit a good shot.

Even the best players on Tour miss five to six greens a round. Unlike you, however, they rarely make five or six bogeys. A solid short game turns potential disaster holes into easy pars.

SECTION 6

YOUR SHORT GAME

Whether it's an approach to a par 5 or a greenside chip, here's how to get it close

Some days your full-swing shots just can't miss; other times you can't hit greens even from a perfect lie with your favorite club in your hands. That's when your short game shows how important it is to keeping your scores down. Those mild-mannered chips, pitches and lobs make up for poor shots in a hurry, taking you from parts unknown to a comfortable spot next to the pin with swings that rarely go above knee height.

There are thousands of ways to get the ball close from short range, but instead of confusing you with a multitude of setup and swing options, this section breaks down your short game into five simple shots: bump-and-run chips; high, medium and low pitches; and lob shots. Mastering these basic short-game plays arms you with enough shotmaking options to tackle anything the course throws at you during your round. Plus, by the time you have these short shots down pat, you'll understand the adjustments you need to make when facing more difficult situations.

Short swings are easy to learn. So if you struggle to get the ball close, pay attention to the Top 100's advice and prepare to see an instant improvement in your scores.

5 THINGS YOU'LL LEARN IN THIS SECTION

- The right way to set up for a chip so that your club automatically catches the ball clean
- How to vary your club selection to produce the correct amount of carry and roll for any situation
- How to pitch the ball close to the pin from the fairway—and even add spin if you want it
- How to pitch higher or lower so you can attack the pin regardless of what's between you and the hole
- The essential keys for pulling off flops and lob shots

TOP 100 SAY

Stick With Your Bump-and-Run

Is the average player better off hitting bump-and-run chips, or learning to chip with a wedge and varying the trajectory?

62%
Change clubs and keep the ball low to the ground at all times

38%
Become a wedge master and vary your trajectory

"It's better to use a wedge and change the trajectory by leaning forward and moving the ball position back to hit it lower. If all you know is a bump-and-run, you're limiting yourself."
—Don Hurter

"Most players have better distance control chipping with a 7- or 8-iron. Stick with your bump-and-run."
—Mike LaBauve

CHIP IT CLOSER

Here's how to make those tough little shots from off the green a piece of cake and get up-and-down every time

How to Hit the Perfect Chip

Borrow from your putting stroke to create solid short shots

As with most shots, you'll hit better chips if your setup position is correct. The goal of your chipping address position is to situate your body, arms, hands and club to create a descending blow without chunking the clubhead into the ground, or striking the ball with the leading edge of the clubface. Your setup and technique are correct if your impact position looks like this.

KEY MOVE

CLUBHEAD LOW
Compare the height of the ball with the height of the clubhead: The ball is high and the clubhead is still very low to the ground. This proves that a downward strike—not an upward flip—gets the ball rolling up the clubface and into the air.

TOE CLOSED
Although your hands should be passive and your left wrist straight, they do need to rotate so that the club turns over on its heel through impact. Try to smoothly rotate the toe of the cub toward your target (don't jerk it) as you swing through the impact area.

INSTRUCTION

How to Set Up for Solid Chips

Get the heel of the club up and the handle forward for a solid, consistent chip stroke

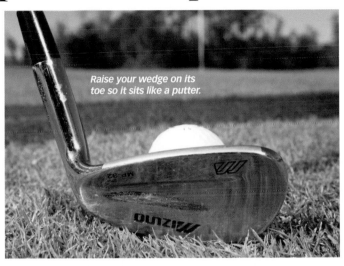

Raise your wedge on its toe so it sits like a putter.

Step 1

Aim the clubface at your target, and then raise the club slightly on its toe. This gives you a more upright lie, which makes your chip swing more of a putting stroke. A putting stroke is easier to control because it moves straight back and through. A flatter lie demands you swing the club on an arc.

Step 2

Move the handle of your club two inches farther toward the target than the front edge of the ball. This de-lofts the clubhead and promotes the downward strike that you're looking for. You can use any wedge with this technique, and even your 8- or 9-iron will work.

Step 3

The butt of your club should point a couple of inches left of the center of your body. Make sure that your shoulders are square to the target line and your weight is over your left foot, and then play the ball off your right big toe.

Step 4

Move the club with your arms and shoulders while keeping your hands and wrists quiet and your weight on your left side. As you swing through the hitting zone, you should feel as though you're striking down on the ball while gently closing the clubface.
—**Todd Sones**

Make a "y" to Chip It Close

You'll catch the ball clean with the handle forward

Fault

You hit your chips fat so they never get close to the flag, or you blade them over the green.

Fix

As you take your address, make sure you set most of your weight over your left foot and move the handle of the club forward. Notice that when you do this your arms and clubshaft form a lower case "y".

Establishing this y and keeping it intact during your chipping motion will allow you to come down sharply on the ball and catch it clean before your clubhead makes contact with the turf. Try to "trap" the ball between your clubface and the ground at impact. This will keep your hands forward of the ball and ensure proper contact.

—**Steve Bosdosh**

Make a "y" at address...

...and maintain it during your swing.

How to Chip From Every Lie

Let your backswing do the work for you

The problem

You assume that one swing will get the job done for every chipping situation. In reality, however, you need at least two: one for lies in the rough and another for tight lies. Here's how to match your swing to the situation and leave your chips closer to the hole.

How to find the right chip plane

Spread some balls around a chipping green, making sure you're left with many different lies. Then, vary your technique to match each shot. If it's available, place a mirror behind you and check that your backswing works to the inside on normal chips and outside on chips from the rough. If you're still struggling, exaggerate each move until you get the results you want.
—**Brian Mogg**

Swing inside from a tight lie

Your goal is to sweep the ball off the turf with a rounded swing. Imagine a shaft stuck in the ground behind your ball and on your target line. Take the clubhead away to the inside of the shaft with very little wrist hinge, as though you were attempting a long putt. Do the same on your forward swing, and release the clubhead toward the target while keeping your hands at thigh height.

Swing outside from the rough

When your ball is sitting down, swing your clubhead outside the shaft on your backswing and hinge your wrists aggressively to get the club up. (Think "low hands, high clubhead.") On your downswing, drop your arms toward the ground and across the ball (left of the target) without releasing your hands. This allows you to dig deep and pop the ball up without fear of catching it thin.

Keep your hands low.

TIP Since this is a shallow swing, expect minimal spin and more roll once the ball hits the turf.

Quickly hinge the club up.

TIP You'll generate extra loft using this technique, so plan to fly the ball at least three quarters of the distance to the flagstick.

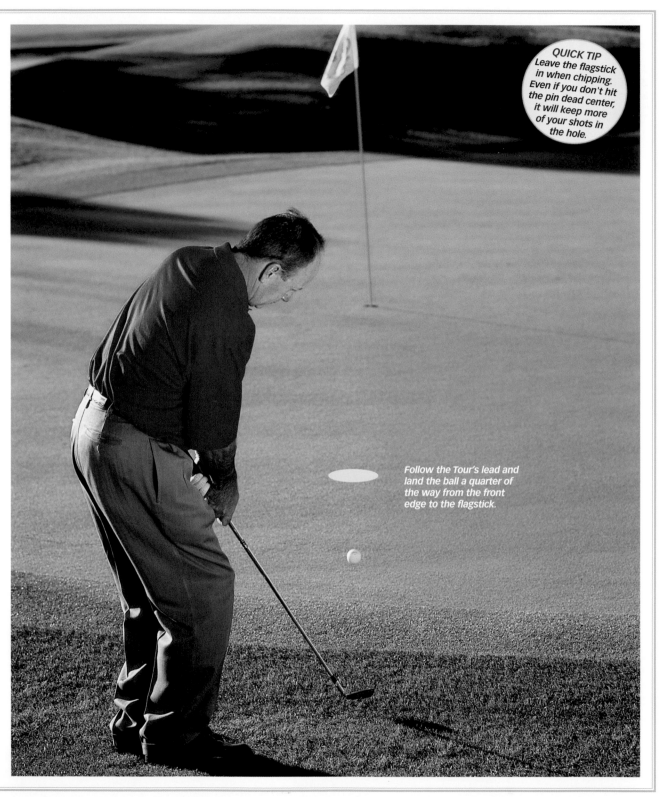

Land the Ball in the Right Spot

Use the Tour's 25 percent rule

Working with CompuSport, a biomechanics research firm, I studied 30 PGA Tour pros hitting shots inside 100 yards. On short shots from just off the green, they consistently landed the ball a quarter of the way from the front edge of the green to the flag. So, if the hole was eight paces from the front, they dropped the ball two paces on.

When they needed more or less flight, the pros changed clubs but kept the landing spot a quarter of the way on. If the green sloped away, they took a more lofted club and used the extra height to counter the faster surface. If the green ran uphill, they used a less lofted club for a hotter roll. But 25 percent was the Tour's golden rule.

—**Fred Griffin**

QUICK TIP
Leave the flagstick in when chipping. Even if you don't hit the pin dead center, it will keep more of your shots in the hole.

Follow the Tour's lead and land the ball a quarter of the way from the front edge to the flagstick.

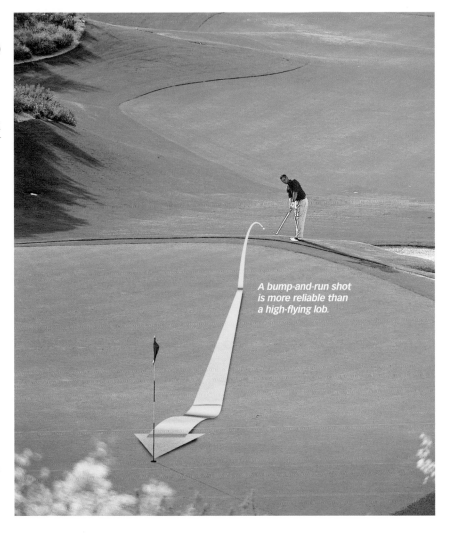

How to Roll It to Tap-In Range

Keep the ball on the ground when you have lots of green in front of you

Unless you have a Tour-level short game or practice flop shots regularly, forget about hoisting one of those high-lofted shots to the hole—it's unnecessary and ups the odds for a miscue. Even if you catch it clean, it will have big-time backspin, so if you land on a slope it will roll back down.

Whenever there's lots of green between you and the hole, get the ball rolling as soon as you can. Chip the ball onto the green and send it toward the cup like it's a putt. It's a lot easier to make solid contact with the short swing you'll need, and your distance control will be a lot better, too.

—**Jim Murphy**

How to pick the right chip stick

● *A sand-wedge chip will roll the same distance as it flies (a 1:1 ratio). A pitching-wedge chip will roll twice as far as it flies (1:2); a 9-iron is 1:3 and so on.*

● *Based on the 25% Rule, if there's 40 feet between you and the pin, an 9-iron is the perfect choice since the shot needs 10 feet of carry and 30 feet of roll.*

A bump-and-run shot is more reliable than a high-flying lob.

Should I Chip With One Club or Many?

If I'm looking to have a great short game, should I always hit bump-and-runs with a 7- or 8-iron or should I use a single club, such as a wedge, all the time?

You need two basic shots—the bump-and-run, and the lofted chip. The bump-and-run is the best for dry, firm ground because it's difficult to predict how a higher shot will bounce once it hits the ground. You're better off keeping it low and letting it roll like a putt. Wet and soft greens demand a wedge so you can fly the shot almost all the way to the hole. You don't need to alter your trajectory too much. Instead, lengthen or shorten your motion depending on the carry distance.

—**Donald Crawley**

Map Out Your Attack

If you can't judge the distance, play to a zone

When you chip, picture the green divided into four sections. Zone 1 is closest to you, Zones 2 and 3 are in the middle, and Zone 4 is the farthest away. No matter where the hole is located, always land the ball in Zone 1 and make it roll to the hole. What club will do the job? If your ball lies just off the green, use this system:

● **Finish in Zone 1:** Sand or lob wedge

● **Roll to Zone 2:** 9-iron or pitching wedge

● **Roll to Zone 3:** 8- or 9-iron

● **Roll to Zone 4:** 7- or 8-iron

—**Eden Foster**

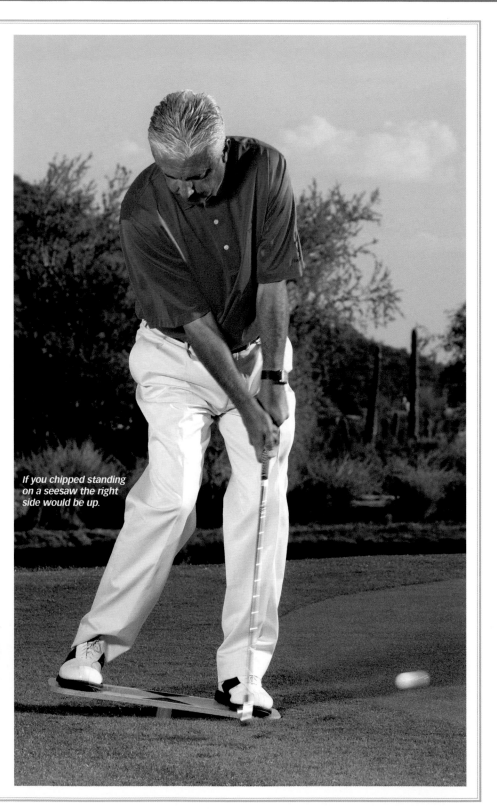

If you chipped standing on a seesaw the right side would be up.

Get on Your Left Side to Chip It Stiff

A proper weight shift will guarantee better contact from tight lies

The problem

When you face a chip from a tight lie you fear skulling it so you hit it fat.

The solution

Pretend you're balanced on a small seesaw. At address, the seesaw should tilt to the left. This means your weight is perfectly positioned so you can hit down on the ball and catch it clean.

How to practice it

Hit chips with an empty plastic water bottle under your right foot. Play the ball slightly back of center, and use the bottle to remind you to shift your weight over to your left leg. Shifting your weight forward and keeping it there during your stroke correctly positions the bottom of your swing arc at the back of the ball—you won't be able to hit the ground behind the ball if you try.

—Bill Forrest

WRONG! | **RIGHT!**

Simply shifting your hips to the left won't get your weight on your left side where it needs to be for clean contact.

Practice chipping with a small plastic bottle under your left foot to remind you to set your weight forward and keep it there.

How to Catch Every Chip Clean

Use this simple drill to play perfect little shots

Fault

You try to lift the ball into the air and end up blading it across the green. Solid chips are the result of hitting down into the back of the ball, not trying to lift it up.

Fix

Here's a drill that will produce the kind of chips you dream about—unless it's those blue corn dealies. You'll need to hit the snack aisle for those.

Balance a club on the top of a water bottle as shown (it's easier than it looks), and place the ball 12 inches behind the middle of the grip. Make your chip stroke without knocking the shaft off the bottle [photo right]. You'll need to descend into the ball and keep your clubhead low to the ground after impact. If you try to scoop the ball or allow the club to pass your hands [photo above], you'll send the club and the bottle flying.

—**Glenn Deck**

Swing down, not up, to avoid a game of pickup sticks.

How to Chip Without Yipping

Be aggressive without hitting it too hard

The next time you face a chip shot, think about your stroke being SAD—Short, Aggressive and Down. The enemies of good chipping are LPU: Long, Passive and Up. Do any of those and you'll CSC—Chunk, Skull or Chili. So here's how you can be SAD about your chipping game in 10 minutes.

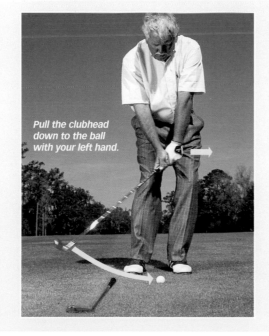

Pull the clubhead down to the ball with your left hand.

Step 1

Take your pitching wedge or 9-iron. Set up with a narrow stance and play the ball about midway between your heels. Lay a second club on the ground one inch outside your right foot as shown. The idea is to swing over this club on the way back and down to the ball.

Step 2

Swing back until your hands are about even with your right pocket. This is all you need—any longer and you'll decelerate on the downswing to compensate.

Feel a firm left wrist at impact.

Step 3

Pull the club aggressively down to impact with your left hand. Your wrists and hands should feel firm—that's how you know you didn't try to scoop at the ball. You'll make a short follow-through and see your ball track to the hole.

—**John Elliott**

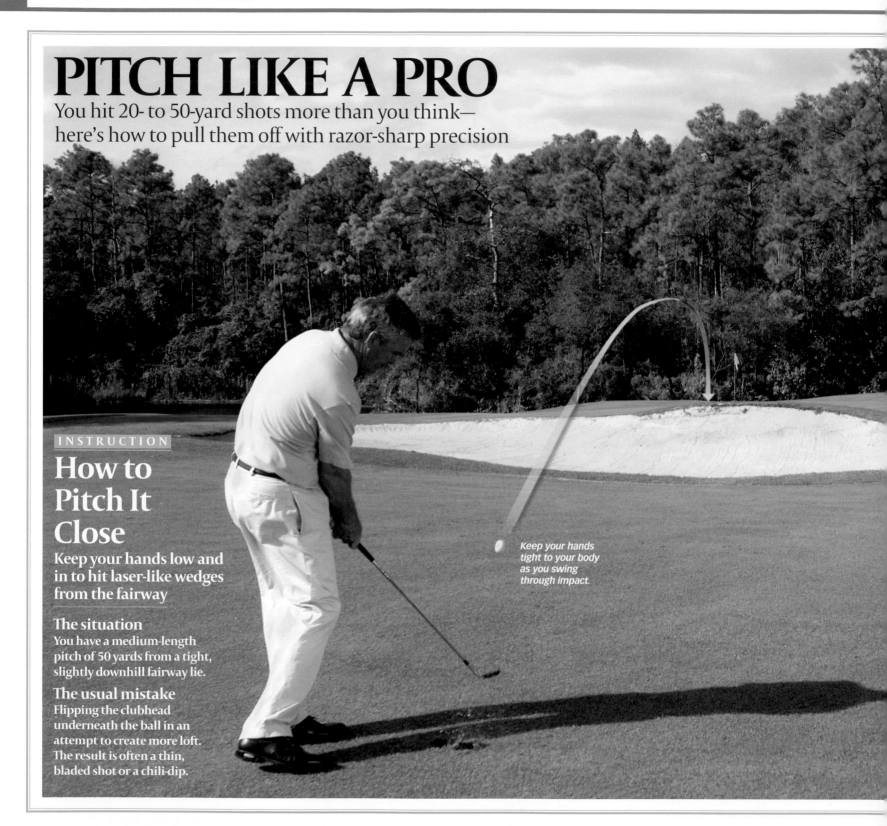

PITCH LIKE A PRO

You hit 20- to 50-yard shots more than you think—
here's how to pull them off with razor-sharp precision

INSTRUCTION

How to Pitch It Close

Keep your hands low and in to hit laser-like wedges from the fairway

The situation
You have a medium-length pitch of 50 yards from a tight, slightly downhill fairway lie.

The usual mistake
Flipping the clubhead underneath the ball in an attempt to create more loft. The result is often a thin, bladed shot or a chili-dip.

Keep your hands tight to your body as you swing through impact.

How to get the technique

Like you've read, you should lead with the handle of the club, not the head. More importantly, keep your clubhead low and tight to your body as you rotate through the shot *[below left]*. The closer the handle is to your body, the easier it is to hold your wrist angles through impact.

The key to avoiding the flip is to use the opposite end of the club than what seems natural, that is, the grip instead of the clubhead. By pulling the butt of the handle in and up to your left, you will turn to square the clubface and drop the clubhead down to the ball. Turn your body—not your hands—and just let the ball get in the way of your rotation.

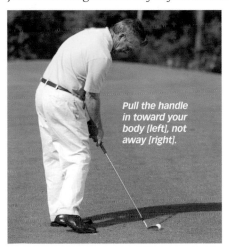

Pull the handle in toward your body [left], not away [right].

WRONG!

Knuckles to the Ground

As you swing through, you should feel as if you're trying to scrape your knuckles along the ground. This sensation will lower the shaft and bring your hands inside, making it nearly impossible to scoop. You can practice this by hitting half-shots, starting with your hands at thigh height. Think about maintaining the relationship between your hands and the clubhead as you swing forward, keeping your hands close to the ground. Pull—don't push—and you'll hit the ball solidly every time.
—**Rick McCord**

Point your knuckles down...

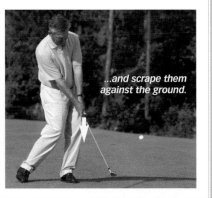

...and scrape them against the ground.

5 More Keys to Solid Pitching

1 Narrow your stance from your normal iron setup so your feet are slightly less than shoulder-width apart.

2 Play the ball in the center of your stance. Move it slightly forward of center for a high, soft-landing shot and back for a lower shot.

3 Allow the length of the shot to dictate the length of your swing. The longer the shot, the longer your arms should swing back and through.

4 Feel like the clubface is sliding across the inside of the ball, not hitting the back of it. An inside approach will keep your right palm facing out to the right, adding loft.

5 Don't limit your follow-through. The length of your swing is not as important as its speed. Let your finish be dictated by the rate of acceleration: the faster your swing, the longer your finish.
—**Rick McCord**

INSTRUCTION

Pitch It High or Low

Here are three shots that travel the same distance on three different trajectories

Not all pitches are equal—sometimes you need more loft to carry an obstacle or to fly the ball onto an upper tier, while other situations require you to hit a low runner so you can use the contour of the green to snuggle your ball up to the hole. So to get it as close as possible on any pitch shot, you must know how to alter the trajectory of the ball. All you need to do is alter your setup and swing length to produce the desired height. Follow the chart below to become an instant shotmaker from 20 yards, and you'll knock it tight regardless of what the course throws at you.

—**Bill Moretti**

Swing along your shoulder line, which will point right of your target due to your closed stance.

LOW TRAJECTORY
Take the clubhead back to knee height and follow-through to your waist.

Strengthen your grip by rotating your hands to the right.

Pitching adjustments (20-yard shot)

	Low shot	Medium shot	High shot
Grip	Stronger (hands rotated to the right)	Standard	Weak (hands rotated to the left)
Stance	Closed shoulders; ball back of center	Square shoulders; ball middle of stance	Open shoulders; ball forward of center
Shaft lean	Butt end of club at middle of left thigh; hands 4 to 6 inches in front of ball	Butt end of club at middle of left thigh; hands slightly forward of ball	Butt end of club at navel; hands 1 to 3 inches behind ball
Swing length	Knee-high to waist-high	Waist-high to waist-high	Chest-high to waist-high
Swing path	Along shoulder line (right of target due to closed stance)	Along shoulder line	Along shoulder line (left of target due to open stance)

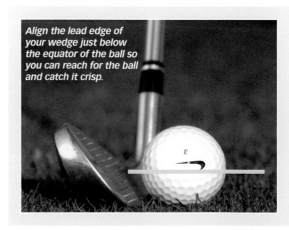

Align the lead edge of your wedge just below the equator of the ball so you can reach for the ball and catch it crisp.

MEDIUM TRAJECTORY
Square shoulders, hands slightly forward, swing waist to waist.

HIGH TRAJECTORY
Weaken grip, open shoulders, swing chest-high to waist-high.

DRILL

Reach for It!

Try this trick to stop blading your chips

Address the ball in a taller posture and align the leading edge of your club just below the equator of the ball. On your forward stroke, stay loose and allow your arms to lengthen. If you do, your club will bottom out in front of the ball like it should. "Underreaching" at address gives you a better margin for error to create crisp contact.

—Tim Mahoney

DRILL

How to be Pitcher Perfect

Hit the shot with your body, not your hands

The problem

Most poor pitch shots result from overactive hands and wrists, so keep them calm and instead pitch the ball with your body. Here's a drill that will teach you to rotate your upper and lower body completely through the shot and produce a more consistent launch angle and extra distance.

The solution

Place a dowel that's at least 24" (or longer) in the hole on top of your grip and lean the shaft forward at address so the dowel is left of your front hip. Then try to pitch the ball by pulling the club through impact with your body turn, not by flipping your wrists.

—Anne Cain

QUICK TIP
For a smoother pitch swing, use a weak grip, with the Vs formed by your thumb and forefinger pointed at your chin.

NO!
Don't stop turning or get handsy.

YES!
Keep your hands passive—pull them through impact with your body turn.

YOU'RE DOING IT WRONG IF...
The dowel smacks the left side of your torso in your forward-swing.

YOU'RE DOING IT RIGHT IF...
You pitch the ball cleanly and the dowel stays left of your body throughout your motion.

Soften Up Your Pitches

How to hit it higher and land it softer

The situation

You're faced with a tricky pitch with an obstacle between you and the pin. You need loft and pinpoint distance control or you won't get up and down.

The standard play

Hit a high, floating lob shot with your 60-degree wedge or a lower pitch with tons of spin to get your ball to stop after a single hop. Problem is, the lob shot is a high-risk alternative and most recreational players can't generate the spin needed to stop the ball on a dime.

The better play

The Super Soft Pitch—a simple shot that adds extra loft to your everyday pitching motion. You'll get a high shot that stops near where it lands without having to make the perfect lob.

—**Donald Crawley**

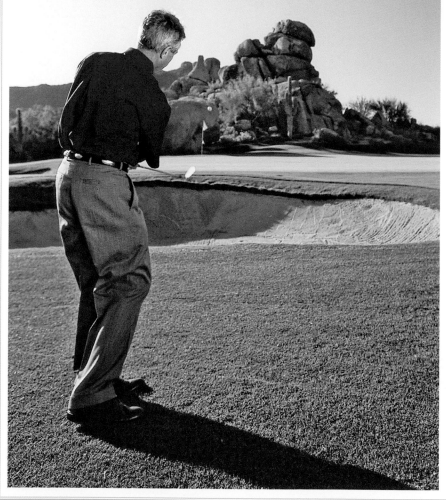

How to play the Super Soft Pitch

The key to hitting the Super Soft Pitch is to pre-set your body in the correct impact position at address. This helps you strike the ball with the right amount of loft. In the past, you've pitched the ball either too low or too high because your poor impact position either added or subtracted loft from your clubface.

Setup

Sole either your 56- or 60-degree wedge on the turf with the face square and pointing directly at your target. (There's no need to open it—that only creates extra bounce and increases the potential for thin contact.)

SHOULDERS
Make sure your shoulders are level and that your arms hang straight down. Ease up your grip pressure—the Super Soft Pitch requires soft hands.

BALL POSITION
Play the ball just slightly back of center and lean your shaft forward. (Be careful not to close your clubface.) Your grip should line up with your sternum about an inch in front of the ball with your weight favoring your front foot.

Swing

Make your backswing by swinging your arms and chest away from the ball using soft hands and an easy hinge of your wrists. Your swing path should feel pretty straight, but with a slight turn so that the toe of the clubhead points straight up once your hands reach knee height.

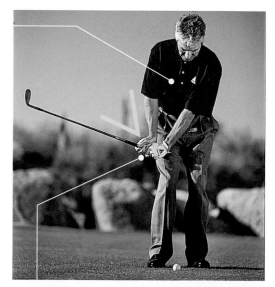

DOWNSWING
Stop your backswing just as your hands pass your right knee. On your downswing, turn toward the target and unhinge your wrists so that you return the clubhead, shaft and weight to the same position they were in at address. When you do this correctly, your club will descend into the bottom of the ball with the correct loft.

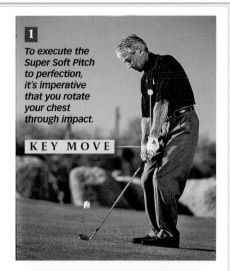

1

To execute the *Super Soft Pitch* to perfection, it's imperative that you rotate your chest through impact.

KEY MOVE

2

You want everything rotating together or you won't be correct at impact.

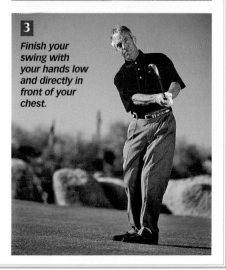

3

Finish your swing with your hands low and directly in front of your chest.

INSTRUCTION

How to Make Your Pitches Bite

Accelerate then stop to get the check, please

If your pitch shots fly straight, but they land on the green without any spin and run past the hole, use the keys below to help your pitches land on your target then grab the green harder than a miner's handshake.

QUICK TIP
The faster you accelerate then stop, the more the ball will run up the face and grab in the grooves. That groove-grab adds spin.

Step 1
On your backswing, point your thumbs at the sky and the butt of the club at the ground.

Step 2
Come down sharply into the ball to get it rolling up the clubface.

Step 3
Once you feel impact, stop your hands abruptly at waist height and keep them and your club low.

CHECKPOINT

For Sale: Extra Spin

The right gear makes for easy checkups

Three tests by Golf Laboratories show that a rusty wedge and a clean, high-spin ball can give you thousands of extra revolutions of spin (www.golflabs.com).

Chart 1 — SPIN RATE RPM (0 to 15,000): UNFINISHED WEDGE, CHROMED WEDGE, UNFINISHED WEDGE 3 SEASONS

Chart 2 — SPIN RATE RPM (0 to 15,000): TITLEIST PRO V1, TOPFLITE EXTREME DISTANCE

Chart 3 — SPIN RATE RPM (0 to 15,000): NORMAL CONDITIONS, MUDDY BALL, WET CONDITIONS

UNFINISHED BUSINESS
New chromed and unfinished 56° sand wedges (same make and model) produced similar rpms, but the same unfinished wedge used over three seasons sent spin rates off the charts.

SPIN BALL WIZARDS
Does a true high-spin ball (like the Titleist Pro V1) spin more than a pure distance model (like the Top-Flite Extreme Distance) off the same wedge? The results speak for themselves.

CLEAN UP YOUR ACT
Mud on the ball reduced spin by 33%, and water (simulated by dunking the club and ball) cut the spin rate by 49%. So if you play under the lift, clean and place rule, take advantage of it!

HOW TO LOB IT

Sometimes you need to carry an obstacle and fly the ball all the way to the flag. These tricks will turn you into a major flopper.

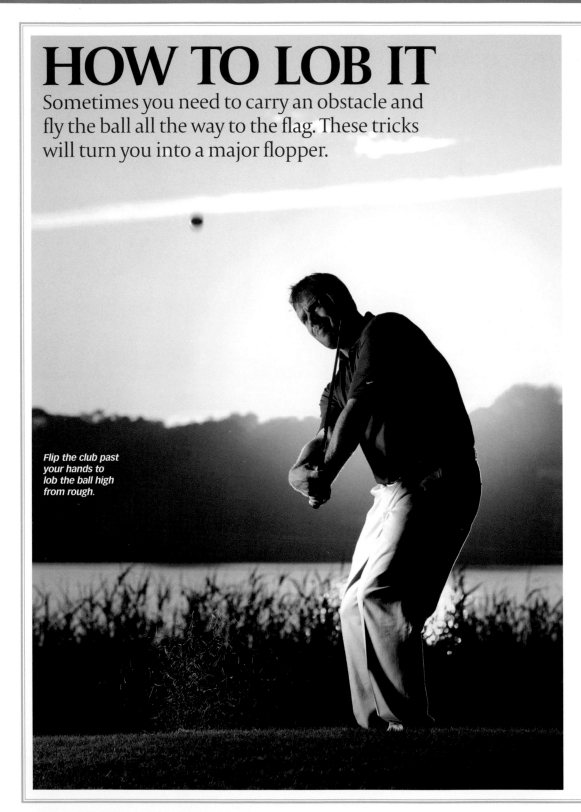

Flip the club past your hands to lob the ball high from rough.

INSTRUCTION

Get Wristy to Lob It From Rough

On this shot, it's OK to make an early release

The mistake you should make

On most shots, wristy impact is a recipe for disaster. However, when you have to pop the ball high and soft, you actually want to flip your wrists.

How to commit it

Set up with a slightly open stance and play the ball slightly back of center. Take your regular pitch backswing, but as you come back down, slow your arms and hips (something you do anyway if you often muff pitch shots) and quickly break your wrists through impact. Don't allow your arms to pass your body. If it helps to think of folding your left wrist or bowing your right, do it. At the finish, your right hand should hide your left. While this is the opposite of traditional short-game advice, it's exactly what you need in this situation.

Why it works

Flipping the club past your hands increases the effective loft of the clubface. So you get extra height on the shot that you normally wouldn't get if you adhered to the standard advice of keeping your hands ahead of the club at impact. Plus, deceleration is common on short swings, so you don't even have to practice this shot. The technique works with any of your wedges, but to hit the ball extra high and help it land soft (don't expect much spin with this technique), use your lob wedge.

Don't try it when...

Your lie is tight. The wrist-break flop shot requires perfect timing and has zero margin of error from a tight lie, so unless you have a fluffy lie in greenside rough, don't attempt this shot.
—Eden Foster

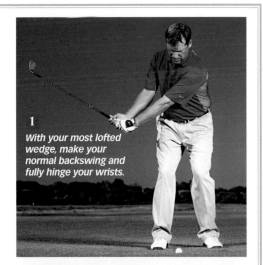

1

With your most lofted wedge, make your normal backswing and fully hinge your wrists.

2

As you approach impact, apply the brakes to your arms and step on the gas with your wrists.

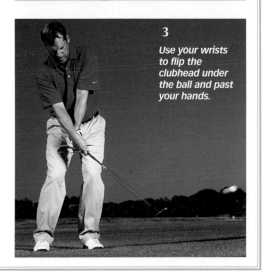

3

Use your wrists to flip the clubhead under the ball and past your hands.

Stay Down to Loft the Ball Up

Keep your focus on the point of impact well after the ball is on its way

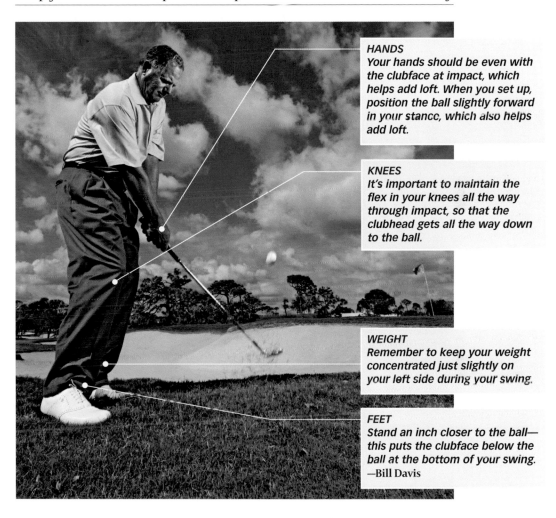

HANDS
Your hands should be even with the clubface at impact, which helps add loft. When you set up, position the ball slightly forward in your stance, which also helps add loft.

KNEES
It's important to maintain the flex in your knees all the way through impact, so that the clubhead gets all the way down to the ball.

WEIGHT
Remember to keep your weight concentrated just slightly on your left side during your swing.

FEET
Stand an inch closer to the ball— this puts the clubface below the ball at the bottom of your swing.
—Bill Davis

Aim for Groove 4

It's the key for lobbing from tight lies

Imagine contacting the ball between the third and fifth grooves up from the bottom of the clubface. This encourages you to make a descending blow, with the shaft leaning forward at impact. Your wrists won't break down, and the ball will climb up the face and into the air.
—**Charlie King**

Hit down on the ball, making contact on the fourth groove to get the ball rolling up the face.

ESCAPING THE SAND

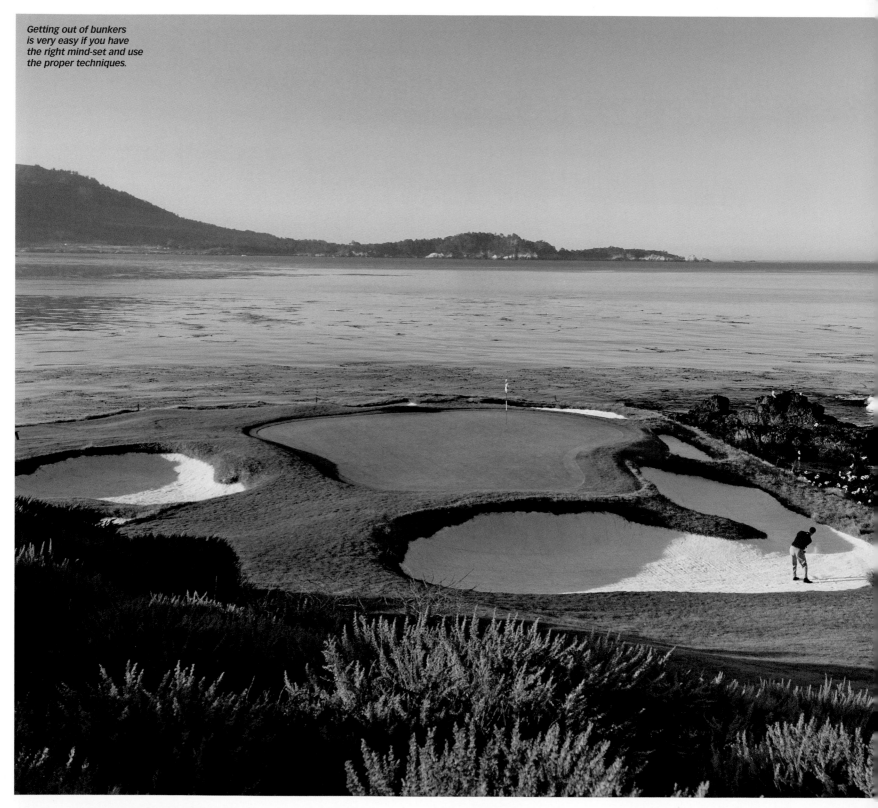

Getting out of bunkers is very easy if you have the right mind-set and use the proper techniques.

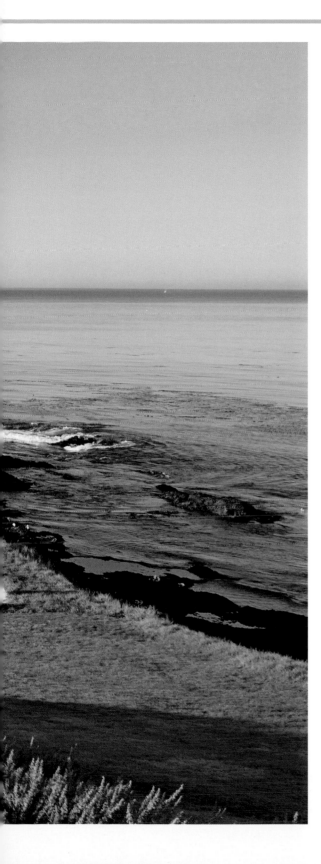

SECTION 7

ESCAPING THE SAND

Bunker shots come in many shapes, lies and levels of difficulty. Here's how to play them all.

There's a big gap between the bunker skills seen on Tour and those on display at your local muni. Most recreational golfers approach a sandy lie like the ball is covered in Kryptonite. Pros, on the other hand, thrive in sand, and would rather hit out of a bunker than chip from the rough. Tour players prefer bunker shots compared to other alternatives when they miss the green because (1) it's an easy shot, and (2) it's something they practice regularly. Unless the lie is very difficult, you can expect a top-tier player to get up and down from a bunker two-thirds of the time.

The goal of this section is to close this gap and help you become more familiar with sand shots and the relatively simple technique needed to get the ball out and onto the green. How simple? It's the only shot where it's okay for you to miss the ball. Plus, the club you use most often from sand comes with a special design trait—bounce—that makes blasting out just that much easier.

The instruction on the following pages will help you conquer any bunker lie imaginable, including the ones that typically send your scores through the roof. Soon, you'll look forward to hitting from sand—just like the pros do.

5 THINGS YOU'LL LEARN IN THIS SECTION

- How to escape greenside bunkers on your first swing
- Adjustments you need to make for different lies and conditions to blast the ball close
- How to take the right amount of sand and correctly use the bounce on your wedges
- How to add height and spin to stop your sand shots from short distances
- Setup and swing keys to handle the most nasty and terrifying bunker situations

The Most Difficult Shot in Golf

In a recent *GOLF Magazine* survey, we asked what shot gives you the most trouble.

40-yard bunker shot: 33%

Approach shot over water: 22%

Other: 26%

Half-wedge shot: 19%

Even Tour pros don't fare well from the sand at this distance, getting up and down less than a third of the time. By comparison, the 2006 PGA Tour average for getting up and down from a greenside bunker was 55 percent.

"On long bunker shots, drop down to an 9- or 8-iron and make a U-shaped swing (instead of the V-shaped swing you make in greenside bunkers). Hit the sand about an inch behind the ball and follow through. Your ball will still ride out on a cushion of sand, but the less-lofted club and rounder swing will fly the ball to the green."

—Dr. Jim Suttie

BUNKER-SHOT BASICS

Proven techniques for getting out of sand
traps on the first try—every time

How to Blast It Close From the Sand

Follow these three
easy steps for
foolproof escapes
from normal lies

12:00

Keep your legs wide and quiet.

Attack from the inside.

Step 1: With the flagstick representing 12:00 on a clock face, open up your stance just slightly, so your feet, hips and shoulders are pointing to 11:30. Aim the leading edge of your sand wedge at the flag.

Step 2: Spread your feet two inches wider than normal. A wider stance helps quiet your legs so you can correctly swing more with your arms. Plus, a wider stance makes it easier to repeat your swing and control your clubhead.

Step 3: These adjustments will help you attack the ball from the inside with the clubface square to the target, so not only will you get out of the bunker, the ball will fly at your target.

—**Scott Sackett**

How to Stop Leaving the Ball in the Bunker

Make a steep swing and a round follow-through to guarantee your next shot is a putt

The problem
You hit a lot of your bunker shots too fat, and many of them stay in the bunker.

Why it's happening
Your swing is too shallow, causing your wrists to uncock too early. This forces you to hit too far behind the ball and chunk the shot.

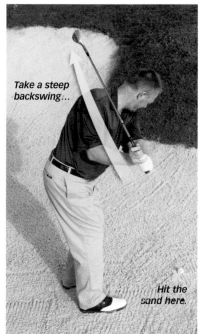

Take a steep backswing...

Hit the sand here.

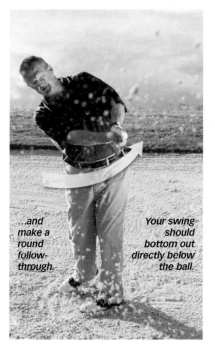

...and make a round follow-through.

Your swing should bottom out directly below the ball.

Fix 1
Make a steeper swing

Position your feet a little left of the target line and take the club straight up and down, contacting the sand just behind the ball. This motion will prevent your wrists from uncocking prematurely on the way back down.

Fix 2
Follow through to your left

After impact, swing your club around your body, left of the target line. Following this path will encourage you to use your body more during your downswing so your hands won't take over and shut down the face.

How to get the right depth

Stick a tee in the sand so that you can see only the top, then place a ball on it. Now play a shot. If you make a steep enough swing, you'll hit the tee around its midpoint down in the sand. You'll know you've done it right if the tee flies out of the sand and your ball floats toward your target.

—**Martin Hall**

DRILL

Play the Sand, Not the Ball

In bunkers, the sand is the target

When you're in a greenside bunker the club should never touch the ball. You want your wedge to toss the sand beneath and behind the ball onto the green. The ball will float out on the whoosh of sand.

You must convince yourself that the ball is an afterthought on these shots. To practice this, stand in the flat part of a practice bunker and place two tees opposite your left instep as shown below.

You don't need a ball. Hinge your wrists quickly on your backswing to create an upright path, then swing down and let your sand wedge hit about two inches behind the tees. Make a full follow-through, finishing with your hands at shoulder height. You'll see that the tees have flown up and toward the target along with the sand you sprayed.

Repeat this drill five times, and see how high and far you can make the tees fly. Then drop a ball down and repeat that swing. With a little practice, escaping bunkers will become an afterthought, too.
—**Mike Malaska**

You want the ball to ride out on a cushion of sand.

Start this drill by placing two tees where the ball should be.

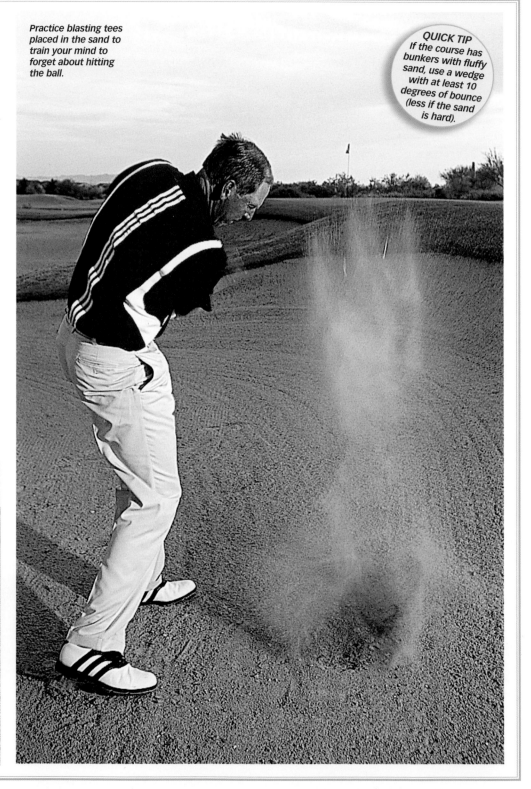

Practice blasting tees placed in the sand to train your mind to forget about hitting the ball.

QUICK TIP
If the course has bunkers with fluffy sand, use a wedge with at least 10 degrees of bounce (less if the sand is hard).

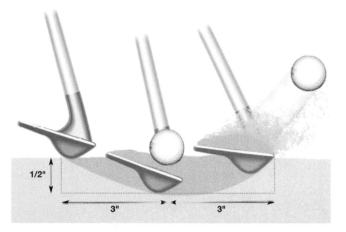

Is Your Divot in the Right Place?

This simple drill gives you the answer

A perfect bunker swing enters the sand about two to three inches behind the ball, skims a half-inch to an inch under the surface, then emerges about three inches in front of where the ball rested. The clubhead never touches the ball itself. The sand carries the ball up and out.

To see if you're doing it correctly, draw parallel lines in the sand about six inches apart, drop a ball between them and make your swing. Check the guide at right to see if you're entering the sand too early, entering the sand too late or taking too large of a divot.

—**Paul Marchand**

1/2"

3" 3"

Imagine a cheese danish with the ball in the center of the cheese, and simply knock out the entire danish. That's how big your divot should be.
—Steve Bosdosh

GREEN →

Check your track marks

PERFECT The club never touched the ball.

TOO DEEP This one was left in the bunker.

ENTERED TOO EARLY Left it in the bunker again.

ENTERED TOO LATE This one was bladed over the green.

How to Use Your Wedge's Bounce

That chunk of metal on the bottom of your wedge is the key to hitting great bunker shots

On most iron shots from the fairway, the leading edge of the club touches the ground first, and then digs into the turf. **On shots from the bunker, the first thing that should enter the sand must be the trailing edge of your wedge.** This allows the bounce (the fat, protruding hunk of metal on the bottom of the club) to glide the club through the sand rather than digging into it and stopping the forward momentum of your clubhead.

Bury a two-by-four that's at least 12 inches long in the sand so that the top is even with the sand's surface. Pile about an inch of sand on the board and place a ball on top. Make your normal bunker swing and try to erase the sand from the board,

making contact an inch or two behind the ball. Try to get the pocket of sand to reach the green. This drill familiarizes you with how bounce feels in action, and also trains you to take divots that are the correct size and depth.
—**Scott Sackett**

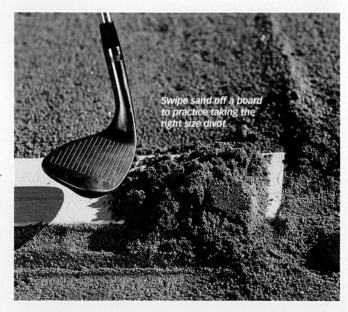

Swipe sand off a board to practice taking the right size divot.

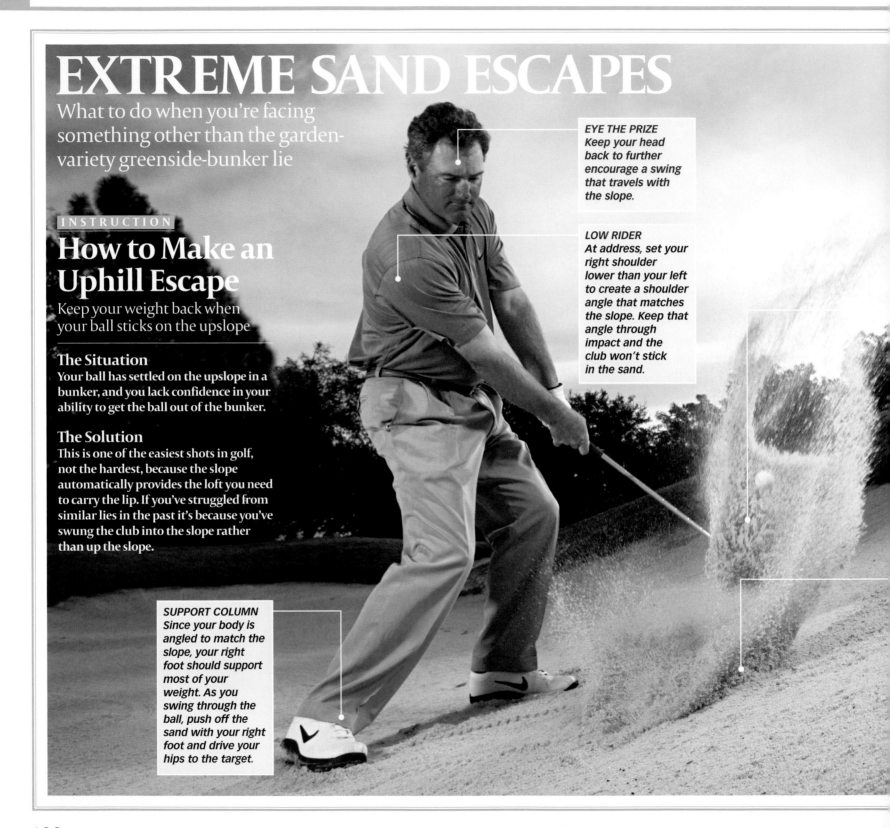

EXTREME SAND ESCAPES

What to do when you're facing something other than the garden-variety greenside-bunker lie

INSTRUCTION

How to Make an Uphill Escape

Keep your weight back when your ball sticks on the upslope

The Situation
Your ball has settled on the upslope in a bunker, and you lack confidence in your ability to get the ball out of the bunker.

The Solution
This is one of the easiest shots in golf, not the hardest, because the slope automatically provides the loft you need to carry the lip. If you've struggled from similar lies in the past it's because you've swung the club into the slope rather than up the slope.

EYE THE PRIZE
Keep your head back to further encourage a swing that travels with the slope.

LOW RIDER
At address, set your right shoulder lower than your left to create a shoulder angle that matches the slope. Keep that angle through impact and the club won't stick in the sand.

SUPPORT COLUMN
Since your body is angled to match the slope, your right foot should support most of your weight. As you swing through the ball, push off the sand with your right foot and drive your hips to the target.

All you need to do to hit a perfect bunker shot (one that settles near the flag and rolls very little) is angle your hips and shoulders to match the slope and make your everyday bunker swing. It's the same principle as hitting from an upslope in the fairway or rough.

—**Brian Mogg**

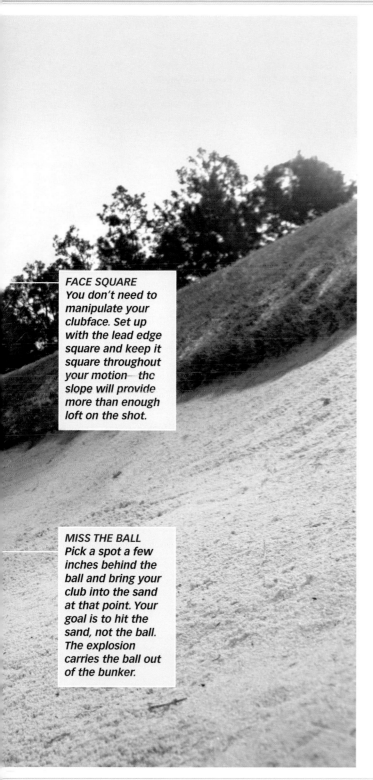

FACE SQUARE
You don't need to manipulate your clubface. Set up with the lead edge square and keep it square throughout your motion—the slope will provide more than enough loft on the shot.

MISS THE BALL
Pick a spot a few inches behind the ball and bring your club into the sand at that point. Your goal is to hit the sand, not the ball. The explosion carries the ball out of the bunker.

"You should feel most of your weight on the ball of your right foot as you blast through the sand."

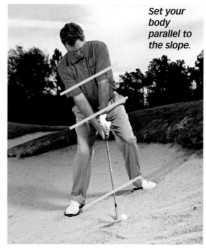

Set your body parallel to the slope.

Step 1
Play the ball in the center and dig your right foot in deep to anchor your swing. Unlike a standard bunker shot where you open the clubface, address the ball with the face square. The slope will give the ball ample lift. Tilt your body so that your shoulders are angled the same as the slope you're standing on. (Lay a club across your chest to check if you're angled correctly.)

Keep your weight back.

Step 2
Pick a spot two inches behind the ball and try to hit the sand at that exact spot. Swing your arms and club up the slope and on the same angle of your hips and shoulders. This produces an ascending path through impact. It's easy to do if you keep your shoulders tilted and your weight back. You should feel most of your weight on the ball of your right foot as you blast through the sand.

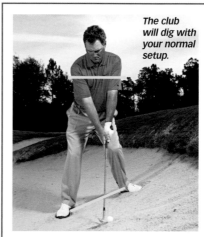

The club will dig with your normal setup.

WRONG!

Don't do this!
From this lie, your typical bunker setup—shoulders level with the flat part of the bunker—will cause the club to dig in rather than glide through the sand, and your ball will stay in the hazard.

Bury Your Club From Buried Lies

For nasty buried lies, your best bet is to go pound sand!

The situation

Your ball is three-quarters buried in loose sand toward the upper part of a steep lip. Even taking a stance won't be easy. You'll have no trouble swinging the club back, but deep sand and the overhanging lip will severely limit your follow-through.

The solution

Realistically, you can't do much more to the ball than dislodge it. But guess what? That's about all you have to do! In fact, you're free to commit the most common bunker error of all time and quit on the shot. More good news? You get to make a violent, no-finish swing and pound that stupid bunker!

How to do it

Step 1: Use whichever of your wedges has the most bounce and open the blade just a bit at address. As you finish settling into your posture, dig your back foot deeper in the sand than your front.

Step 2: Make a full backswing, then slam the club powerfully into the sand an inch or two behind your ball as if you're trying to bury the clubhead.

Step 3: Don't expect any follow-through, just a soft rebound effect as your club emerges lazily from the sand. Meanwhile your ball and a half-cup of sand are already crossing the bunker lip on their way to the green.

Why it works

The difference between this shot and one where you quit on it unintentionally is that, in this instance, you are accelerating the clubhead, not decelerating it. As a result, you can still displace enough sand to get the ball up and out of the bunker on an almost vertical trajectory.

—Eden Foster

QUICK TIP
If the ball is only half-buried, use the same technique, but close the face and don't slam the club into the sand as hard.

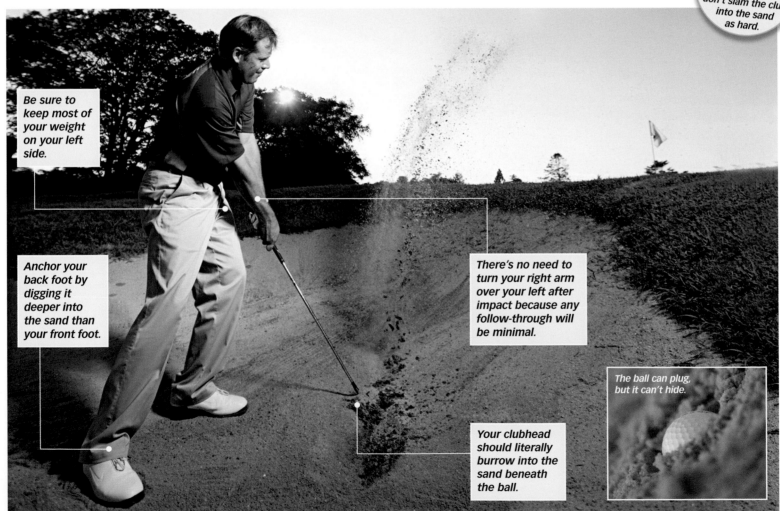

Be sure to keep most of your weight on your left side.

Anchor your back foot by digging it deeper into the sand than your front foot.

There's no need to turn your right arm over your left after impact because any follow-through will be minimal.

Your clubhead should literally burrow into the sand beneath the ball.

The ball can plug, but it can't hide.

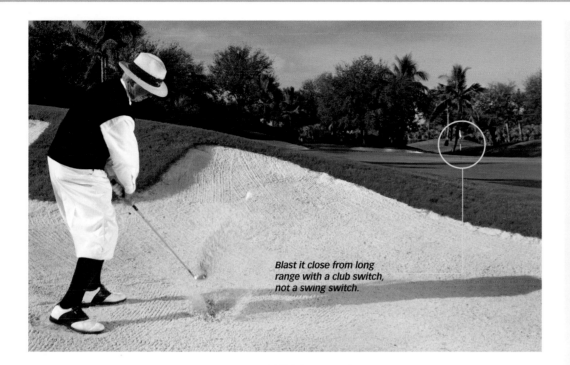

Blast it close from long range with a club switch, not a swing switch.

3 steps to Hit a 40-Yard Sand Shot

Time for an old swing with a new club

The situation

You have a decent lie in a bunker, but you're still 40 yards from the flagstick. This shot sends a shiver through even the best sand players because standard blast techniques won't get the ball all the way to the green, and trying to pick the ball clean with your sand wedge is about as easy as picking your teeth with one.

The solution

Before you start thinking "automatic bogey," realize that this difficult shot is actually very easy to pull off. The secret is to keep your sand wedge in your bag and use an iron with less loft and more length, then treat this shot like you would any other bunker escape.

Step 1: Point your toe line to the left of the flagstick and dig in less with your feet.

Step 2: Rotate the clubface open 45 degrees and lean the shaft away from the pin.

Step 3: Make your everyday bunker swing, being careful to swing the club along your toe line, not toward the flagstick. And instead of blasting through the sand like you would from a greenside bunker, take less sand and try to "skid" your club under the ball.

For a shot of 40 yards, use your 9-iron. Drop down to an 8-iron for a 50-yard shot and use a pitching wedge for a 30-yard shot.

Use the same setup and swing for each club/yardage combination. With a little practice you'll have a much easier time pulling off what's considered one of the hardest shots in golf.
—**Dr. Gary Wiren**

Pop and Roll to the Hole

Splash it low to let the ball run on long bunker shots

Fault: You struggle with distance control from bunkers when the hole is clear across the green. The ball either checks up way short, or you skull it way over the green trying to carry it to the hole.

Fix: You need a lower-flying shot that will run. Instead of an open clubface and stance at address, set them both square to the target line. Try to release the club just like you were hitting a draw—the toe of the club should point up as you follow through and the clubface will rotate closed [photo above]. You'll put less spin on the ball and cause it to run once it hits the green.

How to practice the low runner from sand

Think of tossing the sand over your left shoulder.

Pick up a handful of sand with your right hand and hold it in front of you in the "address" position. Now throw it over your left shoulder. This is the action your right hand should make after impact, because it closes the clubface to create the lower trajectory. Use this thought and you'll have a new shot to save par.
—**Jerry Mowlds**

INSTRUCTION

What to do When You're Up Against the Lip

This bunker buster will do the trick

The situation

Your ball has stopped in the sand a foot or so below the lip.

The solution

Because the ball is sitting on such an extreme upslope, don't feel as though you need to use the most lofted club in your bag—your sand wedge, pitching wedge or even your 9-iron will work just fine. And since the ball is too low on the face for you to keep both feet out of the bunker, you're going to have to get dirty.

Start by stepping down into the bunker so that your back foot is as far below the ball as the ball is below the lip. This will effectively put the ball in the center of your stance. Open the clubface, aim right of your target, and lower your right shoulder to get your shoulders more even with the slope. Then take the club back on a steep, V-shaped path and bring it down hard into the sand just below the ball, driving the heel of the club into the hill. There's no need to make a conscious follow-through—the concussion of the club hitting the sand is what drives the ball out and onto the green.

—Jason Carbone

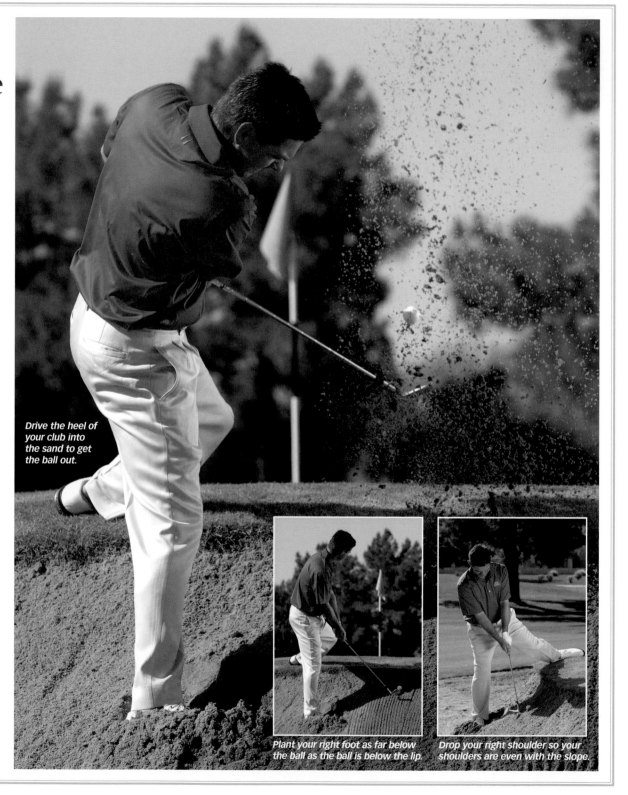

Drive the heel of your club into the sand to get the ball out.

Plant your right foot as far below the ball as the ball is below the lip.

Drop your right shoulder so your shoulders are even with the slope.

How to Stop it Quick From the Sand

No green? No problem!

The situation

You have a good lie in a greenside bunker, but you've short-sided yourself and have just a few paces of green between you and the flag. You need a high, soft sand shot that stops on a dime.

The solution

Here are four easy steps to make it sit.

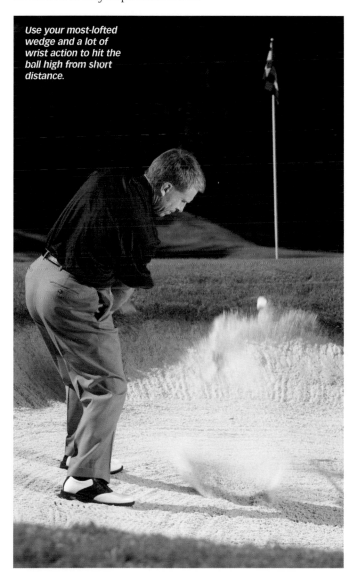

Use your most-lofted wedge and a lot of wrist action to hit the ball high from short distance.

Step 1

Select your most-lofted wedge. Position the ball slightly forward in your stance and move the handle of the club in-line with your right thigh to add extra loft to the clubface.

Step 2

Spread your stance by taking a step out with your right foot and dig both feet into the sand a half-inch for balance. Your shaft should now point just left of the center of your torso.

Step 3

Make sure your shoulder line and shaft line form an angled "T." Your job is to recreate the "T" at impact so that your club enters the sand with the same amount of loft you established at address. Swing your club more with your arms and your wrists, using minimum shoulder movement.

Step 4

Keep your chest pointed down and swing your arms and hands underneath your body. Move onto your left hip through impact to keep the club from releasing past your hands. Try to keep your hands and clubhead low in your follow-through so the clubface stays open.

—**Todd Sones**

A Last Resort: The Drop Shot

Taking your allowable drop might be a better bet than trying to pull off a miracle escape

According to Rule 28 of the USGA Rules of Golf, a player "may deem his ball unplayable at any place on the course except when the ball is in a water hazard." In this case, you have three options, all of which carry a one-stroke penalty:

(a) Play a ball as nearly as possible at the spot from which the original ball was last played.

(b) Drop a ball behind the point where the original ball lay, keeping that point directly between the hole and the spot on which the ball is dropped.

(c) Drop a ball within two club-lengths of the spot where the original ball lay, but not nearer the hole.

If you choose b or c, you must drop the ball within the bunker.

How to Play the Three Hardest Bunker Shots

These lies will kill you if you let them. So don't.

Downhill lie

Why it's so hard: It reduces the loft on your wedge in the situation that you need it most. Be clear about what you're trying to accomplish here. If the hole is cut near you, it's unlikely you'll get it close, so just get the ball out. If the hole is on the other side of the green, you have a chance to run it close because this shot will have almost no spin to it.

Set your shoulders parallel to the slope of the bunker, which will shift your weight over your front foot.

Use your most-lofted wedge to counter the de-lofting effect of the slope.

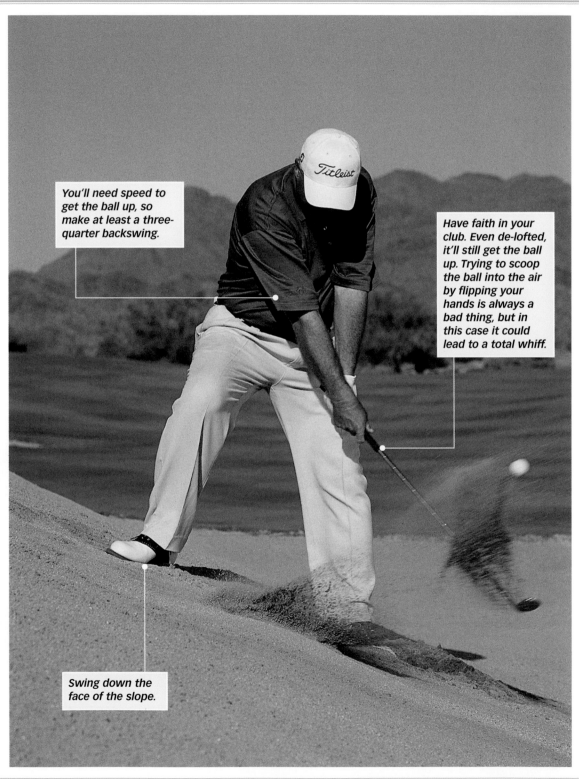

You'll need speed to get the ball up, so make at least a three-quarter backswing.

Have faith in your club. Even de-lofted, it'll still get the ball up. Trying to scoop the ball into the air by flipping your hands is always a bad thing, but in this case it could lead to a total whiff.

Swing down the face of the slope.

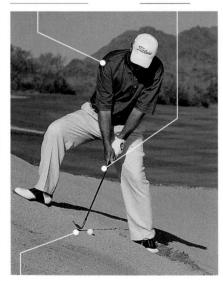

If you can maintain your balance, play the ball opposite your front foot. If that could send you tumbling, play it toward the middle of your stance.

Ball above feet

Why it's so hard: A big heap of sand is keeping the ball from rolling to the bottom of the bunker and you have to blast through it. And this baby will immediately fly left of where you're aimed.

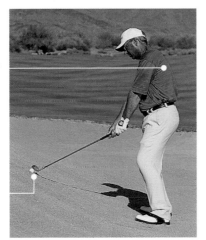

An upright swing will bury your club in the sand, so for one of the rare times in the short game, keep your upper body straight up.

Position the ball just forward of center and choke down on the grip to shorten the club so you don't bury it into the hill.

This shot tends to go left, so aim right of your target. The higher the ball is above your feet, the more right you need to aim.

Make a rounded, baseball-type swing to avoid getting the club stuck.

Accelerate aggressively through the shot and try to throw that sand all the way to your target.

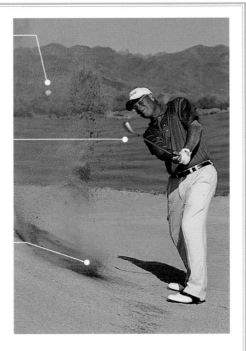

Ball below feet

Why it's so hard: If you don't set up to this shot correctly, you'll wind up doing a somersault into the sand. And if the ball is close to the lip of the bunker, you can easily smack the turf.
—Paul Trittler

Bend your knees and lower your rear end to bring the ball within reach.

Spread your feet wider than shoulder width to create a stable base for your swing.

Position the ball forward in your stance, just inside your front foot.

Keep your lower body quiet to maintain balance.

To avoid hitting too far behind the ball, hinge your wrists quickly on your takeaway, then unhinge them as you swing down.

The steeper the slope, the more the ball will want to go right, so aim well left of your target.

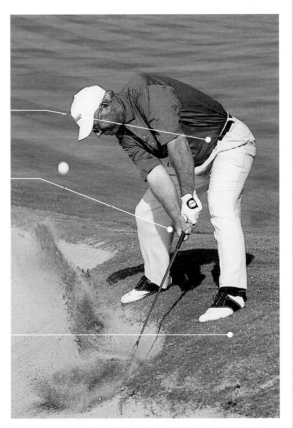

What to Do in Hard or Wet Sand

When the sand is wet...
Add more clubhead speed
Your brain tells you thick wet sand should be more difficult to deal with—you'll get the club stuck in the sand or skull it trying to pick the ball clean. In fact, there's only one adjustment you need to make: swing harder! The sand hasn't changed—it's just heavier, so you need more clubhead speed to displace it. Other than that, keep your technique exactly the same.
—Paul Trittler

When the sand is hard...
Lose your bounce
Hard sand requires two things: (1) a wedge designed with minimal bounce, and (2) the clubface must be wide open when it hits the sand. Less bounce and an open face should allow your club to slide under the ball. When the sand is so shallow that even these adjustments won't work, chip the shot cleanly (ball-first contact). Clean contact requires practice, but it's a good shot to have.
—Dave Pelz

Your scores drop when
your putts do likewise.

SECTION 8

HOLING OUT

It all comes down to the most perplexing part of the game—putting. Here's how to get the ball in the hole in far fewer strokes.

I n the end, the object of the game is to get the ball into the hole. While holing a shot isn't your objective on every swing, it is when you're on the green. Here, the cup becomes your true target for the first time on that hole, so pressure builds. If you miss your landing spot in the fairway by a few yards or hit your approach to a section of the green other than which you planned, it's just a miss. Do the same while putting and that miss turns into a stroke lost forever.

The demands of putting are severe, which is ironic since they involve the simplest move you'll make on the course other than getting out of your golf cart. It boils down to that tiny target and the slips, slides, turns, breaks and bumps between it and where your ball lies. There's a lot to overcome, and a lot of questions to be answered. How fast will it go? How hard should I putt it? Is it downhill or flat? Will it go straight or curve left?

There's a school of thought that says it takes years of experience to answer these questions correctly. The Top 100 Teachers disagree, and over the next several pages they will arm you with everything you need to putt the lights out from any distance. You know what the target is—here are the skills to find it.

5 THINGS YOU'LL LEARN IN THIS SECTION

- How to align your body and aim your putter so your putts start out on the right line
- Find an alternative grip that can compensate for errors in your stroke so your putts still find the hole
- How to study and read greens like a Tour caddie to get the right line and speed
- How to practice and improve your stroke—without getting bored—using the Top 100's best drills
- How to lag putts close so you'll never three-putt again

SETUP AND STROKE BASICS

How to grip your putter, how to aim it and how to swing it to turn knee-knockers and lags into tap-ins

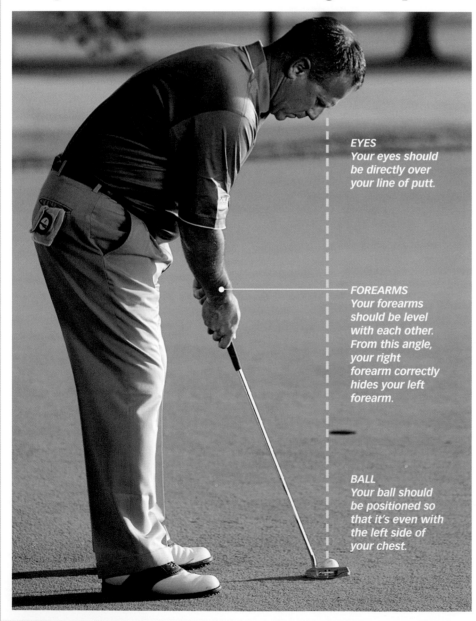

EYES
Your eyes should be directly over your line of putt.

FOREARMS
Your forearms should be level with each other. From this angle, your right forearm correctly hides your left forearm.

BALL
Your ball should be positioned so that it's even with the left side of your chest.

INSTRUCTION

How to Nail Your Alignment

A great putting setup needs eyes and arms

Use the following quick, two-part check to build a solid putting foundation every time.

Check 1: Forearms

Your forearms should be level with each other at address. There are two ways to check this. If there's someone else on the putting green, have him stand behind you along the line of your putt at address and look at your forearms. Your right forearm should hide your left forearm. If you're alone, take your address position and look down at your forearms—if they're level with one another, you're good to go.

Check 2: Eyes

At address, your eyes should be directly over your ball and your line of putt. This is crucial—even if your forearms are correct, if your eyes are too far outside the ball or too far inside the ball, a consistent path will be almost impossible. If you're not sure whether your eyes are over the line at address, check their position by dropping a ball from the bridge of your nose. If your eyes are too far forward, the ball will land outside your ball on the ground. If your eyes are too far inside the line of your putt, the dropped ball will land inside the ball on the ground.
—**Tom Patri**

NO! Your arms are uneven and closed to the line of the putt.

NO! Your arms are uneven and open to the line of the putt.

NO! Your eyes are too far inside the line of putt.

NO! Your eyes are too far outside the line of the putt.

Get Your Putts on the Right Track

Use a CD to make sure your eyes are over the ball

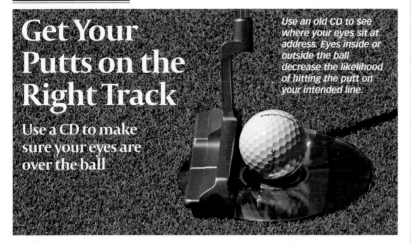

Use an old CD to see where your eyes sit at address. Eyes inside or outside the ball decrease the likelihood of hitting the putt on your intended line.

Fault: You consistently pull or push putts because your eyes are either too far inside the ball at address (causing a push) or too far outside the ball at address (causing a pull).

Fix: Position a ball in the little hole in the middle of an old music CD, shiny side up. Address the ball as if you were going to putt it and check where your eyes reflect on the CD. If your eyes are inside the ball, bend slightly forward from your hips until they move over the middle of the CD. If your eyes are outside the ball, bend slightly back from your hips. Positioning your eyes over the ball gives you the best view of the line and stops pull and push strokes in their tracks.
—**Scott Sackett**

Check Your Launch Angle

Let the hole be the judge

To ensure that you're hitting putts with the correct amount of loft, place a ball about 1½ inches behind a hole and strike it as if you were hitting a 20-foot putt. Contacted with 4 degrees of loft, the ball will glide approximately 6 to 12 inches and thus carry the hole, which is 4¼ inches in diameter. Line up several balls this way and putt them over the hole. If there's too little loft on the putter at impact, the ball likely will hit the hole and pop up. Too much loft and the ball will carry the hole by several inches. You want it to just clear the back lip.
—**Scott Sackett**

Not enough loft

Too much loft

Correct loft

Try a Forward Press for Smoother Putts

A little push forward will keep your putts from skidding off line

A well-hit putt will leave your putterface with topspin, which is desirable because it produces the pure forward roll that keeps your ball tracking toward the hole. If you tilt the shaft away from the target at address and allow it to stay that way through impact, however, you actually add to the loft that is built into your putter. This puts backspin on your ball and causes it to skid, bounce off-line and usually finish short of the hole. Here's how to contact the ball with the correct loft every time.

Step 1

Play the ball even with your nose and press your hands forward until they're even with your shirt logo. This sets up the putterface to contact the ball at or slightly above the equator with the correct amount of loft, rolling it with topspin toward the hole.

Step 2

To get a visual idea of the type of spin you're putting on your putts, draw a line around the ball and start your putts with the line horizontal. If you're putting backspin on the ball, the line will rotate backward—away from your target—just after impact.
—**Michael Breed**

WRONG!

Adding loft at impact creates unwanted backspin and putts that skid and bounce off-line.

RIGHT!

A forward-leaning shaft creates topspin, sending the ball forward on a tight roll. Press the shaft slightly forward at address and maintain this lean throughout your stroke.

How to Make a Money Stroke

One thin dime can change you from a hitter to a stroker

Fault: You stab at the ball with your putter rather than making a smooth stroke, giving you zero speed control.

Fix: Place a dime on the back of your putter as shown and make your normal stroke. If you're stroking your putts using a pure pendulum motion, the dime will stay on the putter, no matter how far back and through you take the putter. If you're stabbing the ball, however, the dime will slide off the back of your club as soon as you transition from the backstroke to the forward stroke. You may not be able to tell if you're decelerating, but a dime will pick it up instantly.

—Dr. Jim Suttie

Deceleration will knock the dime off your putter here...

...while a smooth pendulum stroke will make sure it's on here.

Add Smooth to Your Stroke

Swing from low to high to generate a purer roll

To generate true roll with minimal bouncing or skidding, you must swing the putter slightly upward through impact. Set most of your weight over your right foot and you'll discover that your putter will naturally—and correctly—swing back lower and finish higher. If you address the ball with most of your weight over your left foot, you'll make a descending strike that presses the ball into the turf and causes it to hop off line.

—Eddie Merrins

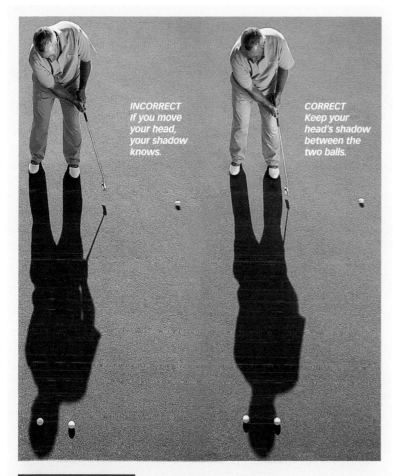

INCORRECT
If you move
your head,
your shadow
knows.

CORRECT
Keep your
head's shadow
between the
two balls.

DRILL

Keep Your Head Still

Your shadow will show you how

Your goal

Contact in the center of the face so the ball starts on the line you've chosen.

How to achieve it

One trait all good putters share is keeping their head still. You can't keep your putter on line if you move your head, nor can you keep your head still if you move the putter on the wrong path. A steady head allows your hands, arms and shoulders to move the putter correctly.

On a sunny day, set up to the ball with your shadow directly in front of you. Place two balls on the green about a foot apart and address another one so that your head's shadow is between the two balls. Make your putting stroke, hold your finish and check your shadow to see if your head moved. If you have difficulty keeping your head still, use more arms and hands in your stroke with less shoulder movement.

—Paul Trittler

CHECKPOINT

How to Control Distance

Keep your wrists out of your stroke

Fault: Your left wrist breaks down at impact, allowing the putterhead to pass your hands. That's why you often hit one putt several feet short of the hole then blow your next attempt three feet past.

Fix: Maintain the triangle formed by your shoulders, arms and hands throughout your stroke, keeping the butt of the grip centered between your forearms. Accelerate the putterhead through impact, matching the length of your through-stroke to that of your backstroke. Then hold your finish to make sure you don't pull out of your posture too soon.

—Scott Sackett

Push Your Putter With Your Palm

The right grip and right technique will help more of your putts find the center of the cup

The shortcut to saving strokes is in the palm of your hand. When you set the putter grip in the palm of your right hand, it gives you a stable, repeatable stroke that will do more for your game than beating balls on the driving range. Here's how to palm your way to better putting.

Step 1: Let your palm be the pilot
Set your putter behind the ball and position the grip in your right palm before placing your left hand on the club. The grip should be in line with your forearm [below, right], and the putter should feel like an extension of your arm. Avoid the fault of gripping the putter in your right fingers [below, left].

Step 2: Put the push on
If your alignment is correct, your right palm will face the target, which is where you want it at impact. Your through-stroke should feel like you're pushing the ball down the target line with your right palm. This stroke will point the clubface at the hole and make it easier for you to release the putterhead for a more consistent roll.

—Dr. David Wright

WRONG!	RIGHT!

A finger hold makes it easy for your stroke to break down; a palm grip gives you extra control.

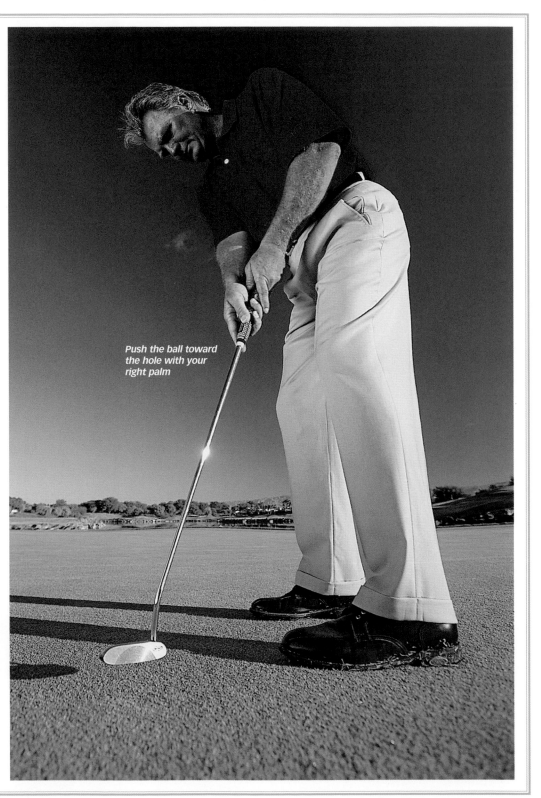

Push the ball toward the hole with your right palm

Make Yours an Alternative Grip

Grips that buck tradition can help solve many putting problems

IF MOST OF YOUR MISSED PUTTS END UP LEFT OF THE HOLE...

Try a saw grip

This putting grip guides your hands and arms like you're sawing wood. If you recall the last time you cut wood, your hands and arms move along the same line as the cut. Similarly, a saw putting stroke swings your putter straight back and forth along your intended target line. There's no rotation so the putterface remains square and your tendency to pull putts disappears.

There are four main variations of the saw grip.

Perpendicular saw
Thumb and last three fingers of the right hand positioned forward of the shaft.

TRY IT If you can't stop releasing your forearms and closing the putterface.

Claw saw
Right hand folded around the grip and right hand and arm in line with the shaft.

TRY IT If your putterface rotates left after impact. The claw saw will keep your putter moving squarely down the line.

Parallel saw
Looks and feels like the standard right-hand position used for sawing wood.

TRY IT If your putter path heads left in your follow-through. This saw grip will smooth your stroke and harness right-hand power.

Vertical saw
Last three fingers of the right hand placed behind but in line with shaft.

TRY IT If you cut putts and often miss right. This grip keeps your putter square and on-line if your left wrist breaks down.
—Dave Pelz

With a regular right-hand-low grip [above], your shoulders tilt at address. A left-hand-low grip levels them out.

IF YOU HAVE DIFFICULTY CONTROLLING THE SPEED OF YOUR PUTTS...

Go left hand low

Gripping your putter with your right hand lower than your left seems to make sense because that's how you hold all of your other clubs. With your putter, however, a right-hand-low grip tends to set your shoulder alignment left and tilt your right shoulder down.

Most golfers aim their shoulders to the left with a standard grip [above]. A left-hand-low grip straightens this out.

A left-hand-low grip promotes good shoulder alignment and an on-line putter path. It also places your right hand in a submissive position behind your left wrist and forearm—this all but eliminates wrist hinge in your follow-through, even if you push too hard with your right hand. Your ability to control speed and distance will improve noticeably.
—Dave Pelz

A split-hand grip keeps your left hand quiet.

IF YOU CAN'T KEEP YOUR PUTTER ON LINE...

Practice with a split-grip

Your left hand is the passive hand, while your right hand is responsible for the movement in your stroke. To understand how this works, try putting with your left hand in its normal position but your right hand at the very bottom of the handle. To make a decent stroke with this grip, you'll see that your left hand must stay quiet while your right hand does almost all the work of taking the club back and then through. The advantage of the split-hand grip is that rather than trying to make your two hands work together in unison, each hand simply has one job to do: Your left hand is the anchor, while your right hand is the mover. This simplifies the stroke and makes it much easier to keep your putter on line.
—Mitchell Spearman

JUDGE LINE, SPEED & BREAK

The best stroke in the world won't get the ball in the hole unless you know how the putt will react to the green once it gets rolling. Try these time-honored techniques for picking the right line.

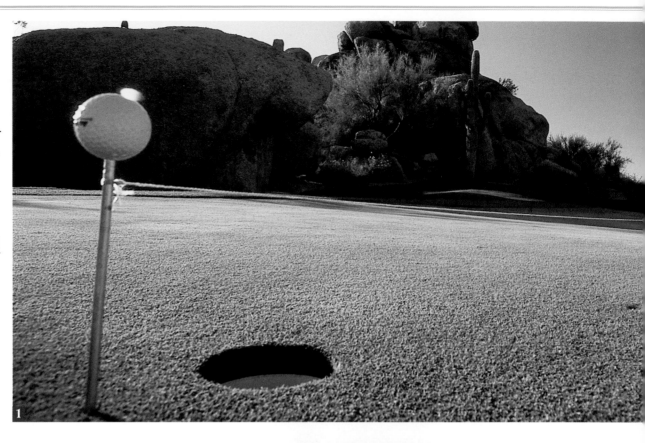

DRILL

How to Stay on Your Line

A five-step plan to get your putts tracking from the start

It's critical to build a setup that gives you the best chance to get your ball rolling in the right direction, because a ball that starts off line stays off line. Here's a five-step plan to correctly position your body and putter on the line you've chosen.
—**Donald Crawley**

Step 1: Find your line
On the practice green, stand behind your ball and imagine how it will roll. Run a raised string along the starting point of the line and burn the image of what your starting line looks like into your brain. This physical representation of your putt line will give you an idea of what a straight line actually looks like.

Step 2: Align your ball
Draw a straight line across the logo on your ball. Use this mark to align your ball along the intended line of the putt by placing it underneath and parallel to the static line. Now you have a reference point to get your putterface pointed in the right direction.

Step 3: Aim your putter
Remove the string and sole your putterhead on the ground. Align the face so that the top edge makes a perpendicular angle with the mark on your ball. This will ensure that your putter starts the ball on the correct line after contact, as long as you don't dramatically open or close the face during your stroke.

Step 4: Set your eyes
Set your eyes over the ball and parallel to your intended line. If you set your eyes to the inside of the ball your stroke will have a tendency to move inside and push your putts; set your eyes outside and you'll likely pull your putts. Either way, you'll miss the putt.

A physical representation of your line can be very helpful.

Step 5: Align your body

Allow your arms to hang straight down from your shoulders, and then place your hands on the grip. Loose, free-hanging arms are needed to create the tension-free stroke that you need to be a consistent putter.

CHECKPOINT

Be a Green-Reading Detective

All the clues to the break are out in the open

While a good course designer will do his best to challenge your green-reading abilities, he'll also leave obvious clues about how the ball will roll on different areas of the green. If you know what to look for, you'll know the general slope of the green even before you get behind your ball.

Clue 1

PUTTS BREAK AWAY FROM HILLS
Don't forget the obvious. Putts will break away from greenside bumps, hills and rises, especially if they're close to the line of your putt.

Clue 2

PUTTS BREAK AWAY FROM THE CLUBHOUSE
While not always true, clubhouses are normally built on the highest point on the course, usually for drainage purposes. Look for home, and you'll get a good idea of the general lay of the land— information that can come in handy when you can't tell exactly which way a putt falls.

Clue 3

PUTTS BREAK TOWARD WATER
For obvious drainage reasons, greens will slope toward the nearest body of water. On oceanside courses, don't underestimate the natural roll of terrain toward the sea—putts break especially hard toward the agua here.

Clue 6

PUTTS BREAK TOWARD COLLECTION AREAS
Those funny, tightly mown greenside spots that your ball finds when you short-side the green are always below the level of the putting surface, and they usually house a drain at the lowest point. If you're putting near one of these collection areas, the break will favor that direction.

Clue 5

PUTTS BREAK AWAY FROM BUNKERS
The last thing a course designer—and especially the superintendent— wants is water draining into a bunker. More often than not, the green slopes away from the sand to avoid extra bunker maintenance.

Clue 4

PUTTS BREAK TOWARD THE SUN
The grass on the green grows all day long, following the path of the sun. In the late afternoon, when the blades are at their longest, greens feature a serious grain toward the setting sun. Your putts will break with the grain. This clue is especially important when playing on long-blade Bermuda grass.

"On the practice green, walk off 10 paces and make a mental note of the stroke it takes to roll putts that distance. Use that as a guide for all putts you face during your round."
—Donald Crawley

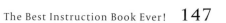

GREEN READING

Here's how to become an expert planner on the greens and get the right line every time

INSTRUCTION

Find the Spine

The first step to reading the green

You've probably heard TV announcers refer to the "fall line" when talking about a certain putt. What they're referring to is the road map to a particular hole position. The "spine" or fall line influences nearly every putt. Think of it as the Rosetta Stone to figuring out your line. Once you identify it, you're on your way to fully understanding the putt you face.

INSTRUCTION

See the Slope

Watch were the water goes

Every green has built-in drainage points, low spots where water can run off. Knowing where they are is the key to finding the spine.

Determine the highest point above the hole and walk to that spot. Imagine you have a hose and you're streaming water in the direction of the hole. The water will funnel toward the hole and follow a certain line as it drains off the green. That line is the spine.

—Fred Griffin

(Special thanks to Mark Sweeney, AimPoint Technologies)

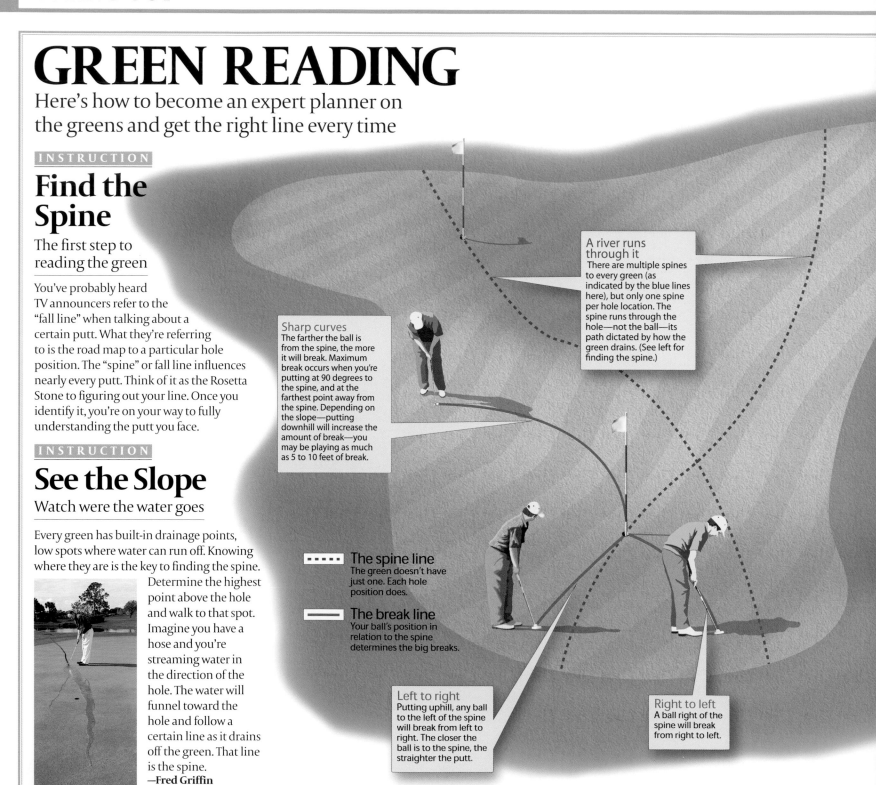

A river runs through it There are multiple spines to every green (as indicated by the blue lines here), but only one spine per hole location. The spine runs through the hole—not the ball—its path dictated by how the green drains. (See left for finding the spine.)

Sharp curves The farther the ball is from the spine, the more it will break. Maximum break occurs when you're putting at 90 degrees to the spine, and at the farthest point away from the spine. Depending on the slope—putting downhill will increase the amount of break—you may be playing as much as 5 to 10 feet of break.

The spine line The green doesn't have just one. Each hole position does.

The break line Your ball's position in relation to the spine determines the big breaks.

Left to right Putting uphill, any ball to the left of the spine will break from left to right. The closer the ball is to the spine, the straighter the putt.

Right to left A ball right of the spine will break from right to left.

Be Your Own Stimpmeter

Try this to get the right speed

Find a flat spot on the practice green of your home course, take a stance that's about 12 inches wide and position the ball just inside your left heel. Swing your putter back so it goes directly in front of the big toe on your right foot. Hit five putts this way and note how far the ball rolls. Do the same thing when you're playing a different course. If the stroke that produces an eight-foot roll on your home course produces a 12-foot roll on the unfamiliar one, you'll know the greens are that much faster and that you should plan on more break.

—Fred Griffin

TOP 100 SAY

Read Greens Like a Caddie

Six things the experts look for when judging slope

1 **The faster the putting surface,** the more break you have to allow for. This is because you'll be hitting the ball much softer and it will take more time to reach the hole. The more uphill it is, the less it will break because a firmer putt takes less time to reach the hole.

2 **If the grass looks shiny** along the line of your putt and darker when you look at the ball from behind the hole, you're putting down grain (that is, the grass is bending toward the sun). Expect a quicker putt and more break.

3 **If the grass looks dark** along the line of your putt, but shiny from behind the hole, you're putting against the grain. The putt will be slower and break less.

4 **Feel the ground with your feet** as you walk on the putting surface. Does the green feel firm (faster) or spongy (slower)? Do your leg muscles feel as if they are walking uphill toward the hole (slower) or downhill (faster)?

5 **Watch the ball of everyone** who putts before you. You'll get a sense what the ball will do near the hole and where it's most sensitive to break. Also note what any ball does when it goes beyond the hole. This gives you the perfect read and speed for any comeback putt.

6 **Make your first read from behind the ball,** looking toward the hole. Crouch down as low as you can to get a better view of the contours. Also, take note of water and drainage areas (putts often break toward these features), or mountains (putts break away from hills). If you're still unsure about your read, walk behind the hole to get a different perspective.

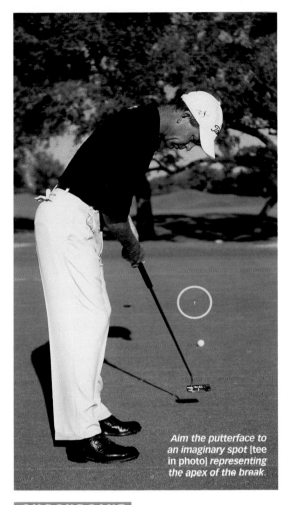

Aim the putterface to an imaginary spot [tee in photo] representing the apex of the break.

Play More Break

You'll make more than you miss if you err on the high side

The problem
You consistently miss on the low side of the hole.

The solution
Once you've chosen a line, pick a spot near the hole that represents the highest point of the break. For instance, if the putt will move a foot from right to left, picture a tee one foot to the right of the cup [above]. Aim the putterface at this spot, align your body perpendicular to the face, and try to die the ball into the high side of the hole. If you're hitting it too hard, move your aiming spot closer to you.
—Mark Wood

THE RIGHT PUTTER FOR YOU

Choosing from the hundreds of putter models on the market is a daunting task.
The following gear tips will help you find a new favorite flatstick.

How to Make a Model Stroke

The secret is in the design of your putter

The myth
Depending on your preference, swing your putterhead straight-back-and-through or on a slight arc.

The truth
The design of your putter— not your preferred putting style— determines the type of path you should trace. Toe-weighted putters are engineered to open and close during your stroke and travel on an arc, and face-balanced models (ones that feature a centered shaft connection or a double-bend shaft) are engineered to remain square and travel on a straight line.

What to do
Match your stroke to your putter, or buy a model that's designed to complement your putting style.

If your putter is face-balanced...
Take it back and through on a straight line keeping the face square all the way.

Allow your arms to hang directly underneath your shoulders.

Bend from your hips more to get your eyes over the target line.

Play the ball slightly forward of center with the putterhead directly below your nose.

If your putter is toe-weighted...
Take it away to the inside of your target line, return it square and finish back on the inside.

Play the ball off your left armpit.

Stand erect, with your eyes inside the target line.

Position your hands in front of your shoulder line.

Face-balanced stroke
Move the putter straight back and through by rocking your shoulders like a teeter-totter. To ingrain the feel of this stroke, place a club across your chest as shown and secure it underneath your armpits. Hit some putts by pointing the triangle formed by the club and your arms away from the target and then to the target.

Toe-weighted stroke
Since your hands are outside your arms, you'll naturally move the putter to the inside. The key is to maintain a free-flowing motion so you don't disturb the integrity of the arc. Practice putting with your left arm only to develop a free-swinging motion. Think of how a gate swings open and shut on its hinges—that's the feeling you're after.
—**Mike Adams**

Is Your Putter Ruining Your Stroke?

If the shaft is too long or short for you, the answer is yes

Your putter is too short...

If you have zero elbow bend

When the handle is so low that your have to straighten your arms to take your grip, it forces you to tip your shoulders up and down to make your stroke. You'll have distance - control problems because you'll make contact with a different amount of loft on every stroke.

Your putter is too long...

If your arms are jammed into your sides at address

When you grip an overly long putter, you're forced to bend your elbows too much, and when you swing your putter your body will get in the way. Choking down will only alter your putter's swingweight and send your tempo out of whack.

Your putter is just right...

If your arms hang under your shoulders when you grip the top of the handle

Look for elbows just under your rib cage with a slight amount of flex, which allows your arms and shoulders to swing the putter under your body without excess wrist and head motion.
—Todd Sones

Choose the Right Type of Hosel

Make sure it benefits your setup and stroke.

Straight-in

If you pull more putts than you push, you'll fare better with a shaft/hosel-in-the-heel design (such as the flare-tip), which will hold off the rotation of the face. If you push putts, try a center-shafted putter (such as the straight-in), which gives you more direct control of the face position through impact.

Slant-neck

If your stroke is of the "straight-back-and-straight through" variety, you'll putt more consistently with a face-balanced putter, or one with a shaft/hosel attachment closer to the center of the head. Most face-balanced putters come with a double-bend shaft, so keep your eyes out for those. On the other hand, if you're more of a "Crenshaw" putter, and like to gently roll the putter on an "inside-to-square-to-inside" stroke, you'll be better off with a hosel/shaft attachment that favors the heel.

Flare-tip

Plumber-neck hosels increase your ability to see how your putter is aligned at address. But they also impact your hand position. If you strive to keep your hands ahead of the putter at impact, which many good putters do, a hosel/shaft offset like a plumber-neck will benefit your stroke.

Double-bend

Plumber-neck

THE NEW WAYS TO PUTT

Tried-and-true techniques never go out of style—unless the ball isn't going into the hole. Then it's time to try something new.

How to Roll With the Right Speed

This drill will give you the right pace for short putts

Fault: You leave short putts short, or they lose their line due to a lack of speed

Fix: Secure a scorecard pencil between two sets of tees in front of the hole as shown at right. Putt a few balls from anywhere from three to five feet from the hole. The idea is to hit these putts with enough force that the ball pops over the pencil and then into the hole. You'll quickly learn that to sink your putts with the proper amount of speed; you can't baby the ball to the hole, nor can you rocket it because too much speed will pop the ball over both the pencil and the hole.

Once you get to the point where you can consistently pop eight out of 10 putts over the pencil and into the hole, remove the pencil and try to sink your putts with the same velocity through the two tees—these putts should always hit somewhere on the back of the cup. Then remove the tees and work on maintaining the same speed and line.

—**Dr. Gary Wiren**

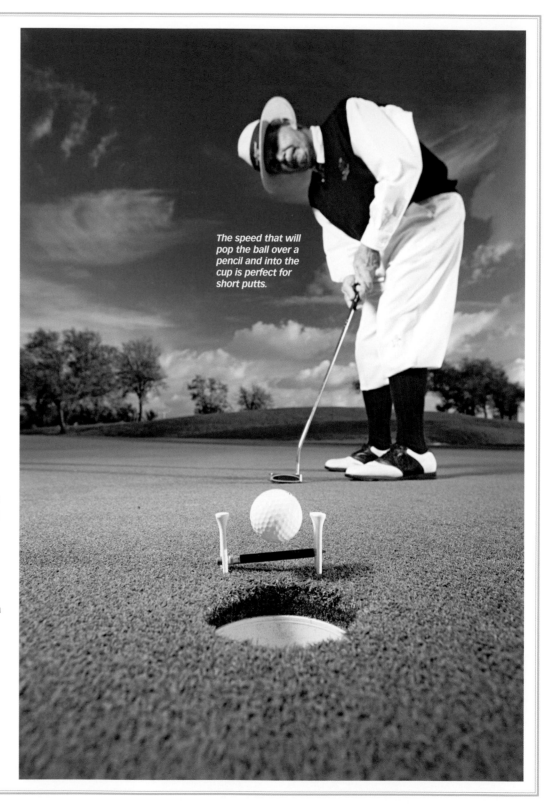

The speed that will pop the ball over a pencil and into the cup is perfect for short putts.

Apply the Right Type of Force

Here's an easy thought to help you hone your distance control from short range

The key to making short putts is getting the ball started on the right line and rolling it with the correct amount of pace. The amount of force you need to generate the correct speed is the same amount of force you'd use to toss a penny to the hole from the same distance. Thinking of the simple image of flipping a penny to the target tells you exactly how hard or soft to stroke your putt, allowing you to shift more of your focus to the hole.

—Eddie Merrins

Pitch a penny to get a feel for correct pace.

How to Putt Under Pressure

Use this drill to turn knee-knockers into kick-ins

On short pressure-packed putts, it's vital to keep your head and body still. If you lift your head to watch the ball you'll pull your shoulders and the putterhead off line, causing the putt to miss to the left. To stay still, try pinching your knees inward. As you stroke, let your ears be your eyes: Listen for the ball to hit the bottom of the hole—that means no peeking!

—Mark Wood

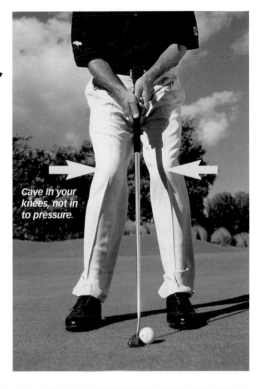

Cave in your knees, not in to pressure.

How to Be a Clutch Putter

Brain-wave analysis proves the less you think, the more you'll make

Missed putt

This is a 10-second snapshot of a golfer's brain activity as he addressed, hit and missed a five-foot putt.

Made putt

This reading was taken over a similar putt that the same golfer made. The quiet readings below reveal a relaxed mind.

These jagged lines show a spike in brain activity before contact, as if he were thinking, "Don't miss!"

This line shows the movement of the golfer's facial muscles, also suggesting major tension.

The inner line indicates the golfer's face was relaxed, while the quiet readings below reveal a relaxed mind.

No, there wasn't an earthquake. The sensors detected the golfer's mental delight as the putt dropped in the hole.

This is your brain on golf

Red numbers are good, but as this MRI of a golf-stressed brain shows, if your head is red, you're dead.

STRESSED BRAIN

CLUTCH BRAIN

Code red!

The red shows intense electrical activation in the ventral medial frontal cortex. That's the part of your brain that recognizes danger and forces your heart rate to increase and muscles to tense up, helping you to survive threatening situations. But tension and a racing heart don't help much on the course. When a nervous golfer stands over a tough shot, this is literally what his fear looks like.

Praisin' the blues

The blue means less brain activity. This is typically a good thing in golf—it means you're not overthinking the shot. You don't want your ventral medial cortex activated when you're putting. An MRI of Tour player's brain would likely show more blue than a Picasso!

—Analysis provided by Dr. Richard Keefe, associate professor of sports medicine at Duke University

Be Firm With Downhillers

Forget the sweet spot— off-center impact keeps you from jabbing at nasty sliders

The situation

You're facing a slick, downhill breaker. The tendency under these circumstances is to make a super-short, jabby stroke.

The solution

You have to impart enough energy into the ball to get it started, but if you quit on the stroke there's a good chance the ball will skip off line. Think back to how dead the impact felt the last time you mistakenly struck a putt off-center toward the toe—and how far short of the hole you ended up. That's your key.

Why it works

By making contact toward the toe, you spill energy instead of transferring it. The ball will start on the line you selected, but only the slope and slickness of the green will act to keep it in motion. Through friction and gravity, the ball tends to die—safely in or near the hole.

How to toe it

Set up to deaden your impact

1. Address this putt so the toe of your putter is aligned with the outside third of the ball.

2. Rehearse a short, slow backswing and a deliberate forward swing. Hold the putter firmly enough to prevent your "toe hit" from opening up the blade.

3. Step up to the ball and make the same stroke. You'll create "dead" impact to offset the slick conditions.
—**Eden Foster**

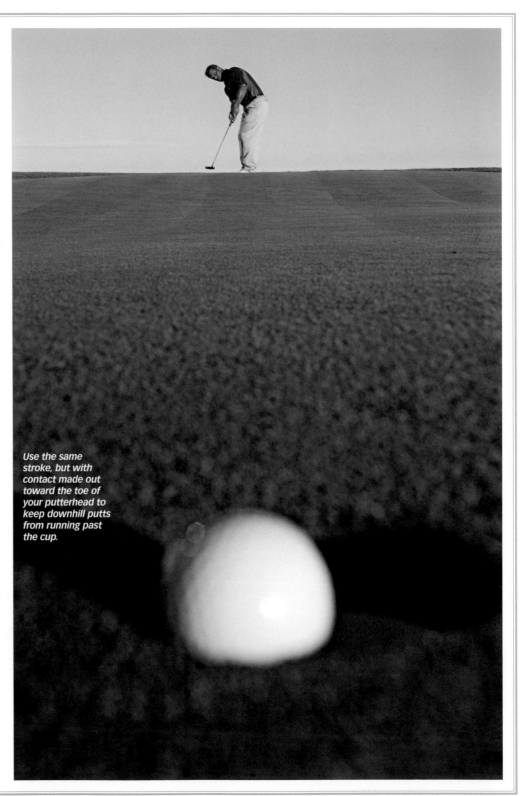

Use the same stroke, but with contact made out toward the toe of your putterhead to keep downhill putts from running past the cup.

How to be Automatic From Mid-Range
These drills will help you make the ones you should

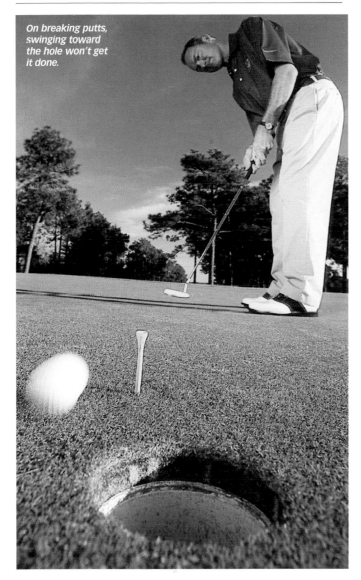

On breaking putts, swinging toward the hole won't get it done.

Line on ball parallel to clubface

2. Track 'em

The fault it fixes: You have no confidence in your stroke.

How to do it: Build confidence in your stroke before you head to the first tee by laying two clubs along the ground so they form a path that ends at the hole, then putt five-footers between the shafts. Seeing the ball drop into the cup, even if it kisses off some steel, will get your mind thinking that you can make everything you look at.

3. Adjust for slope

The fault it fixes: You roll downhill putts way past the roll and come up short when putting uphill.

How to do it: See below to roll it right.

UPHILL
Press a tee under the lip of the hole on the uphill side, then hit your putts firmly enough so they strike the tee before dropping in.

DOWNHILL
Press a tee under the lip on the downhill side of the cup, leaving most of it exposed. Try to make putts without hitting the tee.

4. Line up

The fault it fixes: You push or pull putts.

How to do it: Follow the steps below to learn how to strike the ball with a square putterface.

Step 1
Mark a straight line from the number on the ball through the center of the brand name as shown.

Step 2
Position the line you drew on the ball perpendicular to the target line.

Step 3
At address, set your putterface parallel to the line you drew on the ball.

Step 4
Strive to line up your putterface and the line you drew on the ball on your forward stroke. If you see the logo rolling tightly end over end, you'll know the putter was square. If the logo looks wobbly, keep practicing.
—**Chuck Winstead**

1. Go on a bender

The fault it fixes: Breaking putts give you fits.

How to do it: Commit yourself to aiming at a spot other than the hole on short benders. Place a tee on the edge of the hole at 5 o'clock (the far side of the hole is 12 o'clock) for right-to-left breakers, and 7 o'clock for left-to-right breakers. Try to putt around the tee so the break feeds the ball into the hole. This will force you to pick a spot outside the hole and putt directly at it.

Learn the Pop-Piston Stroke

This unique putting method makes long lags seem like tap-ins

The problem

On long putts, you have difficulty getting the ball to the hole with your Tour-style, back-and-forth pendulum stroke.

The solution

A "pop-piston" stroke will help you get long putts to the hole with ease.

How to do it

Position the ball toward your left toe. Open your stance slightly to accommodate the forward ball position, and keep your eyes over the line of putt.

Place your thumbs on the top of the grip, with your left index finger on top of your right fingers on the target side of the shaft. Anchor your right elbow against your right hip.

Push the putterhead straight back with your left index finger, and keep your right elbow fixed to your right hip. This will ensure that the putterhead stays on line. At the end of your backstroke, your right wrist should be bent back while your left wrist should remain unhinged and in-line with your left forearm.

To start the club forward, use your right palm as a piston and shove everything (hands, arms and putterhead) forward. Your right elbow should straighten as it pushes the putter, but no other individual part of the assembly should move. Straightening your right elbow is a key element of the "piston" forward stroke. It's a natural movement that makes it much easier to gauge distance—especially on long lag putts.

—Dr. T.J. Tomasi

Top: Use your left index finger to push the club back and your right palm to move it forward.

Center: Anchor your right elbow against your right hip.

Bottom: Open your stance and position the ball off your left toe.

"Pop" your putterhead back by hinging your wrists, and use your right arm as a piston to maintain acceleration and centered contact.

QUICK TIP
Look at the target when making practice strokes to match what your eyes see to the motion needed to get the ball there.

DRILL

How to Stop Three-Putting for Good

Try this drill to become a master lagger

The odds of holing a putt longer than 35 feet are not high, but the chance of three-putting from this distance is good. Here's how to avoid those round-killing three-putts

On all putts longer than 35 feet, imagine that the hole is a six-foot circle and try to get the ball within the circumference of it. This makes the putt look much easier, and you'll actually end up holing one every once in a while.

You can also use this circle rule on putts from less than 35 feet, but make sure you get the ball past the cup. I call this region the "Safe Zone." When you're rolling the ball into the Safe Zone, you're rolling it great.

—Dave Pelz

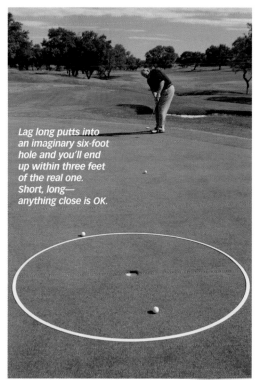

Lag long putts into an imaginary six-foot hole and you'll end up within three feet of the real one. Short, long— anything close is OK.

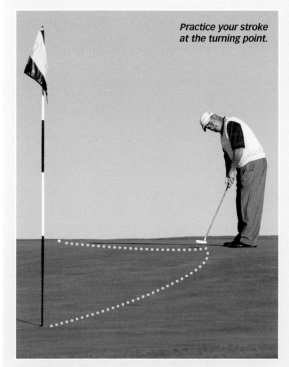

Practice your stroke at the turning point.

INSTRUCTION

Break Breakers Into Two

Hit a tough lag close by cutting its length in half

Don't get overwhelmed by a long, double-breaking putt—simplify it by finding the turning point: the spot where the break changes direction. After a first read, walk to where you think the turning point will be. Make a practice stroke, sensing how the slope will affect the ball as it nears the hole. Then return to the ball and focus on getting it to the turning point at the right speed. You might want to pick out an old ball mark three feet in front of you to make aim easier. Get the ball rolling to the turning point, and gravity will do the rest.

— Peter Kostis

CHECKPOINT

Find Your Putter's Sweet Spot

Play "taps" to hit pure putts

The problem
You know you hit that last putt perfectly, but it wobbled off line.

Why it's happening
Many putters are imperfectly weighted, so your sweet spot might be left or right of center. If that's the case, even putts you hit dead center will lose direction and distance.

The solution
Here's how to tell if your flatstick's at fault—and how to fix it instantly.

STEP 1
Dangle your putter, holding it halfway up the shaft, then take a tee and start tapping the face on the toe, which causes it to twist going back.

STEP 2
The closer you get to your putter's true center, the less twisting you'll see. When you tap it and the toe and heel swing back in perfect sync, that's your sweet spot.

STEP 3
Grab a Sharpie and simply make a line or dot to mark the spot. Use that as your new—and true— sweet spot.

A Better Way to Putt

After analyzing nearly 3,000 putts, our research reveals there's a better way to get the ball into the hole

The conventional wisdom

You should look at the ball for the duration of your putting stroke, and keep your eyes on that spot until well after the ball has been struck.

The unconventional theory

You should look at the hole–not the ball–from the moment you set the club behind the ball until you complete your putting stroke.

The Study

40 players ranging in handicap from eight to 36. They were divided into two 20-person groups, with each group balanced in terms of handicap, age and gender. One was the experimental group. The other was the control group. This control group used the conventional method of looking at the ball while putting throughout the test.

The Experiment

Using the conventional method of looking at the ball, both groups putted nine balls to holes ranging from three feet to 43 feet away. The results were statistically equal. Next, the control group putted one ball to each of nine targets in random order. The experimental group did the same but with one huge change: They were instructed to go through their normal pre-putt routine, but rather than looking at the ball as they made their stroke, they were told to look at the hole.

Then we compared the two groups. How did looking at the hole measure up? The results will surprise you.

The New Way to Putt

1. *Address the ball and place your putter behind it.*

2. *Start looking at the hole, and don't look back at the ball. (We promise it's still there.)*

3. *Hit your putt, and keep looking at the hole until you complete your stroke.*

Rather than looking at the ball as they made their stroke [left], the subjects were told to look at the hole the entire time [right].

The Shocking Results!

● **Long putts end up significantly closer to the hole when you look at the hole while making your stroke**. On average, after all was said and done, on putts between 28 feet and 43 feet in length, the experimental group (those who looked at the hole) had slightly less than 28 inches remaining to the hole.

By comparison, on the same long putts, the control group (those who looked at the ball) left themselves nearly 37 inches remaining to the hole. That means the experimental group was 24 percent closer, nine inches that could be the difference between a two-putt and a three-putt.

● **Looking at the hole may be more effective on short putts, too.** On putts between three feet and eight feet, the experimental group left an average of just under nine inches to the hole. On the same putts, the control group ended up with leaves that averaged 12.5 inches. Strictly speaking, that's not statistically significant, but those inches might be the difference between a routine tap-in and the occasional short miss.

"On average, after all was said and done, on putts between 28 feet and 43 feet in length, the experimental group (those who looked at the hole) had slightly less than 28 inches remaining to the hole."

MORE RESULTS:
Two other facts of note from our research: From 13 to 23 feet, both methods produced similar results. Neither method produced more holed putts from any distance.

Putts end up closer when you look at the hole

(Looking at the ball)
37 inches remaining

28 inches remaining
(Looking at the hole)

28-43 foot putts

That's 24% closer!

Any golfer who's had an important putt burn the lip of the hole knows every inch is precious on the green. This graph clearly shows that looking at the hole, not the ball, will pay off dramatically.

(Looking at the ball)
12 inches remaining

9 inches remaining
(Looking at the hole)

3-8-foot putts

Why it works

There are three main reasons why the new method improves on your old one:

1. You're using both eyes to to see your target, giving you highly accurate depth perception.

2. Maybe it was a fear of whiffing the putt, but testers who looked at the hole maintained their posture like statues.

3. Testers who looked at the hole didn't decelerate through the ball. In other words, they established natural speed control.

—Eric Alpenfels

Are You a Candidate?

Should you look at the hole instead of the ball when you putt?

Take this test and find out:

Q: Do you typically three-putt more than twice per round?
Yes ❏   No ❏

Q: Do you consistently leave yourself a putt of more than five feet after hitting a 25-footer?
Yes ❏   No ❏

Q: Do you take longer than two seconds to pull the trigger after your last look at the hole?
Yes ❏   No ❏

Q: Do you second-guess yourself after you've addressed the ball more than twice per round?
Yes ❏   No ❏

Q: Do you find it hard to strike putts aggressively and avoid decelerating?
Yes ❏   No ❏

Score: *If you answered yes this many times...*

0: We still need a partner for the member-guest, but you're probably too busy playing in the U.S. Open.

1-2: You might think it sounds quirky, but it could be all that's standing between you and breaking your next scoring barrier.

3 or more: You've got nothing to lose.

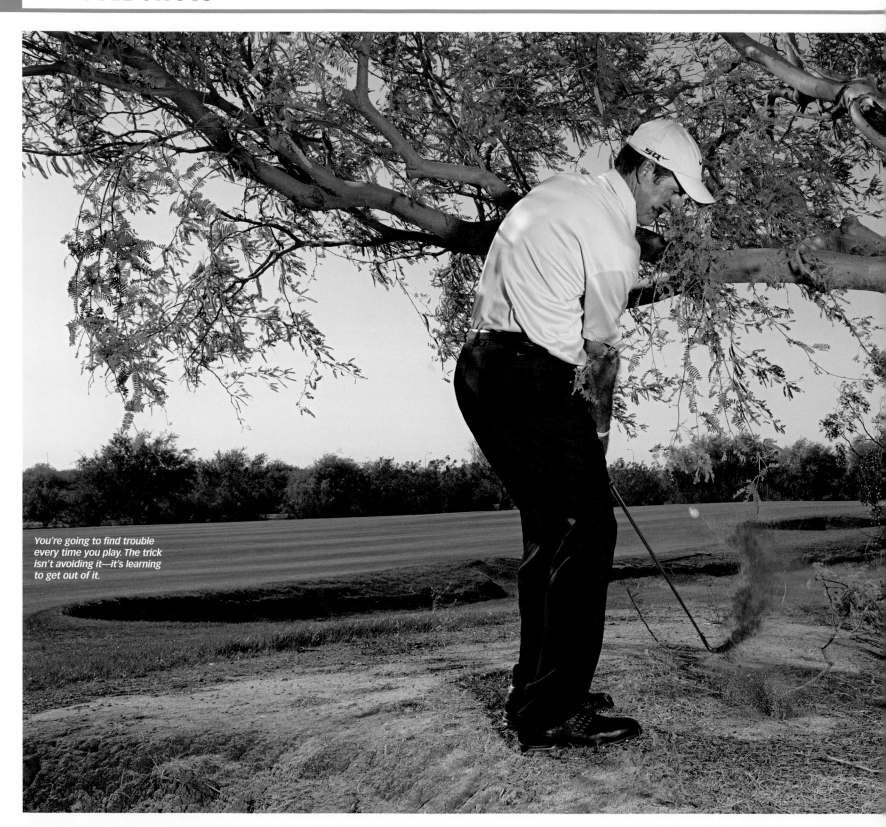

You're going to find trouble every time you play. The trick isn't avoiding it—it's learning to get out of it.

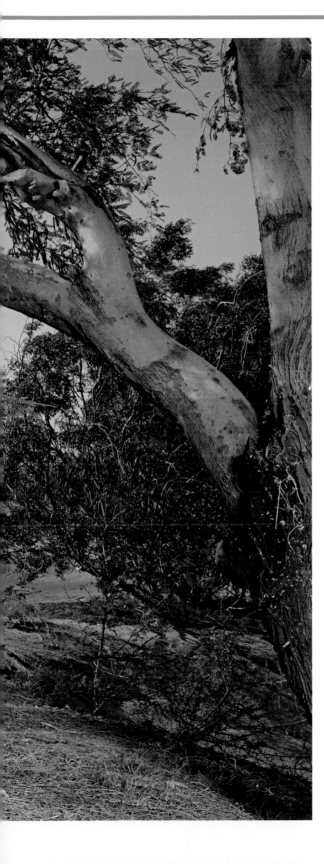

SECTION 9

TROUBLE SHOTS

Even the best-made plans sometimes go haywire. Here's how to get out of any predicament on the course.

Face facts: you'll never play a round when you hit every shot off tightly mown grass with a level lie. Bad shots happen, and even good ones end up in trouble via bad bounces, strange kicks and other "rub of the green" effects that defy explanation but nonetheless are a very real part of the game.

A trouble situation is anything that prohibits you from making your regular swing. Most often it takes the form of an obstacle between you and your target. Other times it's the lie itself, like when your ball comes to rest in ankle-deep rough or in a sand-filled divot. When you think of how many times you alter your technique to accommodate anything but a perfect lie, you realize just how often trouble shots pop up during the normal course of play.

Point is, finding trouble is something every golfer does. The trick is getting out of it. It's bad enough to find trouble, let alone use two or three swings to get back on the fairway or green. Using this section to tackle every possible trouble situation is difficult—there are far too many. Instead, the Top 100 Teachers describe how to overcome the most common forms. Learn and perfect these escapes and you'll be sitting pretty—even when your ball isn't.

5 THINGS YOU'LL LEARN IN THIS SECTION

- How to hit over, under and around trees that block the path to your target
- Three plays to find the fairway on windy days
- How to escape rough with three different clubs
- A secret to setting up on a sidehill lie and adjusting your swing to make clean contact
- How to hit two chips from difficult situations around the green with two unlikely clubs.

How to Avoid Trouble at the Beginning

I'm sick of getting into trouble on the first three holes or so. Is there a way to get my rounds off to better starts?

"If you're tired of relying on trouble shots while your game is still sputtering out of the blocks, try this trick one of my Tour students uses. Instead of ending your pre-round warm-up on the practice putting green, end it on the driving range. To finish up your prep, hit the shots you'll need on the first, second and third holes, from the drive to the approach shot. Hit in reverse order (3rd, 2nd, 1st) so that the first hole is fresh in your mind when you head to the tee. Visualize each fairway, and then go through your normal pre-shot routine (picking out a target, visualizing the shot shape) before hitting each shot. This routine will put you in full scoring mode from the beginning and place less pressure on your trouble game."

—Pat Goss

HOW TO GET OUT OF TROUBLE

Each situation is unique. The key is to get creative and stay confident.

How to Hit Out of Trees

Choke down to keep it low

The situation

You've missed the fairway, and though your lie is good and you're only 100 yards from the green, a low-hanging branch prevents you from playing a wedge shot.

The strategy

Step 1: Stay aggressive—never let a tree or its limbs come between you and a chance for birdie.

Step 2: Determine which is the highest-lofted club in your bag that will keep the ball under the branch.

Step 3: Mix and match your grip (how much you choke down on the handle) and backswing length to produce the appropriate distance.

How to do it

For the shot depicted here, a 6-iron is the highest loft that will keep the ball under the limb. Let's say you normally hit a 6-iron 160 yards. Here's the trick to hitting it the 100 yards you need.

—Dr. Gary Wiren

KEY MOVE
This technique only works if you swing to a full finish. The ball will fly low enough to avoid the trouble and travel far enough to stop safely on the green.

160 yds
Take your normal grip on the end of the handle.

150 yds
Now choke down to the middle of the grip. This takes 10 yards off the shot.

140 yds
If you choke all the way down to the bottom, that subtracts 10 more yards.

140 yds
With a full swing you'll still produce 140 yards—that's too much.

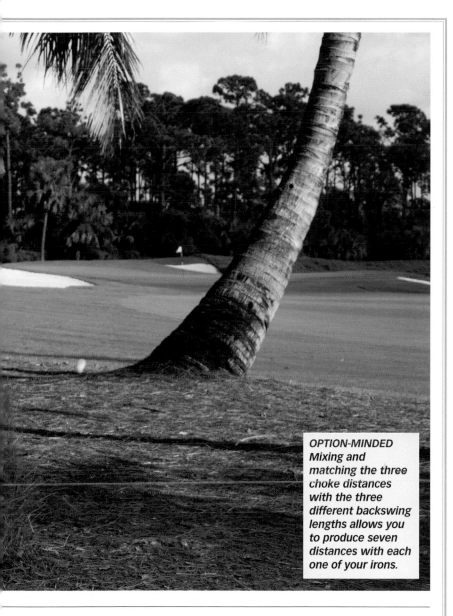

OPTION-MINDED
Mixing and
matching the three
choke distances
with the three
different backswing
lengths allows you
to produce seven
distances with each
one of your irons.

5 120 yds
Shorten
your
backswing
by 10 inches
(hands
chest high)
to hit it 20
yards less.

6 100 yds
Shorten
your
backswing
another 10
inches
(hands at
hip height)
to take off
another 20
yards.

INSTRUCTION

Another Way to Keep It Low

Swing flatter for a low-spin low runner

The play

To keep the ball low and chase it down the fairway, you need to control the three things that make it go up: loft, clubhead speed and backspin. Typically you hit down on the ball with your irons. In this case, you want to flatten out the bottom of your swing.

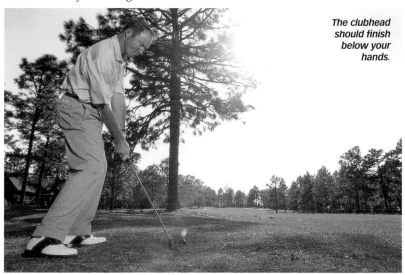

The clubhead
should finish
below your
hands.

How to do it

Use a 5-iron and position the ball two inches back from the middle of your stance. This will tilt the club's shaft forward and de-loft the face.

Step 1

Make a three-quarter-length backswing (hands stopping at chest height) for better control.

Step 3

This is the key move: At impact, don't let your right forearm rotate over your left. Think of this shot as a really long chip and finish with the clubhead below the level of your hands. It might help to squeeze the club a little tighter with your left hand, in order to firm up your left side so your right forearm can't turn over.

Step 3

The low knuckleball produced should run well down the fairway after landing, so, when possible, aim away from any bunkers short of the green. If bunker play is a weakness, plan to hit short of them.

How to practice it

To get a feel for the ideal punch-shot swing, stand your golf bag up about five feet in front of your hitting area and try to hit shots through the legs and under the bag *[above]*. Start with short chips with your 5-iron and work your way up to longer shots. After 10 minutes, repeat the drill using other clubs. With practice, you'll get a feel for how far you can make each club run. If you hit the bag, you've produced too much backspin. To fix that, swing slower.

—Chuck Winstead

How to Hit Over Obstacles

Who put that tree there? Who cares! Here's how to go right over it.

The situation

Let's say you have 150 yards to the green, normally a 7-iron, but you need the loft of an 8-iron to clear the tree. The standard by-the-book advice when you're behind a tree is to play safely out to the fairway. But what if you're down in your match and need to make something happen? With a few tweaks, you should be able to throw your ball up high over that tall boy and keep your momentum going. Take the 7-iron and follow these steps.

MAKE A SLICE MOVE Take dead aim at the tree and set up to the ball as if you were hitting a big, high fade. It's something that should feel familiar to many of you, and will help the ball gain height quickly.

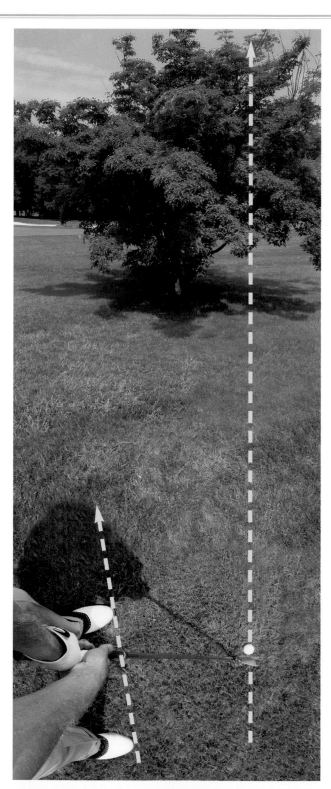

1. Create extra loft

● Widen your stance so the insides of your feet are just outside your shoulders.
● Aim the clubface at the target, then align your feet about 10 degrees open.
● Play the ball an inch more forward than normal. Swing the club along your stance line.
● The extra distance comes from hitting out of the rough. The longer grass causes the shot to come out "hot," with less spin. It will carry farther, and roll.

2. Make a steep backswing

You should feel like the clubhead is outside your hands as it nears hip height in your backswing. Even if the clubhead isn't actually outside your hands, trying to get it there will open the clubface. Your swing will feel steeper than normal, like you're lifting the club straight up as you reach the top. The goal is to produce a downswing with enough force to help the ball jump up in a hurry.

3. Adjust your release position

On a normal shot you release the club so the toe passes the heel and your arms extend the club low past impact *[photo, right]*. This is exactly what you don't want when hitting over a tree. Instead, try to keep the clubface open for as long as possible.
—**Michael Breed**

The Secret To Hitting Off a Sidehill

When the ball's above your feet, use your hand to find the target

The problem

You're not sure how to aim your club when the ball is above your feet.

The solution

When you address a ball that's sitting above your feet, the leading edge of your club may appear to be facing your target, but that doesn't mean the clubface is looking there as well. But there's an easy way to gauge the true direction in which you're aiming from an uneven lie.

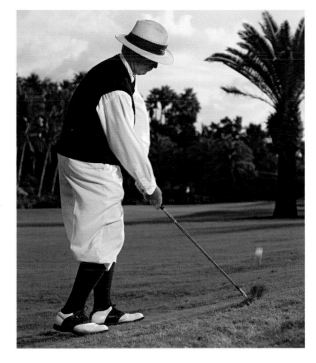

How to line up on target from a sidehill lie

Step 1
Hold the club you're going to use in your left hand, and then match the loft of the clubhead with your right hand.

Step 2
Cock your right elbow so that your right forearm is perfectly horizontal, then hinge your right hand up until it matches the angle of the hill.

Step 3
Place the clubshaft between the ring and middle finger of your right hand so that the shaft forms a right angle with your palm. The butt end of the club will point to exactly where your clubface is actually facing—in this case, left of your target.

Step 4
With the shaft still between your fingers, turn your body until your club points at your target. Your body will face right of the target, but the clubface will point at the target. Sole your club and swing along your toe line.
—Dr. Gary Wiren

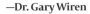

Make a Back-Handed Escape

Here's what to do when an obstacle interferes with your stance

Choose one of your wedges—these have the largest faces and you'll benefit from a broader hitting area since you won't be looking at the ball during contact.

Step 1
Turn your back to the target, stand about a half-foot to the right of the ball and grip your wedge in the middle of the handle. Flip your club around so that the face points at your target with the club resting on its toe.

Step 2
Cock your club up by bending your right elbow (keep your upper arm still). Add just a touch of wrist hinge.

Step 3
Straighten your arm and slap your clubhead into the back of the ball.

This is a trick shot that's actually very easy to pull off with a little practice. Make sure you accelerate all the way to the ball so the club doesn't flip past your hands and hit the ball thin.
—Tom Stickney

Escape Rough With Your Worst Swing

Fix your slice for straighter drives, but keep it in your pocket to save par from nasty lies

The situation

On the tee, you hoist your driver like you're trying to squish a bug on a 10-foot ceiling. On the way back down, you make a severe cut and leave a sizable divot on the tee box. There's no "around" to your swing—it's all up-and-down. The result: a 165-yard slice that lands in a patch of nasty, thick rough.

The silver lining

You're now faced with 200+ yards to the green. You need some distance on your second shot so you can play your third shot close to the pin. The good news: with a mid-iron and that ugly, steep, cut swing you made on the tee, you'll be in business.

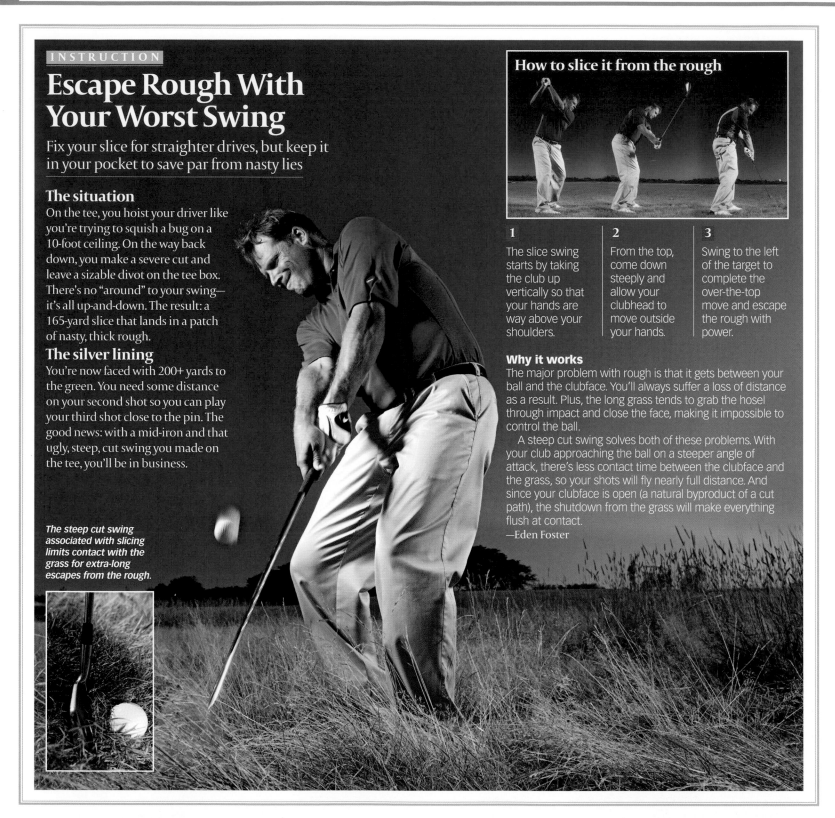

The steep cut swing associated with slicing limits contact with the grass for extra-long escapes from the rough.

How to slice it from the rough

1 The slice swing starts by taking the club up vertically so that your hands are way above your shoulders.

2 From the top, come down steeply and allow your clubhead to move outside your hands.

3 Swing to the left of the target to complete the over-the-top move and escape the rough with power.

Why it works

The major problem with rough is that it gets between your ball and the clubface. You'll always suffer a loss of distance as a result. Plus, the long grass tends to grab the hosel through impact and close the face, making it impossible to control the ball.

A steep cut swing solves both of these problems. With your club approaching the ball on a steeper angle of attack, there's less contact time between the clubface and the grass, so your shots will fly nearly full distance. And since your clubface is open (a natural byproduct of a cut path), the shutdown from the grass will make everything flush at contact.

—Eden Foster

Hosel It From Deep Grass

The part of the club that causes shanks can help you make a great escape from deep lies

Just getting the clubface on the ball in deep rough (never mind moving it forward) can be tough. But here's how to use the whole clubhead—including the hosel—to muscle the ball out of the junk.

Step 1
Stiffen the clubshaft
Choke down about an inch or so on the handle of your sand wedge or pitching wedge. This will help stiffen the shaft (make it stronger) and allow the clubhead to cut through the grass more effectively at impact.

Step 2
Get more mass behind the ball
Sole your club with the face slightly closed and the ball in the "V" formed by the clubface and the hosel. This will get more of the clubhead's weight (most of it is in the hosel) behind the ball at impact, and the opposing clubface and hosel angles will keep your ball on target.

Step 3
Lean the handle forward
Set up with the ball off the inside of your right heel and lean the shaft forward by moving your hands toward the target. This promotes a steeper swing angle, which allows the clubhead to pass through as little grass as possible.

Step 4
Swing up and down sharply
Use extra wrist hinge and keep your follow-through to a minimum, as you would for a buried lie in a bunker. You almost want to feel as though you're leaving the clubhead in the grass.
—**Patti McGowan**

ADD SPEED
Any blast from the tall stuff requires a powerful swing. Get mad and swing hard.

PUSH AND PULL
From the top, pull your left shoulder toward the sky and push your right under your chin.

RELEASE!
Bow your right wrist to make sure your club exits the hitting area on the correct plane.

Use Hybrid Power to Blast It Out

This club gives you distance from the deep stuff

When to use it
Unless the ball is sitting down deep, or if the grass is wet, give your hybrid the green light from rough. Otherwise, swallow your pride, grab your wedge, and hack the ball back to the fairway.

Which one
To make sure you advance the ball safely, opt for your highest-lofted hybrid. More loft will help pop the ball out of deep grass.

Why it works
A hybrid mimics many of the design elements common to modern fairway woods, including a short hosel. This feature alone makes a hybrid a better choice than an iron from the rough. The typical long hosel of an iron is prone to getting tangled up by long grass, which forces the face open or shuts it down through impact.
—**Robert Baker**

INSTRUCTION

How to Attack Doglegs on Windy Days

Play to your strengths to find the fairway

The situation

You're on the tee of a 400-yard par 4 that doglegs to the left and the pin is cut on the far left side of the green. There's tree trouble to the left of the fairway and water up the right side, and a stiff wind is blowing from left to right.

THE TOP 100 SAY

45%—Play your fade and ride the wind

22%—Fight the wind and play a draw

19%—Hit into the wind and let it blow your ball back

14%—Other (long-iron, hybrids, low shots)

Wind direction

BEST SPOT

IF YOU CAN WORK THE BALL...

Play a hold-up draw

Set up: Middle of tee box
Aim: Center of fairway
Swing: Play your everyday draw with a 3-wood (it's easier to shape than a driver). The left-to-right wind and right-to-left shot shape should even out, putting you in the middle.
Pro: Takes water out of play.
Con: Overcook it and you'll be in the trees; undercook it and you're in the drink.

"Always err on the opposite side of a dogleg. You can still make par even if you hit into the water off the tee. If you hit into trees, you still need to waste a shot to get out of them"
—Anne Cain

IF YOU FEAR SHAPING SHOTS...

Play into the wind

Set up: Toward right tee marker
Aim: Left side of fairway
Swing: Don't make any setup or swing adjustments. Make your regular swing with either your driver or 3-wood and hit toward left edge of the fairway. The wind should blow the ball back to the center.
Pro: No need to make any setup or swing adjustments.
Con: Slight loss of distance.

"Most of a hole's yardage occurs before the dogleg—hit only what you need to get past the bend and in the fairway, even if it's an iron."
—Kevin Walker

IF YOU'RE A FADER...

Ride the wind

Set up: Toward right tee marker
Aim: Up the left side
Swing: Hit your driver and start the ball up the edge of the treeline. The combined effects of the left-to-right wind and left-to-right spin should put you in the right side of the fairway.
Pro: Takes the trees out of play
Con: None, unless you really slice it.

"With the pin cut left, position A is the right side of the fairway because it gives you the clearest view of your target. Distance is never as important as hitting to the correct side. If you don't have to hit driver, then don't."
—Mike Adams

How to Chip From a Collection Area

Take the fear out of chipping from ultra-tight lies by using your hybrid

When to use it
From a collection area, or over any mound or tier between you and the pin.

Which one
Use your highest-lofted hybrid to loft the ball over longer grass around the green and to create more forward roll once it lands.

Why it works
The extra weight and longer shaft length of a hybrid allows you to make a smooth, short stroke and still create a lot of distance. The rounded sole shape should quell any fears you may have of hitting the shot fat or thin.

How to do it
Even from distances as far as 100 feet, you have plenty of club in your hand to roll the ball close, so concentrate on making your normal putting stroke. (Yes, practice is recommended to develop distance control and touch.) *Focus on these keys:*

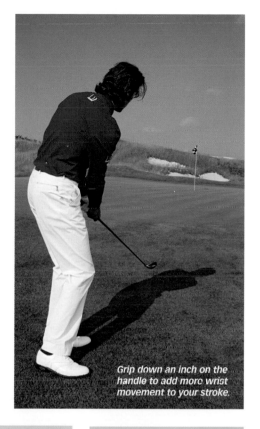

Grip down an inch on the handle to add more wrist movement to your stroke.

Setup
● Play the ball directly under your right eye
● Narrow your stance (heels just inside your shoulders) and set your weight slightly forward
● Sole your club on the ground and set the face square to your target line

Backswing
● Swing the triangle formed by your arms and shoulders in a pendulum motion
● Add a little wrist motion for a touch of feel
● Keep your lower body quiet

Through-swing
● Unhinge your wrists—put back what you took out
● Accelerate! Don't hit the ball, but simply let it get in the way
● Add just a touch of forward knee movement
—**Robert Baker**

Beat the Collar

Hit it thin when you're against it

The situation
The ball is against the collar of the green—the long grass behind the ball makes clean contact almost impossible.

The play
Hit a "bellied wedge," striking the center of the ball (the part that lies above the collar grass) with the leading edge of your sand wedge.

How to do it
At address, push the shaft away from you so that the leading edge lines up diagonally across the ball. This little trick ensures that at least some part of the club's leading edge will strike the ball's equator. Take a couple of practice swings, keeping the clubhead fairly level. Expect the shot to come out hot with no backspin.
—**Bill Moretti**

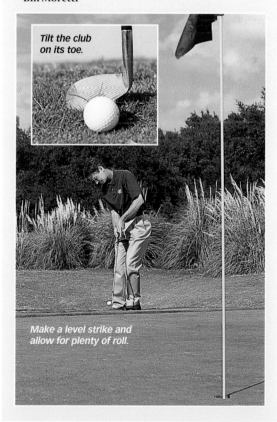

Tilt the club on its toe.

Make a level strike and allow for plenty of roll.

Working on your game won't stop you from never hitting a bad shot again, but it will stop you from hitting the same bad shot twice during play.

SECTION 10

FLAWS AND FIXES

How to make sure you don't make the same mistake twice when bad habits creep into your swing

I t doesn't matter who you are, how long you've been playing or how low your handicap is—you're going to hit bad shots in every round. The key to turning poor rounds into good ones (and good ones into great ones) is to not hit the same bad shot more than once. Since bad shots always come in groups, you can save loads of strokes by stopping a negative trend before it builds momentum.

Owning the ability to quick-fix your game on the course is the hallmark of any great player. Granted, you need practice to completely eradicate flaws in your technique, but Band Aid fixes can and do work, or at the very least can stop the bleeding during your bad rounds.

In this section, the Top 100 Teachers address the 12 most common swing flaws. Their fixes are simple—you can use them during play or as the foundation for a practice session dedicated to completely working out your kinks. That's the way to make sure your fixes stick. A dozen flaws may sound like a lot to you, but these are only the tip of the fault iceberg. Luckily, fixing these takes care of much of the rest. In fact, eliminating just half of these disaster shots will make your next round a nice, low number.

---

5 THINGS YOU'LL LEARN IN THIS SECTION

- How to stop short-game errors like hitting your pitch shots thin and hitting your chip shots fat
- How to get a feel for distance and avoid three-putting
- Self-diagnose your bunker problems
- How to swing on plane more consistently and three ways to fix your slice—and one to fix your hook
- How to stop topping your drives and hit for more power off the tee

---

YOUR GAME

What Makes Your Shots Curve?

There are nine different ways to approach a golf ball, which result in nine possible ball flights. Here are the path/face combinations that cause them. Look for yours to discover exactly what you should be working on.

1 Straight: Swing path along target line, clubface square

2 Hook: Path along line, face closed

3 Slice: Path along line, face open

4 Pull: Path out to in, face square to path

5 Pull-hook: Path out to in, face closed to path

6 Pull-slice: Path out to in, face open to path

7 Push: Path in to out, face square to path

8 Push-hook: Path in to out, face closed to path

9 Push-slice: Path in to out, face open to path

A fade is a controlled pull-slice; a draw a controlled push-hook.

Stop Skulling Your Pitch Shots

Use this drill to make a descending blow

Cause

The ball is too far forward in your stance and your weight is too far back.

Fix

Using your pitching wedge, center the ball and set your feet six inches apart. With your weight forward and your head ahead of the ball, stick the toe of your right shoe into the ground. Then, instead of soling the club, hold it at the ball's equator *[below]*. Start back from there.

Why it works

This setup keeps your weight forward, encouraging a descending blow. Once you see for yourself that hitting down sends the ball up, you'll stop scooping. As for not soling the club, you'll naturally compensate for starting with the clubhead above the ball by extending your arms and swinging down—a key to avoiding thin contact.

—Mike Malaska

Stop the skulls by practicing leaning into the shot.

QUICK TIP
Always play the ball back in your stance on short shots to guarantee catching the ball first and the ground second.

DRILL

Stop Three-Putting

This drill helps you find the elusive touch you need in just minutes

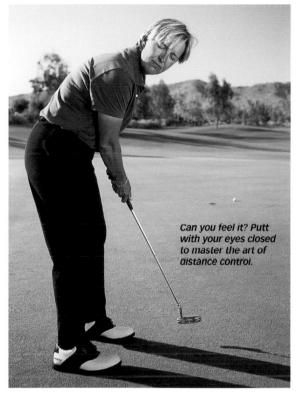

Can you feel it? Putt with your eyes closed to master the art of distance control.

Cause

You lack an innate sense of feel for putting distance. While your eyes are great for sending signals to your brain that tell you how long or short a stroke to make for a given distance, there's more to it than trusting your peepers. Mastering the art of distance control is about trusting yourself and your stroke.

Fix

Place a ball 10 feet from the hole and put your glove in the cup (to take away sound). Survey the putt. Once you think you have a feel for the distance, turn your head away from your target and close your eyes.

Stroke the putt and continue looking away until you can estimate where your ball ended up. Look up to see how closely your estimate matched the actual distance. Your goal is to create a perfect match.

Make this drill part of your practice routine (varying the distance and break each time), and you won't have to rely on mechanics to putt the ball a given distance—your feel will do it for you.

—**Pia Nilsson**

Face First

A major key to consistently putting the ball the correct distance is making consistent contact in the center of your putterface. Contact out toward the toe or heel results in far less energy transfer, which also explains why you roll your ball way past the hole on one putt and then roll it way short the next, even with the same stroke.

To improve your contact consistency, wrap two rubber bands around the left and right sides of your putter's sweet spot. Practicing with the bands on your putter instantly tells you when you fail to stroke the ball in the center of your face. You'll feel a "thud" rather than a "click," meaning you missed the center and hit one of the bands. For feel putters, it's either centered contact or bust.

—**Lynn Marriott**

Hitting the ball on the sweet spot is the key to distance control.

Why Can't I Chip?

Whether you chunk 'em or skull 'em, here are four common chipping errors and four ways to get it close

1 AM I TOO WRISTY?
Your arms and shoulders should move back and through as one piece. Get too wristy and you could chunk it or thin it.

TEST
Take a practice swing, follow through and freeze! Your left wrist should be fairly straight, not bent.

FIX No. 1
Practice with a pencil under a wristwatch on your left hand. That helps keep both wrists firm, not flippy.

YES!
NO?

2 IS IT MY BALL POSITION?
You may be playing the ball too far forward in your stance—the club bottoms out early, leading to chunks.

TEST
Address the ball, then step backwards 12 inches and swing. If the club strikes grass before the spot where the ball was, bingo!

FIX No. 2
Easy. Just move the ball back in your stance to where your club bottoms out, which is generally off your right foot.

YES!
NO?

3 AM I LOCKING MY RIGHT KNEE?
Your legs should be quiet. Locking your right knee leads to lifting your head. Common result? Skulled shots.

TEST
Board the sol train. With the sun on your back, hit some chips and watch your shadow. If your head rises, you're likely straightening your knee.

FIX No. 3
Get left! Your weight should be forward, so shift about 75 percent of your weight to your left leg, and chip away.

YES!
NO?

4 AM I SCOOPING THE BALL?
It's tempting to try to scoop the ball, instead of making a descending blow. But that's a recipe for blading it.

TEST
Take a practice swing and hold your follow-through. The clubhead should be just a foot off the ground. If it's much higher, you're in scoop city!

FIX No. 4
Place a penny an inch in front of the ball on the target line and hit the ball and the penny in one motion. That promotes the correct strike.

—**Rick Grayson**

INSTRUCTION

Stop Pulling Your Shots

Maintain your forward bend to hit straighter shots

Cause

You're losing your "power angle." Your power angle is the one formed between your upper and lower body at the top of your backswing with your spine—the top half of the angle—tilted 5 to 15 degrees away from your target. The only way to create your power angle is to take your club to the top while maintaining the forward bend in your hips from address.

Fix

Get into a powerful setup by bending at your hips so that your bottom rib feels like it's being pulled in closer to your belt buckle. Maintain the distance from your bottom rib to your belt line as you turn and swing to the top. You've done it right if your spine angles away from the target with your head behind the ball and your weight is set in your left hip.

Make your first move down a turn of your left hip back toward the target. Feel like your lower body is separating from your upper body and leading your downswing. A chain reaction should now occur from the ground up—lower body, torso, arms and then club whip through impact at max speed.

Why it works

Keeping your forward bend intact not only creates solid posture at the top, it also allows you to start your downswing correctly by turning your hips without prematurely firing your upper body. Conversely, swinging hard from the top with your shoulders destroys your power angle. You've done it wrong if your head is even or ahead of the ball and your hips are as open as your shoulders. Expect pulls, tops and slices from this position.

—Dave Phillips

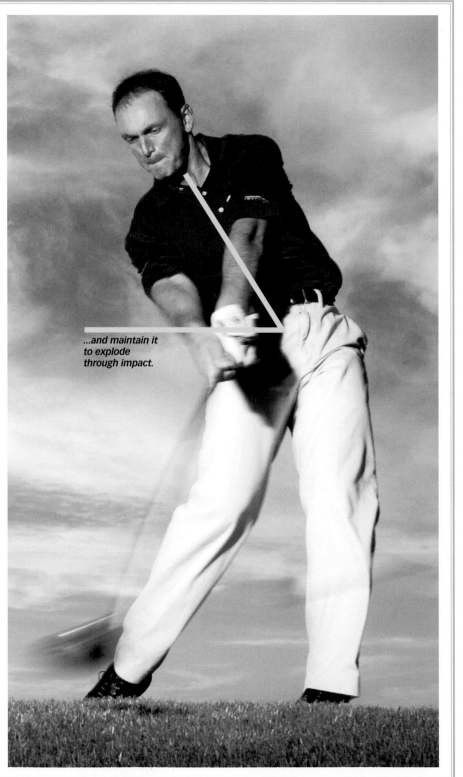

...and maintain it to explode through impact.

Create your power angle on your backswing...

...increase it on your downswing...

DRILL

Stop Swinging Off Plane

Take this quick test to get your swing back on track

Cause

Your inconsistent ballstriking is the result of never getting your club on the correct plane. For most golfers, this has been a difficult thing to gauge—until now.

Fix

Grip a mid-iron in just your left hand and, with your right hand, hold a second mid-iron by its hosel. Take your normal address and position the grip of the club in your right hand about six inches behind the clubhead of the one in your left [*photo, far right*]. Swing both clubs slowly to the top, doing your best to keep them exactly six inches apart all the way.

If both of the shafts feel light in your hands and are still parallel (use a mirror or ask a friend to watch you), you found the correct plane—ingrain that feel.

Why it works

If you make the common mistake of swinging too much around your back (below the correct plane) rather than up around your shoulders, gravity will cause one or both clubs to feel heavy as they hang behind your back.
—**Brad Redding**

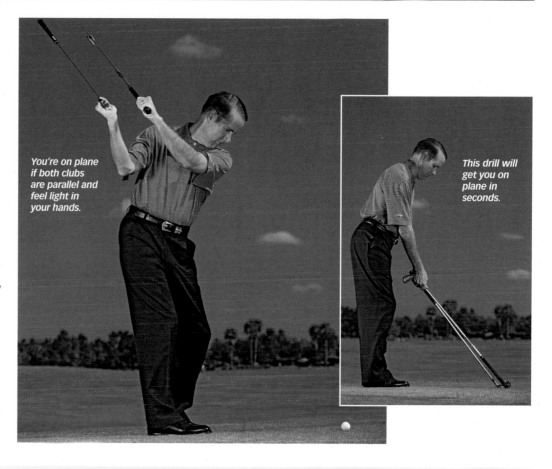

You're on plane if both clubs are parallel and feel light in your hands.

This drill will get you on plane in seconds.

SELF-TEST

Why Can't I Hit a Fairway?

Here are three common causes of wild tee shots—and three ways to split the fairway

1 AM I SWINGING TOO HARD?
Don't swing so you almost fly out of your FootJoys. That throws you off-balance and your swing out of whack.

TEST
Swing! Then hold your finish for five seconds. If you need to take a step, you're off-balance.

→ NO? YES! →

FIX No. 1
Try this drill: Set up, then point your left foot at the target. This promotes a shorter, more controlled backswing, which leads to better balance.

2 AM I SLIDING MY HIPS?
With longer clubs, it can be tempting to slide your hips in your downswing, instead of rotating them, Grayson says. That throws the clubhead off its path.

TEST
Make a backswing and stop at the top. If you feel most of your weight on the right side of your right foot, you're sliding your hips.

→ NO? YES! →

FIX No. 2
Hit the range and bust some drives while keeping your feet together. This makes sliding impossible and forces you to rotate through impact.

3 IS MY DRIVER SHAFT TOO LONG?
Probably. More than half of everyday players are using a shaft that's too long for them.

TEST
A push slice is the common result of a too-long driver. The longer shaft is harder to square at impact.

FIX No. 3
Get fitted. In the meantime, choke down about a half-inch or so.
—**Rick Grayson**

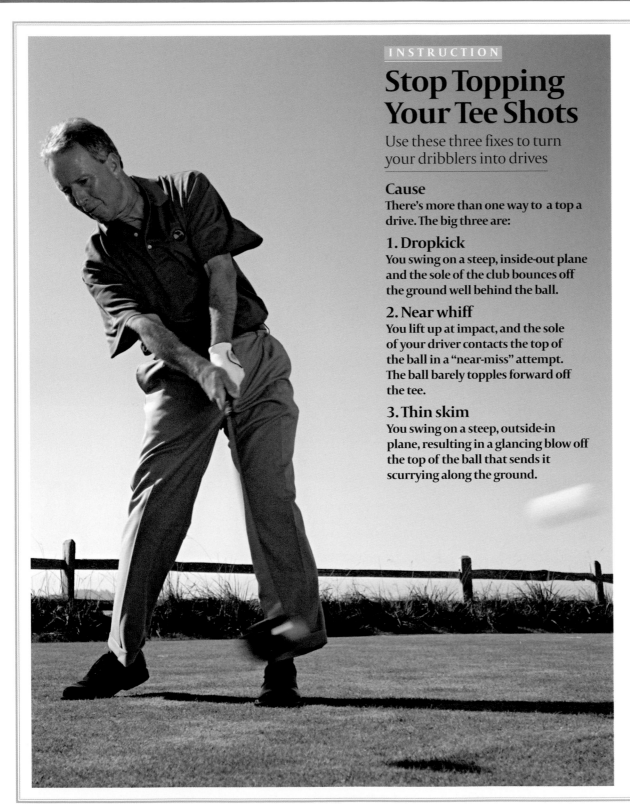

Stop Topping Your Tee Shots

Use these three fixes to turn your dribblers into drives

Cause

There's more than one way to a top a drive. The big three are:

1. Dropkick

You swing on a steep, inside-out plane and the sole of the club bounces off the ground well behind the ball.

2. Near whiff

You lift up at impact, and the sole of your driver contacts the top of the ball in a "near-miss" attempt. The ball barely topples forward off the tee.

3. Thin skim

You swing on a steep, outside-in plane, resulting in a glancing blow off the top of the ball that sends it scurrying along the ground.

Fix 1: Dropkick
Your swing is steep and too inside-out

An inside-out swing plane in and of itself can be a good thing. It promotes a draw, which will help you add distance. It's when you overdo it that you create the dropkick. On your downswing, strive to contact the inside lower quadrant of the ball, but rotate your hands so that the club exits the hitting area on a line that parallels your target line. Try to "throw" the clubhead at your target.

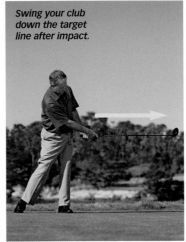

Swing your club down the target line after impact.

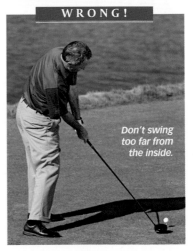

Don't swing too far from the inside.

Fix 2: Near whiff
You raise up at impact

To ensure that you stay down and through the ball, keep your knees flexed—but relaxed—throughout your swing, and keep your right heel on the ground for as long as possible. Also, resist the urge to "slap" at the ball, and instead focus on swinging through it, with your right shoulder turning under your chin through the hitting area. You don't need to help the ball into the air—the club will do that for you.

Fix 3: Thin Skim
Your swing is steep and too outside-in

To stop your right shoulder from pulling your clubhead across the line, address the ball with your right shoulder lower than your left, and bend your right elbow so that it sits closer to your torso than your left. These fixes will help you make the correct turn and will keep your shoulder movement in check, helping your club to remain on plane.

—Laird Small

Maintain your knee flex to keep from lifting up.

Set your right shoulder low to help keep your club on plane.

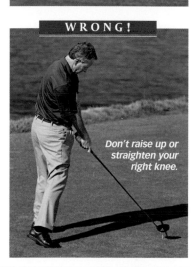

WRONG!

Don't raise up or straighten your right knee.

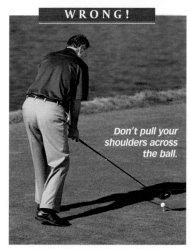

WRONG!

Don't pull your shoulders across the ball.

Why Can't I Escape the Sand?

Here are four common causes for bunker blues— and four easy ways to make a great escape

1 AM I HITTING TOO FAR BEHIND THE BALL?
Hitting four, five or six inches behind the ball is too far. The club should enter the sand about two inches behind for greenside shots.

TEST
Draw a line in the sand up to your ball, perpendicular to the target. Measure where your divot starts. More than 3 inches behind is too far.

FIX No. 1
Visualize your ball resting on the center of a dollar bill. When you swing, your club should enter the back of the dollar and exit the front, creating a bill-shaped divot.

NO? YES!

2 AM I FAILING TO SHIFT MY WEIGHT?
Swinging just with your arms, and not shifting your weight, decelerates the club. The ugly outcome: bladed shots.

TEST
Swing! Now check your feet. Is your leading foot flat in the finish position? That means you're not pivoting your weight toward

FIX No. 2
Take practice swings until you can splash sand onto the green. That forces you to make an aggressive, full-body swing.

NO? YES!

3 AM I TOO HANDSY?
In a greenside bunker, it's tempting to flip your wrist instead of making a full turn. But you'll lose the "pop" needed to escape.

TEST
If most of your shots barely sneak over the lip, you're all hands.

FIX No. 3
Be a one-armed bunker bandit! To promote a full turn back and through, choke down to the middle of the grip with your right hand and hit one-armed shots.

—Rick Grayson

Stop Slicing

Try these three drills to eliminate your banana ball for good

Drill 1: Square up before you start up

Check your address position in a mirror. If your right hand is on top of the grip (instead of on the side), you're set up to produce a slice. Take your right hand off the grip, let your right arm hang loose at your side, then smoothly move it up toward the handle and retake your grip *[photo, far right]*.

Why it works

It encourages a stronger right-hand hold for greater clubhead control, and it sets your shoulders square to your target line. Notice how the right-hand-on-top position *[right]* forces my shoulders to open, pre-programming a slice swing.

—**Michael Breed**

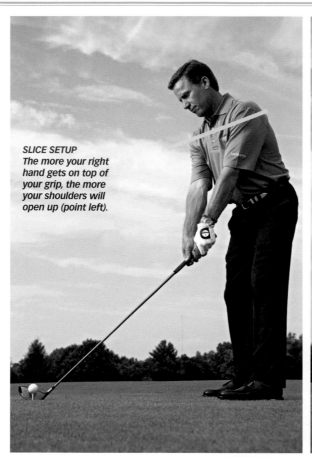

SLICE SETUP
The more your right hand gets on top of your grip, the more your shoulders will open up (point left).

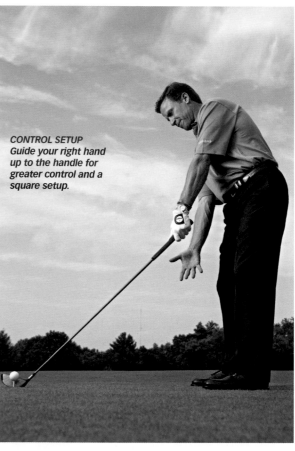

CONTROL SETUP
Guide your right hand up to the handle for greater control and a square setup.

Drill 2: Hit a Homerun

(1) Address a ball in the middle of your stance, then leaving your right foot in place move your left foot back until your feet touch, (2) swing to the top and on the way down move your left foot back to its original position, and (3) make contact with both feet on the ground.

Why it works

This baseball-type swing forces you to begin your downswing with your lower body, which sets up an inside-out sequence (legs, shoulders, arms, hands and clubhead).

—**Darrell Kestner**

Drill 3:
Tell time

Save long-term swing fixes for the practice range and concentrate on this emergency cure. As you swing through impact, make a conscious effort to square up your clubface. If you're wearing a watch on your left wrist, try to allow an imaginary person standing behind you to see what time it is immediately following impact. It's a good trigger to remind you to rotate your forearms through the hitting area to prevent leaving the clubface open. Aim 10 yards right of your intended target in case the ball hooks a little.

After your round, forget this quick fix and try to determine the real cause of your slice. Most likely it's an outside-in downswing path. That requires more than a Band-Aid. But the watch trick works and can definitely help you turn a bad driving day into a decent scoring day.
—**Tom Stickney**

QUICK TIP
If you still slice no matter what you do, try an offset driver. This design gives you more time to square the face.

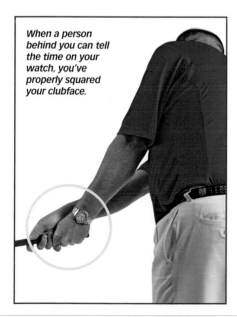

When a person behind you can tell the time on your watch, you've properly squared your clubface.

Rotate your forearms through impact

Stop Hooking the Ball

Think like the Karate Kid to chop this ugly shot

Cause
At impact, your clubface points to the left of both your target and your swing path.

Fix
Imagine you're making a karate chop at a board with the side, or heel, of your left hand on your downswing. This is the swing thought that helped Billy Casper get his hook under control. By leading with the side of your left hand, you delay the rotation of your forearms just enough to prevent the toe of the club from passing the heel too early. Thus, you can't turn the face over.

Why it works
Think of it this way: The back of your left hand mirrors the position of your clubface at impact, so if you can keep your knuckles pointing right of the target, your clubface will look that way, too. If the face looks right, there's no way you can curl the ball to the left.
—**Martin Hall**

Lead with the left side of your left hand—like you would when you make a karate chop—to reel in your hooks.

Stop Hitting Your Irons Fat

Strike the ball then take a walk

Cause
Your clubhead bottoms out behind the ball.

Fix
Try the "strike and stride." Take your normal setup with a 5-iron. Swing to the top, then step toward the target with your right foot as you start down [right]—a move made famous by Gary Player.

Why it works
As you step, your weight will shift onto your front foot. This moves the bottom of your swing arc forward so the clubhead strikes the ball before it hits the ground. The proof is in your divot, which will start on the target side of the ball.
—**Martin Hall**

Stranding weight on your right side places the bottom of your swing arc behind the ball.

Step forward on your downswing to move the bottom of your swing arc in the right place.

Imagining a football field will help your distance control

INSTRUCTION

Stop Missing With Your Wedges

Here's how to hit it tight when you're left with an awkward distance to the hole

Set up open to your target line on wedge shots for a better turn.

Cause
You can't figure out how far to carry the ball and how far back to swing the club.

Fix
Visualize a football field on the fairway.

Why it works
By imagining lines every 10 yards from your ball to the hole, you'll focus on the exact distance to help you play the right shot. If the pin is in front, try to land your ball on the front fringe. If it's all the way back, you'll want to land it about halfway onto the green. Once you know how far you want to carry it, you'll control the distance with the length of your backswing.

—Carol Preisinger

DRILL

Stop Chunking Your Chips

If you're tired of sticking the club in the ground, then try practicing blindfolded

Cause
You dip your head down at impact.

Fix
Address the ball with your chipping club. Hold your chin as high as possible and extend your arms down to the ball.

● Wrap a handkerchief or T-shirt around your eyes. Once it's secure, re-position the club behind the ball and address the ball again. (You might have to peek to check.)

● Chip the ball. Keep your head and upper body high through the motion.

● Remove the blindfold. We'll bet you a five-spot that your ball is closer to the hole than your usual chip.

Why it works
The blindfold eliminates the "hit impulse" which causes you to focus too much on the ball and dip your chin in an effort to scoop it into the air.

—Rick Barry

THE TOP 100 TEACHERS IN AMERICA

A quick look at the nation's most exclusive— and talented—team of teaching experts

GOLF MAGAZINE TOP 100 TEACHERS IN AMERICA

MIKE ADAMS
Facility: Hamilton Farms G.C., Gladstone, N.J.
Website: www.mikeadamsgolf.com
Teaching since: 1977
Top 100 since: 1996
See Mike's tips on pages 59, 81, 90, 150 and 168

ROB AKINS
Facility: Ridgeway C.C., Germantown, Tenn.
Website: www.robakinsgolf.com
Teaching since: 1987
Top 100 since: 2001

ERIC ALPENFELS
Facility: The Pinehurst G.A., Pinehurst, N.C.
Website: www.pinehurst.com
Teaching since: 1984
Top 100 since: 2001
See Eric's tips on pages 30, 91, 158

TODD ANDERSON
Facility: Sea Island Golf Learning Ctr., St. Simons Island, Ga.
Website: www.seaisland.com
Teaching since: 1984
Top 100 since: 2003
See Todd's tips on pages 54 and 92

ROBERT BAKER
Facility: Miami Beach G.C., Miami Beach, Fla.
Website: www.logicalgolf.com
Teaching since: 1989
Top 100 since: 1999
See Robert's tips on pages 57, 65, 74, 75, 94, 95, 167 and 169

RICK BARRY
Facility: Sea Pines Resort, Hilton Head Island, S.C.
Website: www.seapines.com
Teaching since: 1976
Top 100 since: 2005
See Rick's tips on page 181

MIKE BENDER
Facility: Mike Bender G.A. at Timacuan C.C., Lake Mary, Fla.
Website: www.mikebender.com
Teaching since: 1990
Top 100 since: 1996
See Mike's tips on page 54

STEVE BOSDOSH
Facility: The Members Club at Four Streams
Website: www.fourstreams.com
Teaching since: 1983
Top 100 since: 2001
See Steve's tips on pages 45, 110 and 129

MICHAEL BREED
Facility: Sunningdale C.C., Scarsdale, N.Y.
Website: None
Teaching since: 1986
Top 100 since: 2003
See Mike's tips on pages 28, 49, 70, 77, 79, 85, 103, 141, 164 and 178

BRAD BREWER
Facility: Brad Brewer G.A. at Shingle Creek Resort, Orlando, Fla.
Website: www.bradbrewer.com
Teaching since: 1984
Top 100 since: 2007
See Brad's tips on page 36

HENRY BRUNTON
Facility: Henry Brunton Golf, Maple, Ontario
Website: www.henrybrunton.com
Teaching since: 1985
Top 100 since: 2005

ANNE CAIN
Facility: Anne Cain G.A. at Amelia Island G.C., Amelia Island, Fla.
Website: www.annecaingolf.com
Teaching since: 1995
Top 100 since: 2007
See Anne's tips on pages 119 and 168

JASON CARBONE
Facility: Jim McLean G.S. at The Wigwam, Litchfield Park, Ariz.
Website: www.jimmclean.com/usa/wigwam
Teaching since: 1993
Top 100 since: 2007
See Jason's tips on pages 23, 42 and 134

DONALD CRAWLEY
Facility: The Boulders Golf Academy, Carefree, Ariz.
Website: www.golfsimplified.com
Teaching since: 1974
Top 100 since: 1999
See Donald's tips on pages 39, 113, 120, 146 and 147

JOHN DAHL
Facility: Oxbow C.C., Oxbow, N.D.
Website: www.oxbowcc.com
Teaching since: 1974
Top 100 since: 2003
See John's tips on pages 62 and 101

BILL DAVIS
Facility: Jupiter Hills Club, Tequesta, Fla.
Website: www.jupiterhillsclub.org
Teaching since: 1973
Top 100 since: 1996
See Bill's tips on page 123

MIKE DAVIS
Facility: Stallion Mountain C.C., Las Vegas, Nev.
Website: www.waltersgolf.com
Teaching since: 1970
Top 100 since: 2007
See Mike's tips on page 46

GLENN DECK
Facility: Pelican Hill G.A., Newport Coast, Calif.
Website: www.pelicanhill.com
Teaching since: 1983
Top 100 since: 2003
See Glenn's tips on page 115

DOM DiJULIA
Facility: Dom DiJulia G.S. at Jericho Nat'l G.C., New Hope, Pa.
Website: www.dijuliagolf.com
Teaching since: 1990
Top 100 since: 2007
See Dom's tips on page 61

JOHN ELLIOT, JR.
Facility: Golden Ocala Golf & Equestrian Club, Ocala, Fla.
Website: www.goldenocala.com
Teaching since: 1970
Top 100 since: 1996
See John's tips on pages 14, 48, 58, 61, 100 and 115

BILL FORREST
Facility: Troon Country Club, Scottsdale, Ariz.
Website: www.trooncc.com
Teaching since: 1978
Top 100 since: 2007
See Bill's tips on page 114

EDEN FOSTER
Facility: Maidstone Club, East Hampton, N.Y.
Website: www.maidstoneclub.com
Teaching since: 1988
Top 100 since: 2003
See Eden's tips on pages 113, 122, 132, 154 and 166

JANE FROST
Facility: Sandwich Hollows G.C., Sandwich, Mass.
Website: www.janefrostgolfschools.com
Teaching since: 1982
Top 100 since: 1996
See Jane's tips on page 19

BRYAN GATHRIGHT
Facility: Oak Hills C.C., San Antonio, Tex.
Website: www.oakhillscc.com
Teaching since: 1987
Top 100 since: 2001
See Bryan's tips on page 93

DAVID GLENZ
Facility: David Glenz G.A., Franklin, N.J.
Website: www.davidglenz.com
Teaching since: 1978
Top 100 since: 1996
See David's tips on pages 24 and 63

PATRICK GOSS
Facility: Northwestern University, Evanston, Ill.
Website: www.northwestern.edu/athletics
Teaching since: 1993
Top 100 since: 2007
See Patrick's tips on page 161

RICK GRAYSON
Facility: Connie Morris Golf Learning Center, Springfield, Mo.
Website: www.rickgraysongolf.com
Teaching since: 1976
Top 100 since: 1996
See Rick's tips on pages 79, 173, 175 and 177

FRED GRIFFIN
Facility: Grand Cypress Academy of Golf, Orlando, Fla.
Website: www.grandcypress.com
Teaching since: 1980
Top 100 since: 1996
See Fred's tips on pages 42, 54, 70, 112, 148 and 149

RON GRING
Facility: Gring Golf, Daphne, Ala.
Website: www.gringgolf.com
Teaching since: 1978
Top 100 since: 2003
See Ron's tips on page 15

ROGER GUNN
Facility: Tierra Rejada G.C., Moorpark, Calif.
Website: www.golflevels.com
Teaching since: 1993
Top 100 since: 2007
See Roger's tips on page 42

MARTIN HALL
Facility: Ibis Golf & C.C., West Palm Beach, Fla.
Website: www.ibisgolf.com
Teaching since: 1978
Top 100 since: 1996
See Martin's tips on pages 38, 40, 73, 78, 85, 127, 179 and 180

BRUCE HAMILTON
Facility: Spanish Hills C.C., Camarillo, Calif.
Website: www.spanishhills.com
Teaching since: 1973
Top 100 since: 1996
See Bruce's tips on pages 41, 46 and 48

HANK HANEY
Facility: Hank Haney Golf Ranch, McKinney, Tex.
Website: www.hankhaney.com
Teaching since: 1977
Top 100 since: 1996

JIM HARDY
Facility: Jim Hardy Golf, Houston, Tex.
Website: www.jimhardygolf.com
Teaching since: 1966
Top 100 since: 1996
See Jim's tips on page 16

BUTCH HARMON, JR.
Facility: Butch Harmon School of Golf, Henderson, Nev.
Website: www.butchharmon.com
Teaching since: 1965
Top 100 since: 1996

CRAIG HARMON
Facility: Oak Hill C.C., Rochester, N.Y.
Website: www.oakhillcc.com
Teaching since: 1968
Top 100 since: 1996
See Craig's tips on page 23

SHAWN HUMPHRIES
Facility: Cowboys G.C., Grapevine, Tex.
Website: www.shawnhumphries.com
Teaching since: 1988
Top 100 since: 2005
See Shawn's tips on pages 25, 32, 39, 52 and 102

DON HURTER
Facility: Castle Pines G.C., Castle Rock, Colo.
Website: None
Teaching since: 1987
Top 100 since: 2003
See Don's tips on pages 24, 50 and 107

ED IBARGUEN
Facility: Duke University G.C., Durham, N.C.
Website: www.golf.duke.edu
Teaching since: 1979
Top 100 since: 2001
See Ed's tips on page 17

HANK JOHNSON
Facility: Greystone G.C., Birmingham, Ala.
Website: www.greystonecc.com
Teaching since: 1969
Top 100 since: 1999

DARRELL KESTNER
Facility: Deepdale G.C., Manhasset, N.Y.
Website: www.deepdalegolfclub.com
Teaching since: 1980
Top 100 since: 1996
See Darrell's tips on pages 44, 49 and 178

CHARLIE KING
Facility: Reynolds Plantation, Greensboro, Ga.
Website: www.reynoldsgolfacademy.com
Teaching since: 1989
Top 100 since: 2003
See Charlie's tips on pages 53 and 123

PETER KOSTIS
Facility: Kostis/McCord Learning Center, Scottsdale, Ariz.
Website: www.kostismccordlearning.com
Teaching since: 1971
Top 100 since: 1996
See Peter's tips on pages 83 and 157

DON KOTNIK
Facility: Toledo Country Club, Toledo, Ohio
Website: www.toledocountryclub.com
Teaching since: 1969
Top 100 since: 2005
See Don's tips on page 104

PETER KRAUSE
Facility: Windsong Farm G.C., Independence, Minn.
Website: www.peterkrausegolf.com
Teaching since: 1981
Top 100 since: 1999
See Peter's tips on page 11

MIKE LaBAUVE
Facility: Westin Kierland Resort and Spa, Scottsdale, Ariz.
Website: www.kierlandresort.com
Teaching since: 1980
Top 100 since: 1996
See Mike's tips on pages 66 and 107

SANDY LaBAUVE
Facility: Westin Kierland Resort and Spa, Scottsdale, Ariz.
Website: www.kierlandresort.com
Teaching since: 1984
Top 100 since: 1996
See Sandy's tips on pages 32 and 75

ROD LIDENBERG
Facility: Prestwick G.C., Woodbury, Minn.
Website: www.pgamasterpro.com
Teaching since: 1972
Top 100 since: 2007
See Rod's tips on page 15

MIKE LOPUSZYNSKI
Facility: David Glenz G.A., Franklin, N.J.
Website: www.davidglenz.com
Teaching since: 1987
Top 100 since: 1996
See Mike's tips on page 11

JACK LUMPKIN
Facility: Sea Island Golf Learning Ctr., St. Simons Island, Ga.
Website: www.seaisland.com
Teaching since: 1958
Top 100 since: 1996

KEITH LYFORD
Facility: Auburn C.C., Auburn, Calif.
Website: www.lyfordgolf.net
Teaching since: 1982
Top 100 since: 1999
See Keith's tips on page 103

BILL MADONNA
Facility: Bill Madonna G.A, Orlando, Fla.
Website: www.marriottworldcenter.com
Teaching since: 1971
Top 100 since: 1996
See Bill's tips on pages 32 and 71

TIM MAHONEY
Facility: Talking Stick G.C., Scottsdale, Ariz.
Website: www.timmahoneygolf.com
Teaching since: 1980
Top 100 since: 1996
See Tim's tips on page 44, 73, 76, 77, 91, 93 and 119

MIKE MALASKA
Facility: Superstition Mtn. G. & C.C., Superstition Mtn., Ariz.
Website: www.malaskagolf.com
Teaching since: 1982
Top 100 since: 1996
See Mike's tips on pages 64, 71, 128 and 172

PAUL MARCHAND
Facility: Shadow Hawk G.C., Richmond, Tex.
Website: www.golfspan.com
Teaching since: 1981
Top 100 since: 1996
See Paul's tips on page 129

LYNN MARRIOTT
Facility: Legacy Golf Resort, Phoenix, Ariz.
Website: www.golf54.com
Teaching since: 1982
Top 100 since: 1996
See Lynn's tips on page 173

RICK MARTINO
Facility: PGA Village, Port St. Lucie, Fla.
Website: www.pgavillage.com
Teaching since: 1970
Top 100 since: 2003
See Rick's tips on page 73

CONTRIBUTORS

RICK McCORD
Facility: McCord G.A. at Orange Lake Resort, Kissimmee, Fla.
Website: www.themccordgolfacademy.com
Teaching since: 1973
Top 100 since: 1996
See Rick's tips on pages 18, 50, 84 and 116

GERALD McCULLAGH
Facility: Univ. of Minn. Le Bolstad G.C., Falcon Heights, Minn.
Website: www.uofmgolf.com
Teaching since: 1967
Top 100 since: 1996
See Gerald's tips on pages 15 and 42

MIKE McGETRICK
Facility: Mike McGetrick G.A., Denver, Colo.
Website: www.mcgetrickgolf.com
Teaching since: 1983
Top 100 since: 1996

PATTI McGOWAN
Facility: Knack 4 Golf, Orlando, Fla.
Website: www.knack4golf.com
Teaching since: 1986
Top 100 since: 1996
See Patti's tips on page 167

JIM McLEAN
Facility: Jim McLean G.S. at Doral Golf Resort, Miami, Fla.
Website: www.jimmclean.com
Teaching since: 1975
Top 100 since: 1996

BRIAN MOGG
Facility: Golden Bear G.C. at Keene's Pointe, Windermere, Fla.
Website: www.moggperformance.com
Teaching since: 1992
Top 100 since: 2005
See Brian's tips on pages 22, 35, 84, 111, 121 and 130

BILL MORETTI
Facility: Academy of Golf at the Hills of Lakeway, Austin, Tex.
Website: www.golfdynamics.com
Teaching since: 1979
Top 100 since: 1996
See Bill's tips on pages 118 and 169

JERRY MOWLDS
Facility: Pumpkin Ridge G.C., North Plains, Ore.
Website: www.pumpkinridge.com
Teaching since: 1970
Top 100 since: 1996
See Jerry's tips on pages 99 and 133

JIM MURPHY
Facility: Sugar Creek C.C., Sugar Land, Tex.
Website: www.jimmurphygolf.com
Teaching since: 1984
Top 100 since: 2003
See Jim's tips on pages 82 and 113

TOM NESS
Facility: Golf Academy at Chateau Elan Resort, Braselton, Ga.
Website: www.chateauelanatlanta.com
Teaching since: 1972
Top 100 since: 2007

PIA NILSSON
Facility: Legacy Golf Resort, Phoenix, Ariz.
Website: www.golf54.com
Teaching since: 1987
Top 100 since: 2001
See Pia's tips on pages 60 and 173

DAN PASQUARIELLO
Facility: Pebble Beach G.A., Pebble Beach, Calif.
Website: www.pebblebeach.com
Teaching since: 1970
Top 100 since: 2007
See Dan's tips on page 50

TOM PATRI
Facility: Friar's Head G.C., Baiting Hollow, N.Y.
Website: www.tompatri.com
Teaching since: 1981
Top 100 since: 2001
See Tom's tips on page 140

BRUCE PATTERSON
Facility: Butler National G.C., Oak Brook, Ill.
Website: None
Teaching since: 1980
Top 100 since: 2005
See Bruce's tips on page 11

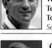
MIKE PERPICH
Facility: RiverPines Golf, Alpharetta, Ga.
Website: www.mikeperpich.com
Teaching since: 1976
Top 100 since: 2001
See Mike's tips on page 84

GALE PETERSON
Facility: Sea Island Golf Learning Ctr., St. Simons Island, Ga.
Website: www.seaisland.com
Teaching since: 1978
Top 100 since: 1996
See Gale's tips on page 15

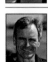
DAVID PHILLIPS
Facility: Titleist Performance Institute, Oceanside, Calif.
Website: www.titleistperformanceinstitute.com
Teaching since: 1989
Top 100 since: 2001
See David's tips on pages 13, 19 and 174

CAROL PREISINGER
Facility: Kiawah Island Club G.A., Kiawah Island, S.C.
Website: www.kiawahislandclub.com
Teaching since: 1986
Top 100 since: 2005
See Carol's tips on pages 19, 93 and 181

KIP PUTERBAUGH
Facility: The Aviara G.A., Carlsbad, Calif.
Website: www.aviaragolfacademy.com
Teaching since: 1972
Top 100 since: 1996
See Kip's tips on pages 32 and 98

NANCY QUARCELINO
Facility: King's Creek G.C., Spring Hill, Tenn.
Website: www.qsog.com
Teaching since: 1979
Top 100 since: 2003
See Nancy's tips on page 26

CARL RABITO
Facility: Rabito Golf at Bolingbrook G.C., Bolingbrook, Ill.
Website: www.rabitogolf.com
Teaching since: 1987
Top 100 since: 2007
See Carl's tips on page 36

DANA RADER
Facility: Ballantyne Resort, Charlotte, N.C.
Website: www.danarader.com
Teaching since: 1980
Top 100 since: 1996
See Dana's tips on page 50

BRAD REDDING
Facility: The Resort Club at Grande Dunes, Myrtle Beach, S.C.
Website: www.bradreddinggolf.com
Teaching since: 1984
Top 100 since: 2001
See Brad's tips on pages 34, 36 and 175

DEAN REINMUTH
Facility: Dean Reinmuth G.S., San Diego, Calif.
Website: www.deanofgolf.com
Teaching since: 1978
Top 100 since: 1996

BRADY RIGGS
Facility: Woodley Lakes G.C., Van Nuys, Calif.
Website: www.bradyriggs.com
Teaching since: 1990
Top 100 since: 2007
See Brady's tips on pages 41 and 54

SCOTT SACKETT
Facility: PGA Tour G.A., St. Augustine, Fla.
Website: www.scottsackett.com
Teaching since: 1985
Top 100 since: 1999
See Scott's tips on pages 36, 59, 126, 129, 141 and 143

TED SHEFTIC
Facility: Bridges G.C., Abbottstown, Pa.
Website: www.tedsheftic.com
Teaching since: 1966
Top 100 since: 2003
See Ted's tips on page 80

LAIRD SMALL
Facility: Pebble Beach G.A., Pebble Beach, Calif.
Website: www.pebblebeach.com
Teaching since: 1977
Top 100 since: 1996
See Laird's tips on pages 56 and 176

RANDY SMITH
Facility: Royal Oaks C.C., Dallas, Tex.
Website: www.roccdallas.com
Teaching since: 1973
Top 100 since: 2001

RICK SMITH
Facility: Rick Smith Golf Academy at Tiburon, Naples, Fla.
Website: www.ricksmith.com
Teaching since: 1977
Top 100 since: 1996

TODD SONES
Facility: White Deer Run G.C., Vernon Hills, Ill.
Website: www.toddsones.com
Teaching since: 1982
Top 100 since: 1996
See Todd's tips on pages 72, 108, 135, 147 and 151

CHARLES SORRELL
Facility: Sorrell School of Golf, Stockbridge, Ga.
Website: www.sorrellgolf.com
Teaching since: 1966
Top 100 since: 1996
See Charles' tips on page 102

MITCHELL SPEARMAN
Facility: Manhattan Woods G.C., West Nyack, N.Y.
Website: www.mitchellspearman.com
Teaching since: 1979
Top 100 since: 1996
See Mitchell's tips on pages 27, 89 and 145

TOM F. STICKNEY II
Facility: The Club at Cordillera, Edwards, Colo.
Website: www.tomstickneygolf.com
Teaching since: 1990
Top 100 since: 2007
See Tom's tips on pages 46, 165 and 179

JON TATTERSALL
Facility: Golf Performance Partners, Atlanta, Ga
Website: www.golfpp.com
Teaching since: 1986
Top 100 since: 2007
See Jon's tips on pages 34, 81 and 84

DR. T.J. TOMASI
Facility: Nantucket G.C., Siasconset, Mass.
Website: www.tjtomasi.com
Teaching since: 1975
Top 100 since: 1999
See T.J.'s tips on pages 21 and 156

PAUL TRITTLER
Facility: Kostis/McCord Learning Ctr., Scottsdale, Ariz.
Website: www.kostismccordlearning.com
Teaching since: 1983
Top 100 since: 1999
See Paul's tips on pages 85, 136, 137 and 143

J.D. TURNER
Facility: The Turner Golf Group, Savannah, Ga.
Website: www.jdturnergolf.com
Teaching since: 1965
Top 100 since: 1996
See J.D.'s tips on page 101

KEVIN WALKER
Facility: Nantucket G.C., Siasconset, Mass.
Website: None
Teaching since: 1979
Top 100 since: 1996
See Kevin's tips on pages 26, 45 and 168

CARL WELTY, JR.
Facility: Jim McLean G.S. at PGA West, La Quinta, Calif.
Website: www.jimmclean.com/usa/pga-west
Teaching since: 1965
Top 100 since: 1996
See Carl's tips on page 19

CHUCK WINSTEAD
Facility: The University Club, Baton Rouge, La.
Website: www.universityclubbr.com
Teaching since: 1993
Top 100 since: 2005
See Chuck's tips on pages 155 and 163

MARK WOOD
Facility: Cornerstone Club, Montrose, Colo.
Website: www.cornerstonecolorado.com
Teaching since: 1984
Top 100 since: 1999
See Mark's tips on pages 89, 149 and 153

DR. DAVID WRIGHT
Facility: Arroyo Trabuco Golf Club
Website: www.wrightbalance.com
Teaching since: 1982
Top 100 since: 2005
See David's tips on pages 21, 27, 105 and 144

Get more information on GOLF Magazine's Top 100 Teachers and the Top Teachers by Region, plus exclusive video tips and drills at

GOLF.com

EMERITUS

The master class of the Top 100 Teachers in America provide over a half-millennium's worth of instruction know-how

JIMMY BALLARD
Facility: Ballard Swing Connection, Key Largo, Fla.
Website: www.jimmyballard.com
Teaching since: 1960
Top 100 since: 1996
See Mr. Ballard's tips on page 81

PEGGY KIRK BELL
Facility: Pine Needles Resort, Southern Pines, N.C.
Website: www.pineneedles-midpines.com
Teaching since: 1958
Top 100 since: 1996
See Ms. Kirk Bell's tips on page 42

CHUCK COOK
Facility: Chuck Cook G.A. at Barton Creek C.C., Austin, Tex.
Website: www.bartoncreek.com
Teaching since: 1975
Top 100 since: 1996

MANUEL DE LA TORRE
Facility: Milwaukee C.C., River Hills, Wis.
Website: www.manueldelatorregolf.com
Teaching since: 1948
Top 100 since: 1996
See Mr. de la Torre's tips on page 97

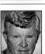

JIM FLICK
Facility: Jim Flick Golf, Carlsbad, Calif.
Website: www.jimflick.com
Teaching since: 1954
Top 100 since: 1996

MICHAEL HEBRON
Facility: Smithtown Landing G.C., Smithtown, N.Y.
Website: www.mikehebron.com
Teaching since: 1967
Top 100 since: 1996
See Mr. Hebron's tips on pages 33, 37, 43, 47, 51 and 55

DAVID LEADBETTER
Facility: David Leadbetter G.A., Champions Gate, Fla.
Website: www.davidleadbetter.com
Teaching since: 1976
Top 100 since: 1996

EDDIE MERRINS
Facility: Bel-Air C.C., Los Angeles, Calif.
Website: www.eddiemerrins.com
Teaching since: 1957
Top 100 since: 1996
See Mr. Merrin's tip on page 153

DAVE PELZ
Facility: Dave Pelz Scoring Game School, Austin, Tex.
Website: www.pelzgolf.com
Teaching since: 1976
Top 100 since: 1996
See Mr. Pelz's tips on pages 12, 13, 104, 137, 145 and 157

PHIL RITSON
Facility: Orange County National, Winter Garden, Fla.
Website: www.ocngolf.com
Teaching since: 1950
Top 100 since: 1996
See Mr. Ritson's tips on page 79

PHIL RODGERS
Facility: Carlton Oaks C.C., San Diego, Calif.
Website: None
Teaching since: 1977
Top 100 since: 1996

CRAIG SHANKLAND
Facility: Craig Shankland G.S., Daytona Beach, Fla.
Website: None
Teaching since: 1957
Top 100 since: 1996
See Mr. Shankland's tips on page 70

DR. JIM SUTTIE
Facility: Suttie Academies at TwinEagles, Naples, Fla.
Website: www.jimsuttie.com
Teaching since: 1972
Top 100 since: 1996
See Dr. Suttie's tips on pages 125 and 142

BOB TOSKI
Facility: Toski-Battersby Golf Learning Ctr., Coconut Creek, Fla.
Website: www.learn-golf.com
Teaching since: 1956
Top 100 since: 1996
See Mr. Toski's tips on page 23

DR. GARY WIREN
Facility: Trump International G.C., West Palm Beach, Fla.
Website: www.garywiren.com
Teaching since: 1955
Top 100 since: 1996
See Dr. Wiren's tips on pages 46, 133, 152, 162 and 165

TOP 100 BY THE NUMBERS

29.23
Average years of teaching experience

20
Top 100 Teachers who have been named PGA National Teacher of the Year

6
Top 100 Teachers who have been inducted into the PGA Golf Professional Hall of Fame

28,000
Members of the PGA of America's 41 sections eligible for Top 100 Status

0.4%
Percentage of those who are Top 100 Teachers

GLOSSARY

Unfamiliar with some of the jargon used by the Top 100? Consult this glossary so you don't miss a single tip.

Above Plane
Swinging your club above the plane defined by your shoulders.

Across the Line
Pointing the shaft right of the target at the top of your backswing.

Address
The position you take prior to hitting a shot. According to the Rules of Golf, you've completely addressed the ball when you've taken your stance and grounded your club.

Aim Line
An invisible line that runs from your ball to your target. See also Target Line.

Alignment
The position of your body relative to the target line.

Angle of Attack
The angle at which your clubhead descends toward the ball on your downswing. A steep angle of attack is the result of an upright swing and a shallow angle of attack comes from a flatter swing.

Apron
The closely mown area encircling a putting green.

Back Lip
The edge of the bunker that's farthest from the green.

Backspin
Ball spin in the direction away from the target.

Ball Flight
The path and trajectory of the ball from impact to when it hits the ground.

Ball Mark
An indentation made in the putting surface where your shot lands on the green.

Ball Marker
A token or a small coin used to spot the position of the ball on the green prior to lifting it.

Ball Position
The location of the ball relative to your stance width. A ball positioned toward your front foot is said to be more forward.

Ballooned
A ball flight defined by an unreasonably high trajectory.

Banana Ball
A slice.

Baseball Grip
Holding the club with all ten fingers.

Beach
A sand hazard.

Below Plane
Swinging your club below the plane defined by your shoulders.

Bend
The curve on a shot created by sidespin.

Bent Grass
A type of grass characterized by thin blades, found on most courses with varying seasonal climates.

Bermuda Grass
Type of grass found on most courses located in warmer or tropical climates. Characterized by thick blades and grainy surface.

Bite
The ability of the ball to stop—rather than roll—when it lands.

Bladed shot
To hit the ball with the leading edge of your iron. See also Skull.

Blast
A shot made from a bunker that displaces a noticeable amount of sand.

Block
A straight shot played severely to the right; similar to a Push.

Bounce
The angle formed between the leading edge of the clubhead and the lowest part of the sole. Clubs with higher bounce angles tend not to dig into the turf and clubs with lower bounce angles tend to dig into the turf.

Break
The curve the ball makes as it rolls toward the hole on the putting green. Break also refers to the general slope of a green.

Bump-and-Run
A shot intentionally hit low and short of your target that rolls substantially after it hits the ground.

Bunker
A sand-filled hazard.

Buried Lie
The lie of the ball, typically in a sand bunker, in which most of the ball sits below the surface. See also Fried Egg.

Butt End
The part of the shaft farthest away from the clubhead.

Carpet
A slang term referring to the putting green or fairway.

Carry
The distance the ball flies in the air.

Cast
Unhinging your wrists too early in the downswing.

Center-Shafted
A putter with a hosel at its center.

Check Up
A shot that spins and stops once it hits the green.

Chicken Wing
A bent right elbow in the release position. Associated with hitting a slice.

Chili-Dip
A shot in which you hit behind the ball, not moving it very far. See also Fat Shot.

Chip
A short, lofted shot hit near the green.

Choke
To play badly under pressure.

Choke Down
Gripping the club farther down the handle than normal.

Chop
To hit the ball with a hacking motion.

Chunk
A shot in which you hit behind the ball, not advancing it very far. See also Fat Shot or Chili-Dip.

Closed Clubface
Your clubface points left of the target when you address the ball, or left of the path on which you swing your club.

Closed Stance
Addressing the ball so that your toe line points to the right of the target.

Clubface
The area of the club on which contact with the ball is made.

Coil
The degree to which your shoulders turn relative to your hips. More shoulder than hip turn usually means more coil and power.

Collar
A closely mown area surrounding the putting green. See also Fringe.

Cross Wind
A wind blowing across a hole or the course.

Cross-Bunker
A lengthy bunker in the fairway and perpendicular to the line of play.

Cross-Handed Grip
Placing your left hand below your right on the handle when putting. See also Left-Hand Low.

Crown
The top side of your driver, fairway wood or hybrid.

Cut Shot
A shot that moves from left to right.

Dance Floor
The green.

De-Loft
Subtracting from the loft built into the clubface by leaning the shaft forward or closing the face at impact.

Dimple
Depression on a golf ball designed to help get the ball airborne and maintain its flight.

Divot
A chunk of grass taken up by the club during impact. It also refers to the resulting void.

Dogleg
A hole that bends left or right.

Double Cross
A shot that flies in the opposite direction of the shot you intended to play.

Double-Breaker
A putt the curves in more than one direction during its roll to the hole.

Downswing
The motion of swinging your club from the top position to the point of impact.

Drain
To sink a putt.

Draw
A shot that starts straight, or slightly right, and arcs gently to the left.

Duck Hook
A shot that starts straight and curves to the left of target. See also Snap Hook.

Duff
To mis-hit a shot by hitting the ground behind the ball and then top the ball.

Duffer
An unskilled golfer.

Elevated Green
A green that sits above your position in the fairway.

Extension
Stretching your arms through and after impact.

Face-Balanced
A weighting system applied to putters that helps keep the putterface square to the target during your stroke.

Fade
A shot that generally tends to curve to the right.

Fat Shot
When your club hits the ground behind the ball. This results in high or low shots with a loss of distance. See also Chunk or Chili-Dip.

First Cut
Term given to a section of rough (or higher grass) directly bordering a fairway.

Flagstick
A movable marker to show the location of the hole.

Flare Out
To rotate your feet on their heels so that they angle away from the center of your stance.

Flat Swing
Swinging your club under the plane defined by your shoulders.

Flex
A measurement of how much a shaft will bend during your swing. Stiffer shafts bend less than softer ones.

Flier
A shot that flies substantially longer than desired, usually as a result of too much grass between the clubface and ball. Flyers are more common from the rough than from the shorter fairway grass, and are most commonly hit from a Flier Lie.

Flight
The path of the ball through the air.

Flop Shot
A short shot played with an open stance and an open clubface, designed to travel very high in the air and land softly on the green.

Flub
A poorly hit shot usually caused by hitting the ground before the ball.

Fluffy Lie
A ball that's sitting up in grass.

Follow-Through
The continuation of your swing after the ball has been hit.

Forward Bend
The degree to which you bend toward the ball from your hips at address.

Forward Press
Moving your hands toward the target while your club is soled on the ground.

Fried Egg
A lie in a sand bunker in which most of the ball is below the surface of the sand. See also Buried Lie.

Fringe
The grass that borders a putting green. The fringe is typically higher than the grass on the green, but lower than the grass on the fairway. See also Collar.

Gap Wedge
A utility wedge with less loft than a sand wedge and more loft than a pitching wedge.

Grain
The direction in which the blades of grass on a green grow.

Greenside
Adjacent to the putting green.

Grip
The manner in which you place your hands on the club. It also refers to the

top part of the club or the material on which you place your hands at the top of the shaft.

Grip Pressure
How tightly you hold the club.

Grooves
The lines cut into a clubface to help impart spin. They are either V-shaped or U-shaped with a maximum allowable width of .035 inches.

Hacker
A derogatory term given to a player of lesser ability.

Hardpan
An area of the course not covered by grass and defined by hard-packed dirt.

Hazard
Any obstruction on a golf course such as a lake, pond, fence or bunker.

Heel
The part of the club head closest to the hosel.

Hole High
A ball that sits even with the hole but off to one side.

Hook
A shot that starts straight or slightly to the right or left then curves dramatically to the left.

Hosel
The area of the club into which the shaft enters.

Hoseled Shot
A shank.

Hot Spot
The area on your driver clubface between the sweet spot and the crown that's said to deliver the greatest amount of energy transfer.

Impact
The moment the clubface meets the ball.

Inside-Out
Swinging from inside the target line to the outside of the target line through impact. Inside-Out swings typically result in either pushes, draws or hooks, depending on the position of the clubface at impact.

Interlocking Grip
A type of grip where the little finger of your left hand is intertwined with the index finger of your right hand.

Knock-Down
A shot intentionally played low to keep the ball under the wind.

Lag Putt
A lengthy putt, or one designed to simply get close to the hole so the next putt is easily made.

Laid Off
Pointing the shaft away from the target line at the top of the swing.

Launch Angle
The angle on which the ball comes off the clubface following impact.

Launch Monitor
A device that measures and computes various swing parameters, such as speed and clubface angle, as well as shot data such as distance and direction.

Leading Edge
The bottom portion of the clubhead closest to the ball when soled at address.

Left-Hand Low
Placing your left hand below your right on the handle when putting. See also Cross-Handed Grip.

Lie Angle
The angle formed between the shaft and the ground when the club is soled at address (measured in degrees).

Lip Out
A putt that hits the edge of the hole and does not go in.

Lob Shot
A high, soft shot generally played near the green with a high-lofted wedge.

Lob Wedge
The highest-lofted wedge in your bag. Designed to hit lob shots, flops and to escape bunkers.

Loft Angle
The angle of the club's face.

Long Irons
Your 1-, 2-, 3 and 4-irons.

Mid-Irons
Your 5-, 6-, and 7-irons.

Offset
The distance from the front of the hosel to the leading edge of the clubface. More offset gives you more time to square the clubface.

Open Clubface
Your clubface points right of the target when you address the ball, or right of the path on which your club is swung.

Open Stance
Addressing the ball so that your toe line points to the left of the target.

Outside-In
Swinging from outside the target line to the inside of the target line through impact. Outside-in swings typically result in either pulls, fades or slices, depending on the position of the club face at impact.

Over the Top
Swinging outside-in.

Overlapping Grip
A type of grip where the little finger of your right hand overlaps the space between the forefinger and second finger of your left hand.

Over-Swinging
Swinging the club past parallel at the top of your backswing.

Pace
The speed at which your putt rolls to the hole.

Path
An imaginary line created by the arc of your swing.

Pick
To catch the ball cleanly at impact without hitting the ground.

Pin
The flagstick.

Pin High
A ball that sits even with the pin but off to one side. Same as Hole High.

Pivot
The rotation of your shoulders, torso and hips during your swing.

Plugged Lie
See Buried Lie.

Pop-Up
An unintentional high, short shot hit with a driver or fairway wood.

Pull
A shot that's hit straight but left of the target.

Pull-Hook
A shot that starts left of target and then curves dramatically to the left.

Pull-Slice
A shot that starts left of target and then curves dramatically to the right.

Punch Shot
A shot played intentionally low to avoid wind, trees or other obstacles.

Punch-Out
A low shot played from trees designed to get the ball back into play.

Push
A shot that's hit straight but right of the target. Similar to a Block.

Push-Hook
A shot that starts right of target and then curves dramatically to the left.

Push-Slice
A shot that starts right of target and then curves dramatically to the right.

Reading the Green
Determining the path the ball will follow during its roll to the hole by analyzing the contour and texture of the putting surface.

Release
The point in the downswing where you unhinge your wrists.

Reverse Pivot
Swinging to the top of your backswing without shifting your weight to your right foot. Associated with slicing.

Rough
The grass bordering the fairway that's higher and generally more coarse than the grass in the fairway.

Sand Save
Escaping a sand bunker then making the ensuing putt.

Sand Wedge
An iron with a heavy sole and increased bounce that's used primarily to get out of sand bunkers.

Saw Grip
An alternative putting grip that allows you to move your hands along the line of putt during your stroke. The Saw Grip is said to reduce the tendency to putt from outside-in and pull the ball left of the hole.

Scoop
Improperly hitting up into the ball in an attempt to lift it into the air. Scooping is the opposite of Trapping and leads to a variety of bad shots.

Scoring Irons
Your short irons and wedges.

Shallow
A flat swing plane.

Shank
A shot that's struck on the hosel area of the golf club. The resulting ball flight is generally straight to the right. See also Hoseled Shot.

Short Game
The part of the game comprised of chipping and pitching.

Short Irons
Your 8-, 9- and pitching irons.

Short-Sided
Missing the green on the side that leaves you with the smallest amount of distance between you and the flagstick.

Shotmaker
A player with the ability to hit a variety of shots.

Sidehill Lie
A lie with the ball either above or below your feet.

Skull
To strike the top of the ball with an ascending, glancing blow. See also Bladed Shot.

Slice
A shot that tends to start to the left of the target and curve to the right of the target.

Snap Hook
A shot that starts quickly to the left and angles sharply downwards and further to the left. See also Duck Hook.

Sole
The bottom of the clubhead.

Spine tilt
The degree to which your spine angles away from the target.

Square Clubface
Your clubface points directly at the target when you address the ball, or in the direction of the path on which your club is swung.

Stance
The position of your feet at address.

Stimpmeter
An apparatus used to measure the speed of a green. Greens with a higher "stimp" are said to be faster.

Swaying
Leaning away from the target during the backswing while turning very little.

Sweet Spot
The dead center of the clubface.

Swing Width
The radius of your swing measured from your hands to the clubhead. A wider swing is associated with more speed.

Takeaway
The start of your backswing.

Tap-In
A very short putt.

Texas Wedge
A slang term for your putter.

Thin
To hit the ball above its equator.

Through the Green
All areas of the course, except for the teeing ground, putting green and hazards.

Tight Fairway
A narrow fairway.

Tight lie
A lie on very short fairway grass or on hard-packed sand or dirt. The opposite of a Fluffy Lie.

Toe
The part of the clubhead furthest away from the hosel. A ball hit here is said to be "toed."

Top Position
The end of the backswing.

Topped Shot
A shot that does not get airborne as a result of a hitting the top of the ball.

Trailing Edge
The portion of the sole farthest away from the ball at address.

Trajectory
The flight path of the ball.

Transition
The change in momentum from backswing to downswing.

Trapped
Your clubhead is too far to the inside or behind your body on your downswing.

Trapping
Correctly pinching the ball against the turf at impact with the face of your iron.

Underclub
Selecting less club than necessary to produce the needed distance.

Unplayable Lie
A ball hit into a position that does not allow you to make contact or establish a safe stance.

Up-and-Down
A situation in which you miss the green, but need only one shot and one putt to finish the hole.

Weight Shift
Moving your weight backwards and forwards during your swing.

Worm Burner
A poor shot characterized by the ball not getting airborne.

Yips
The condition, either mental or physical, in which a golfer cannot make short putts. A short putt that is missed badly is said to be "yipped."

ACKNOWLEDGEMENTS

Time Inc. HOME ENTERTAINMENT

PUBLISHER
Richard Fraiman

GENERAL MANAGER
Steven Sandonato

EXECUTIVE DIRECTOR, MARKETING SERVICES
Carol Pittard

DIRECTOR, RETAIL & SPECIAL SALES
Tom Mifsud

DIRECTOR, NEW PRODUCT DEVELOPMENT
Peter Harper

ASSISTANT DIRECTOR, BRAND MARKETING
Laura Adam

ASSISTANT GENERAL COUNSEL
Dasha Smith Dwin

BOOK PRODUCTION MANAGER
Jonathan Polsky

DESIGN & PREPRESS MANAGER
Anne-Michelle Gallero

MARKETING MANAGER
Alexandra Bliss

THANK YOU

Bozena Bannett, Kevin Beard, Steve Beslow,
Glenn Buonocore, Dr. Richard Coop, Caroline DeOliveira,
Noelle Ewen, Suzanne Janso, Robert Marasco,
Jessica Marksbury, Patrice Peelen-Wenz,
Brooke Reger, Jesse Reiter, Josh Sanburn,
Mary Sarro-Waite, Rob Sauerhaft, Roger Sauerhaft,
Ilene Schreider, Adriana Tierno, Alex Voznesenskiy,
Kris Widger, Ken Yagoda

GOLF MAGAZINE

EDITOR
David M. Clarke

CREATIVE DIRECTOR
Paul Crawford

DEPUTY EDITOR
Michael Corcoran

ART DIRECTOR
Paul Ewen

MANAGING EDITOR (INSTRUCTION)
David DeNunzio

PRODUCTION EDITOR
Michael Walker Jr.

EDITOR AT LARGE
Connell Barrett

SENIOR EDITOR
Gary Perkinson

DEPUTY ART DIRECTOR
Karen Ha

ASSOCIATE PHOTO EDITOR
Carrie Boretz

PUBLISHER
Charles R. Kammerer

ASSOCIATE PUBLISHER
Edward Z. Hughes

DIRECTOR OF BUSINESS DEVELOPMENT
Brad J. Felenstein

GENERAL MANAGER
Peter Greer

NATIONAL DIRECTOR OF ONLINE SALES
Helen Har

VICE PRESIDENT OF CONSUMER MARKETING
Mike Wywoda

Sports Illustrated

GOLF Magazine is published in conjunction
with *Sports Illustrated*

PRESIDENT/PUBLISHER
Mark Ford

EDITOR
Terry McDonell

VICE PRESIDENT, GENERAL MANAGER
Oliver Knowlton

PRESIDENT, SI DIGITAL
Jeff Price

DEPUTY MANAGING EDITOR
David Bauer

EXECUTIVE EDITORS
Michael Bevans
Rob Fleder
Charlie Leerhsen

CHIEF MARKETING OFFICER
Andrew R. Judelson

ASSOCIATE PUBLISHER
Richard A. Raskopf

ASSISTANT MANAGING EDITORS
Neil Cohen (SI Presents)
James P. Herre (Golf Plus)
Craig Neff

GOLF.com

EXECUTIVE EDITOR
Charlie Hanger

DEPUTY EDITOR
David Dusek

MANAGING EDITOR
Eamon Lynch

BOOK DESIGN

PAUL EWEN

PHOTOGRAPHY

BOB ATKINS:
8 (ML, MR), 9 (ML, M), 13 (R), 16, 20, 26 (R), 32 (FL), 41 (B), 46 (R), 56, 57 (L), 60, 62, 63 (L), 64, 65 (L), 66-67, 71 (R), 75 (BR), 76, 77 (T), 79 (B), 81 (B), 85 (MR), 86-87, 101 (B), 103 (B), 105, 113 (T), 115 (T), 120, 121 (L), 123 (R), 124-125, 128, 129 (M), 133 (R), 138-139, 143 (L), 144, 146-147, 155, 158-159, 163 (R), 173, 174, 176-177

NEIL BECKERMAN:
45 (R), 89 (T), 94-95, 167 (R), 169 (L), 178 (T)

D2 PRODUCTIONS:
8 (FR), 9 (MR), 96-97, 114, 134, 141 (TL), 160-161

SAM GREENWOOD:
26 (L), 32 (ML), 34 (L), 36 (FL), 40, 42 (R), 46 (L), 50 (R), 54 (FR), 70 (UR), 73 (BL), 101 (T), 129 (B), 141 (BL), 149 (R), 153 (TR), 180

LEONARD KAMSLER:
12, 13 (L), 25, 27, 28-29, 32 (MR, FR), 38-39 (M), 52-53, 70 (L), 71 (BL), 77 (B), 79 (T), 85 (BR), 91 (R), 93 (M), 103 (T), 104, 113 (B), 140, 141 (R), 143 (R), 145, 157 (T), 164

RUSSELL KIRK:
36 (ML), 70 (BR), 72, 73 (T), 80, 82, 142 (BR), 181

SCHECTER LEE:
6-7, 45 (L), 49 (BR), 100, 129 (TR)

GREG LORD:
17, 29 (R), 87, 157 (R)

SCOTT MCDERMOTT:
89 (BR)

ANGUS MURRAY:
3, 8 (FL, M), 9 (FL, FR), 10-11, 14-15, 18, 22-23, 24 (R), 30, 31 (L, B), 33, 34 (R), 36 (MR, FR), 37, 38 (L), 41 (T), 42 (M), 43, 44 (B), 46 (M), 47, 48, 49 (L, TR), 50 (M), 51, 54 (MR), 55, 57 (R), 58-59, 61, 63 (BR), 65 (R), 68, 73 (MR), 74, 75 (TR), 78, 81 (T), 84, 85 (L), 90, 92, 93 (L), 100, 106-107, 108-109, 111, 115 (B), 116-117, 119, 121 (T), 122, 123 (L), 127, 130-131, 132, 133 (L), 135, 142, 150-151, 152, 154, 162, 163 (L), 165, 166, 170-171, 175, 178 (B), 179, 192

GARY NEWKIRK:
88, 89 (L), 98-99, 136-137, 153 (TL), 172

KEICHI SATO:
169 (BR)

FRED VUICH:
24 (L), 31 (R), 35, 39 (FR), 44 (T), 50 (L), 54 (FL, ML), 73 (BR), 83, 91 (L), 93 (R), 112, 126, 148, 149 (L), 157 (BL), 167 (L)

ILLUSTRATIONS

KEVIN BEARD:
19, 21, 69, 77, 81, 83, 84, 95, 97, 121, 125, 159

PHIL FRANKE:
118-119, 151, 156

ROBIN GRIGGS:
27, 53, 67, 102-103, 147, 148, 168

KAREN HA:
79, 173, 175, 177

PETE SUCHESKI:
105

IAN WARPOLE:
129